iShoogle - pinching sweaters on your phone
multi-gesture touchscreen fabric simulator using natural on-fabric gestures to communicate textile qualities

Dr Pawel Michal Orzechowski

Submitted for the degree of Doctor of Philosophy

Heriot-Watt University, Edinburgh

School of Mathematical and Computer Sciences

May 2016

The Copyright Statement:

The copyright in this thesis is owned by the author. Any quotation from the thesis or use of any of the information contained in it must acknowledge this thesis as the source of the quotation or information.

Abstract

The inability to touch fabrics online frustrates consumers, who are used to evaluating physical textiles by engaging in complex, natural gestural interactions. When customers interact with physical fabrics, they combine cross-modal information about the fabric's look, sound and handle to build an impression of its physical qualities. But whenever an interaction with a fabric is limited (i.e. when watching clothes online) there is a perceptual gap between the fabric qualities perceived digitally and the actual fabric qualities that a person would perceive when interacting with the physical fabric. The goal of this thesis was to create a fabric simulator that minimized this perceptual gap, enabling accurate perception of the qualities of fabrics presented digitally.

We designed iShoogle, a multi-gesture touch-screen sound-enabled fabric simulator that aimed to create an accurate representation of fabric qualities without the need for touching the physical fabric swatch. iShoogle uses on-screen gestures (inspired by natural on-fabric movements e.g. Crunching) to control pre-recorded videos and audio of fabrics being deformed (e.g. being Crunched). iShoogle creates an illusion of direct video manipulation and also direct manipulation of the displayed fabric.

This thesis describes the results of nine studies leading towards the development and evaluation of iShoogle. In the first three studies, we combined expert and non-expert textile-descriptive words and grouped them into eight dimensions labelled with terms Crisp, Hard, Soft, Textured, Flexible, Furry, Rough and Smooth. These terms were used to rate fabric qualities throughout the thesis. We observed natural on-fabric gestures during a fabric handling study (Study 4) and used the results to design iShoogle's on-screen gestures. In Study 5 we examined iShoogle's performance and speed in a fabric handling task and in Study 6 we investigated users' preferences for sound playback interactivity. iShoogle's accuracy was then evaluated in the last three studies by comparing participants' ratings of textile qualities when using iShoogle with ratings produced when handling physical swatches. We also described the recording and processing techniques for the video and audio content that iShoogle used. Finally, we described the iShoogle iPhone app that was released to the general public.

Our evaluation studies showed that iShoogle significantly improved the accuracy of fabric perception in at least some cases. Further research could investigate which fabric qualities and which fabrics are particularly suited to be represented with iShoogle.

Dedication

To all the future PhD students:

I wish you more luck than I had.

Had I known how much this thesis will cost me, I would have never started, but now that it lays printed and bound in front of me (and you) I am proud of what I achieved and who I have become.

I know that I truly contributed something completely new to the world and that it was all built on hard work of mine, the team surrounding me and those inspiring people who published before me and provided me with inspiration.

Over these hard seven years I have learned about polar extremes.

I saw how kind and helpful people can be without any ulterior motivation. I also learned how pride, jealousy and disrespect leads some people to crush others in their path in the name of career and gain. I have seen how my body and my mind took me through years of hard work, brilliant thoughts and immense concentration. But I also saw my body and my mind crumble and cripple me, taking away all that was dear to me and leaving scars that I am yet to learn how to wear with pride.

If I could give you three guidelines, they would be:

Take care of yourself – Nothing is worth ruining your health, friendships, dreams, beliefs or sanity. It is a myth that people who disregard themselves achieve more.

Meet your favourite authors in real life – I wish you that overwhelming pleasure of feeling the union of minds with fellow scientists when working with them and reading their work.

Collaborate and publish – Keeping progress to oneself is a bitter and lonely trap. Surround yourself with people you like working with, create new content and share it.

I also wish you as much blessing as I had. Life is wonderful.

Pawel

Thank You

Thanks to my love and inspiration Kasia Banas

Thanks to my mentors and colleagues: Mike Chantler, Judy Robertson, Nadine Marcus, Lisa Francis, Fiona Houston, Michael Heron, Pauline Belford, Murdoch Jamie Gabbay, Nadia Berthouse, Penelope Watkins, Patrick Green, Bob Thomson, Wojciech Tomalczyk, Witold Zakrzacki, Eugeniusz Łuba, Tom Methven, Stefano Padilla, Douglas Atkinson, Bruna Petreca, Valerie Queva, Valerie Gibson, Hannah Cornish.

Thanks to my amazing friends: Genna, Irina, Estefania, Ewan, Magda, Ainsley, Gustaf, Shaz, Belen, Arek, Celine, Anna Dere, Joisan, Jacek, Kat, Kel, Aoife, Rhi, Rea, Caro, Jules, Jo, Sylvain and all the others who were there for me.

Thanks to my family: Gabriela, Andrzej, Jasia, Janeczka, Kamila, Michal, Piotr, Aga, Sawa, Lew, Bozena, Rysiek, Milosz, Karolina, Jagoda, Danusia, Karolina, Marcin, Ula, Jacek and Jasio.

Acknowledgements

Some work described in this thesis was run alongside of DIGITAL SENSORIA (EP/H007083/2) project and other research conducted by TEXTURE LAB under IMRC (EP/F02553X/1).

Additional funding was received from Google Inc. as a part of Google EMEA Scholarship for Students with Disabilities 2012.

Substantial part of this thesis was dictated to the Nuance's Dragon Dictate voice recognition software.

Acknowledgements were made wherever appropriate.

Table Of Contents

1. **Thesis Introduction** 1
   1.1 Problem Statement 1
   1.2 Perspective 3
   1.3 Research Questions 6
   1.4 Scope 8
   1.5 Thesis Outline 14
2. **Words Describing Textile Qualities** 17
   2.1 Introduction 17
   2.2 Literature Review 20
   2.3 Organisation Of This Chapter 32
   2.4 Study 1 – Evaluating The Expert Word Set And Its Familiarity 35
   2.5 Study 2 – Words Used By Non-Expert Participants To Communicate Fabric Qualities 40
   2.6 Combining Non-Expert And Expert Word Sets 60
   2.7 Study 3 – Clustering The Final Word Set 68
   2.8 Using Fabric Quality Terms To Communicate Textile Qualities 92
   2.9 Chapter Conclusion 96
   2.10 Chapter Contributions 99
3. **Gestures Used For Evaluating Fabric Qualities** 103
   3.1 Introduction 103
   3.2 Literature Review 106
   3.3 Organisation Of This Chapter 115
   3.4 Study 4 – On-Fabric Gestures Performed While Evaluating Fabric Qualities 116
   3.5 Study Results 123
   3.6 Chapter Conclusion 142
   3.7 Chapter Contributions 146
4. **iShoogle – Multi-Gesture Textile Simulator Interface: Visuals, Interaction and Sound** 150
   4.1 Introduction 150
   4.2 Literature Review 152
   4.3 Organisation Of This Chapter 170

4.4   Design Of The iShoogle Interface 171
  4.5   Extending iShoogle With Sound Stimuli 210
  4.6   Chapter Conclusions 216
  4.7   Chapter Contributions 222

5. **Evaluation Of iShoogle Interface In Terms Of Gesture Performance And Sound Interactivity** 225
  5.1   Introduction 225
  5.2   Literature Review 228
  5.3   Study 5 – Gesture Performance, Learning Curve And Cognitive Load 228
  5.4   Study 6 – Evaluation Of Interactive Sound Extension Of iShoogle 251
  5.5   Chapter Conclusion 258
  5.6   Chapter Contributions 261

6. **Impact Of iShoogle's Visual And Sound Elements On Accurate Perception Of Fabric Qualities** 264
  6.1   Introduction 264
  6.2   Literature Review 266
  6.3   Organisation Of This Chapter 275
  6.4   Study 7 – Impact Of Presentation And Interaction On Perceived Fabric Qualities 276
  6.5   Study 8 – The Impact Of Sound On Perceived Qualities Of Fabrics 286
  6.6   Chapter Conclusion 304
  6.7   Chapter Contributions 306

7. **Thesis Discussion and Conclusion** 309
  7.1   Synopsis And Discussion 309
  7.2   Strengths And Limitations 315
  7.3   Future Directions 322
  7.4   Conclusions 325

8. **Appendices** 329
  Appendix I.   Private communications with Douglas Atkinson – Literature Review Of Words That Fabric Experts User 329
  Appendix II.   Words used by two or less out of 28 participants and hence discarded 334

Appendix III. Four Fabrics Used For Testing iShoogle.........338
Appendix IV. Area Independent Method For Creating Annotation Scheme For A New Area Of Research......................340

9. Bibliography...343

Terms Glossary

Textile Qualities – textile qualities and attributes that can be perceived with senses and described with words.

Textile Hand / Handle – textile qualities evaluated with use of touch.

Non-Experts – people who were never trained in handling textiles or describing textile qualities and only who have experience of handling fabrics in everyday life.

Non-Expert Words – words used by non-experts to describe textile qualities.

Experts – people professionally engaged with the textile industry and trained in handling fabrics and describing them.

Expert Words – words used by experts to describe textile qualities.

Evaluating textiles by non-experts – interacting with fabrics in various ways to perceive and understand their qualities. These qualities would not be objective and measured with use of evaluation tools, but rather they would be subjective perceptions of textile qualities.

Describing textiles – using words to communicate evaluated textile qualities.

Textile-Descriptive Words – words used to describe textile qualities.

Textile-Descriptive Term – higher level textile-descriptive word that represent a group of other textile descriptive words of a similar meaning.

Quality Rating Scale – a rating scale described by a textile-descriptive term that can be used for describing fabric qualities.

Textile Quality Icon – a drawing or a symbol representing a textile quality. Icons were placed next to each quality rating scale on a questionnaire.

Active Dictionaries – all the words spoken or written by a person, recalled by them from the memory without being prompted or hinted to use these particular words.

Passive Dictionary – all the words recognised and understood by a person, but not limited to words that a person would use actively when not prompted.

Digitised Fabric – a fabric interacted with via a digital interface (image, video, textile simulator) rather than by handling a physical swatch.

Recording Rig – a suite of hardware and software used to record video or audio of the digitised fabric. Recording rig includes positions of lights, microphones cameras and other equipment as well as treatment of the recorded material with software (e.g. filters, post-processing).

Physical Original of the Digitised Fabric – a physical swatch used to record media (image, video) that was subsequently used in an interface as a digitised fabric.

Rating Accuracy – the difference between fabric qualities perceived when interacting with a digitised fabric via a digital simulator and qualities perceived when interacting with the original physical swatch. Rating accuracy is measured by rating the same fabric twice (in a digital and physical form) on a quality rating scale, and comparing the results. Low difference in ratings signifies high accuracy.

Realistic communication of fabric qualities – a communication of fabric qualities (e.g. with a digital interface) that produces high rating accuracy (digital and physical fabric ratings are similar).

On-Fabric gestures – gestures performed by people interacting with a swatch of physical fabric directly with their hands to evaluate its textile qualities.

On-Screen gestures – gestures performed while interacting with a touchscreen as a method of communicating with software interface and recognised by that software.

Neutral state of the interface – a state of the digital interface (visual, sound etc.) before user interacts with it.

Table Of Tables

Figure 1 – Organisation of this thesis. 13

Figure 2 – Participant arranges cards with 69 professional words into three stacks, corresponding to words being Used, Unused or Unknown in relation to fabrics in Study 1. 37

Figure 3 – Histogram of how many participants used each word. Words used by fewer than three participants were discarded. 45

Figure 4 – Comparison of Know, Use and Agree scores of expert words, ordered by the Know score. 67

Figure 5 – Agree and Use scores of all spoken (expert and non-expert) words. Words with top 50 Use scores. 67

Figure 6 – Agree and Use scores of all spoken (expert and non-expert) words. Words with 51st to 100th of highest Use scores. 68

Figure 7 – Conceptual diagram of textile qualities rating space. This graph demonstrates a method of combining a number of synonymous scales describing textile qualities into one scale for simplicity. Above graph does not represent real data, but rather a concept of reducing number of dimensions. 70

Figure 8 – Flashcards with words clustered into groups by a participant in a Lab setting in Study 3. Image below shows which words participant chose as most representative for each group. 73

Figure 9 – Online word sorting interface – Setup. Participants were introduced to the sorting task with two simple examples (not related to fabrics). 74

Figure 10 – Online word sorting interface – Result. Once participants joined all words into groups (by drag-and-dropping them onto each other), they were asked to star the most representative word within each group. Image for interface demonstration only (not a real user's sorting data).......... 75

Figure 11 – Average distances similarity matrix - darker means more similar, numbers on intersections of words describe how many tens of participants grouped them together (out of 138). 77

Figure 12 – Dendrogram of similarity matrix for word sorting results separated into 8 groups. 79

Figure 13 – Palette graph - another way to represent similarity data of the above dendrogram separated into 12 groups 80

Figure 14 – Modified image used by P. M. Orzechowski et al. (2011) – a simplified dendrogram of word meaning similarity. Number of * indicated representativeness of the word 81

Figure 15 – Means and error bars of 3 groups of word sorting with and without cheaters – measure of distance from average. 88

Figure 16 – Distance from average ratings across three setups in word sorting Study 3 89

Figure 17 – The set of 8 textile quality words that were used in further studies. 93

Figure 18 – A histogram of ratings of real fabrics when ratings were made on a 1-7 scale and a 1-100 scale. Eyeballing distribution indicated they were comparable 95

Figure 19 – Gesture recording video setup (left) and the view from the camera (right). This was the largest fabric sample we used (40x40cm) but most of other samples were smaller (on average 30x30cm). 118

Figure 20 – Patterns that have emerged from the pilot scheme. First hand-drawn draft – handwriting was replaced and colours added for readability. 127

Figure 21 – Final on-fabric gesture dictionary. 130

Figure 22 – Average total number of times each gesture was used by a participant during handling of 11 fabrics (over the average of 11 minutes). 134

Figure 23 – An attempt on annotating 50 seconds of recording with both gestures and words. 138

Figure 24 – Frequency of different gestures on Soft and Rough fabrics. The error bar on depicts Standard Error. 141

Figure 25 – Design space and textile simulator requirements. Modified graph from work described by Whitworth and Ahmad (2014) (in section 2.3). 175

Figure 26 – To satisfy most important requirements haptics, physics simulation and 3D animations were not used and were replaced by gesture controlled stop motion animation and interactive sound. 182

Figure 27 – All the on-screen gestures derived from the on-fabric gestures identified in Chapter 3. All gestures were translated into touch-screen recognisable gestures, but only gestures with * were used in further studies. 189

Figure 28 – Combining gesture recognisers - number of gestures and the direction of movement were the primary means of deciding the type of gesture triggered. When number of fingers changed during the gesture, the gesture was changed. 192

Figure 29 – Network of movie frames and a common frame. 196

Figure 30 – ShoogleIt.com website and examples of usage of shoogle videos with either horizontal or vertical drag interaction. 198

Figure 31 – ShoogleIt Builder. Frame editing screen. Here users could add, remove and reorder frames as well as crop and edit them to achieve seamless playback of shoogle videos.... 199

Figure 32 – ShoogleIt Builder. Output settings screen. Here users could select direction of drag, playback and loop modes and initial video frame. 200

Figure 33 – High Fidelity and Low Fidelity camera recording setup. 203

Figure 34 – Gestures in iShoogle interface. 209

Figure 35 – Fabric samples used to record videos and sound samples for our studies. See Appendix III for larger photos of these fabrics. 212

Figure 36 – Microphone setup and movements used in recording three sounds of fabric sound stimuli: Scratching, Crunching and Rustling. 213

Figure 37 – Stain designs and their presence on different task complexity levels. 238

Figure 38 – Stains were present in full size on one frame only, but were also displayed on four neighbouring frames in smaller sizes. 239

Figure 39 – Stain study: tutorials and an image of interface in use. 240

Figure 40 – Stain study, example of a Slider interface performing Crunch deformation (left) and a gesture interface performing Pinch deformation (right). 241

Figure 41 – Average self-reported cognitive load on a 1-7 scale. Data for three task complexity levels for two interfaces. Error bars depict standard error. 249

Figure 42 – Example of side-by-side shoogle interfaces. During each trial participant decided which sound was more realistic after horizontally pinching both interfaces. 253

Figure 43 – Images used by P. M. Orzechowski et al. (2011) from left to right: Participant using interface on one iPad and rating fabrics on the other iPad; diagram of our two iPad setup and rating sliders; example of what Latex looked like when displayed on the screen. 281

Figure 44 – Rating Accuracy (the difference between fabric quality ratings of a swatch and digital version of the same fabric) across the 4 interfaces. For scale, accuracy is presented as average absolute distance of physical and digital ratings as if they were presented on 1-7 scale. 283

Figure 45 – Study 9. Software and the questionnaire. 295

Figure 46 – Study 9. Handling the swatch and experimental setup. 297

Figure 47 – Did sound improve or undermine the communication of fabric qualities? Asterisks indicate statistical significance. 303

Table Of Figures

Figure 1 – Organisation of this thesis. 13

Figure 2 – Participant arranges cards with 69 professional words into three stacks, corresponding to words being Used, Unused or Unknown in relation to fabrics in Study 1. 37

Figure 3 – Histogram of how many participants used each word. Words used by fewer than three participants were discarded. 45

Figure 4 – Comparison of Know, Use and Agree scores of expert words, ordered by the Know score. 67

Figure 5 – Agree and Use scores of all spoken (expert and non-expert) words. Words with top 50 Use scores. 67

Figure 6 – Agree and Use scores of all spoken (expert and non-expert) words. Words with 51st to 100th of highest Use scores. 68

Figure 7 – Conceptual diagram of textile qualities rating space. This graph demonstrates a method of combining a number of synonymous scales describing textile qualities into one scale for simplicity. Above graph does not represent real data, but rather a concept of reducing number of dimensions. 70

Figure 8 – Flashcards with words clustered into groups by a participant in a Lab setting in Study 3. Image below shows which words participant chose as most representative for each group. 73

Figure 9 – Online word sorting interface – Setup. Participants were introduced to the sorting task with two simple examples (not related to fabrics). 74

Figure 10 – Online word sorting interface – Result. Once participants joined all words into groups (by drag-and-dropping them onto each other), they were asked to star the most representative word within each group. Image for interface demonstration only (not a real user's sorting data).......... 75

Figure 11 – Average distances similarity matrix - darker means more similar, numbers on intersections of words describe how many tens of participants grouped them together (out of 138). 77

Figure 12 – Dendrogram of similarity matrix for word sorting results separated into 8 groups. 79

Figure 13 – Palette graph - another way to represent similarity data of the above dendrogram separated into 12 groups 80

Figure 14 – Modified image used by P. M. Orzechowski et al. (2011) – a simplified dendrogram of word meaning similarity. Number of * indicated representativeness of the word 81

Figure 15 – Means and error bars of 3 groups of word sorting with and without cheaters – measure of distance from average. 88

Figure 16 – Distance from average ratings across three setups in word sorting Study 3. 89

Figure 17 – The set of 8 textile quality words that were used in further studies. 93

Figure 18 – A histogram of ratings of real fabrics when ratings were made on a 1-7 scale and a 1-100 scale. Eyeballing distribution indicated they were comparable 95

Figure 19 – Gesture recording video setup (left) and the view from the camera (right). This was the largest fabric sample we used (40x40cm) but most of other samples were smaller (on average 30x30cm). 118

Figure 20 – Patterns that have emerged from the pilot scheme. First hand-drawn draft – handwriting was replaced and colours added for readability. 127

Figure 21 – Final on-fabric gesture dictionary. 130

Figure 22 – Average total number of times each gesture was used by a participant during handling of 11 fabrics (over the average of 11 minutes). 134

Figure 23 – An attempt on annotating 50 seconds of recording with both gestures and words. 138

Figure 24 – Frequency of different gestures on Soft and Rough fabrics. The error bar on depicts Standard Error. 141

Figure 25 – Design space and textile simulator requirements. Modified graph from work described by Whitworth and Ahmad (2014) (in section 2.3). 175

Figure 26 – To satisfy most important requirements haptics, physics simulation and 3D animations were not used and were replaced by gesture controlled stop motion animation and interactive sound. 182

Figure 27 – All the on-screen gestures derived from the on-fabric gestures identified in Chapter 3. All gestures were translated into touch-screen recognisable gestures, but only gestures with * were used in further studies. 189

Figure 28 – Combining gesture recognisers - number of gestures and the direction of movement were the primary means of deciding the type of gesture triggered. When number of fingers changed during the gesture, the gesture was changed. 192

Figure 29 – Network of movie frames and a common frame. 196

Figure 30 – ShoogleIt.com website and examples of usage of shoogle videos with either horizontal or vertical drag interaction. 198

Figure 31 – ShoogleIt Builder. Frame editing screen. Here users could add, remove and reorder frames as well as crop and edit them to achieve seamless playback of shoogle videos.... 199

Figure 32 – ShoogleIt Builder. Output settings screen. Here users could select direction of drag, playback and loop modes and initial video frame. 200

Figure 33 – High Fidelity and Low Fidelity camera recording setup. 203

Figure 34 – Gestures in iShoogle interface. 209

Figure 35 – Fabric samples used to record videos and sound samples for our studies. See Appendix III for larger photos of these fabrics. 212

Figure 36 – Microphone setup and movements used in recording three sounds of fabric sound stimuli: Scratching, Crunching and Rustling. 213

Figure 37 – Stain designs and their presence on different task complexity levels. 238

Figure 38 – Stains were present in full size on one frame only, but were also displayed on four neighbouring frames in smaller sizes. 239

Figure 39 – Stain study: tutorials and an image of interface in use. 240

Figure 40 – Stain study, example of a Slider interface performing Crunch deformation (left) and a gesture interface performing Pinch deformation (right). 241

Figure 41 – Average self-reported cognitive load on a 1-7 scale. Data for three task complexity levels for two interfaces. Error bars depict standard error. 249

Figure 42 – Example of side-by-side shoogle interfaces. During each trial participant decided which sound was more realistic after horizontally pinching both interfaces. 253

Figure 43 – Images used by P. M. Orzechowski et al. (2011) from left to right: Participant using interface on one iPad and rating fabrics on the other iPad; diagram of our two iPad setup and rating sliders; example of what Latex looked like when displayed on the screen. 281

Figure 44 – Rating Accuracy (the difference between fabric quality ratings of a swatch and digital version of the same fabric) across the 4 interfaces. For scale, accuracy is presented as average absolute distance of physical and digital ratings as if they were presented on 1-7 scale. 283

Figure 45 – Study 9. Software and the questionnaire. 295

Figure 46 – Study 9. Handling the swatch and experimental setup. 297

Figure 47 – Did sound improve or undermine the communication of fabric qualities? Asterisks indicate statistical significance. 303

Table Of Studies

Study 1
Recognition of expert words. Which expert words did non-experts know and use? 35

Study 2
Word generation while handling fabrics. What words did participants use when asked to describe fabrics that they were handling? 40

Study 3
Word Grouping Study. Which words from the expert set have similar meanings? 60

Study 4
Natural on-fabric gestures used for fabric handling. What on-fabric gestures did non-experts use to evaluate fabric qualities? 116

Study 5
Acceptability of the interactive sound in iShoogle interface. Which sound playback did participants prefer to interact with: static playback, or playback influenced by user's actions? 228

Study 6
Performance of gesture and non-gesture interfaces. Can participants use iShoogle to find fabric defects as quickly, accurately and with as little effort as when using an alternative interface? 251

Study 7
Evaluating fabric qualities with various visual interfaces. Can one-gesture iShoogle communicate fabric qualities more accurately than alternative visual interfaces? 276

Study 8
Impact of sound types on perceived qualities. What are the difference in perceived fabric qualities when presenting iShoogle with correct and incorrect sound? 286

Study 9
Impact of sound and silence on perceived fabric qualities. How does the presence of sound impact perceived fabric qualities? 292

Author's Publications

Videos of the iShoogle interface are available at the author's website http://www.macs.hw.ac.uk/texturelab/people/pawel-michal-orzechowski/

P. M. Orzechowski (2010) – Orzechowski, P. M. (2010). *Interactive mobile presentation of textiles.* Paper presented at the Proceedings of the 12th International Conference on Human Computer Interaction with Mobile Devices and Services.

P. M. Orzechowski et al. (2011) – Orzechowski, P. M., Atkinson, D., Padilla, S., Methven, T. S., Baurley, S., & Chantler, M. (2011). *Interactivity to enhance perception: does increased interactivity in mobile visual presentation tools facilitate more accurate rating of textile properties?* Paper presented at the Proceedings of the 13th International Conference on Human Computer Interaction with Mobile Devices and Services.

Methven, Orzechowski, and Chantler (2011) – Methven, T., Orzechowski, P., & Chantler, M. (2011). A Comparison of Crowd-Sourcing vs. Traditional Techniques for Deriving Consumer Terms. Paper presented at Digital Engagement

P. M. Orzechowski et al. (2012) – Orzechowski, P. M., Padilla, S., Atkinson, D., Chantler, M., Baurley, S., Bianchi-Berthouze, N., . . . Petreca, B. B. (2012). *iShoogle: a textile archiving and simulation tool.* Paper presented at the Proceedings of the 26th Annual BCS Conference on Human Computer Interaction (HCI 2012).

Padilla, Orzechowski, and Chantler (2012) – Padilla, S., Orzechowski, P. M., & Chantler, M. J. (2012). *Digital tools for the creative industries.* Paper presented at Digital Futures.

P. M. Orzechowski et al. (2012) - Orzechowski, P., Padilla, S., Atkinson, D., Baurley, S., & Chantler, M. (2012). *Are single images sufficient to communicate qualities of texture-rich products?* Paper presented at Perception.

P. M. Orzechowski et al. (2012) – Orzechowski, P., Padilla, S., Atkinson, D., Chantler, M. J., Baurley, S., Berthouze, B.-N., . . . Petreca, B. (2012). *Archiving and simulation of fabrics with multi-gesture interfaces.* Paper presented at the Proceedings of HCI.

Atkinson et al. (2013) – Atkinson, D., Orzechowski, P., Petreca, B., Bianchi-Berthouze, N., Watkins, P., Baurley, S., . . . Chantler, M. (2013). *Tactile perceptions of digital textiles: a design research approach.* Paper presented at the Proceedings of the SIGCHI Conference on Human Factors in Computing Systems.

1. Thesis Introduction

1.1 Problem Statement

Digitally Communicating Goods' Qualities –
Scalable, Distributed, Convenient

With increasing penetration of the Internet, almost every area of commerce is moving its operations online. Selling goods online makes it possible to operate with fewer physical outlets and reduced costs. These advantages are most visible when operations grow and need to scale up. When goods can be previewed and purchased online, the price of serving each customer is almost independent of the number of customers (who each cover costs of their own device). This stands in contrast to traditional offline commerce, in which to serve more customers, a brand would need larger premises and more staff.

In digital commerce each shopper has their own outlet, which means that the cost and effort of shopping can be distributed between all shoppers. For example, the location and time to do shopping can be chosen at the customer's convenience, while risks and costs (associated with running a high street shop) are minimised for the seller. What is more, numerous shopping outlets (websites, apps) are available on the same device, providing the customer with the convenience of a larger choice and, what follows, better purchases as described by Häubl and Trifts (2000).

The Problem – Online Shopping Does Not Work For Fabrics, Because People Evaluate Textiles By Touching And Feeling Them

The 'touch and feel' qualities of textiles seem to take an important role in consumers' clothes purchasing decisions, as analysed by Levin, Levin, and Heath (2003), possibly because we touch our clothes constantly when wearing them. Depending on the function and type of garments, different types of qualities such as Soft, Flexible or Sturdy are desirable. For instance customers might expect jeans to be sturdy and a scarf to be soft, but not the opposite.

In a physical shop customers can touch the garment and evaluate these qualities; however, in an online outlet, they need to estimate fabric qualities based on the provided description and media (e.g. images, videos) of fabrics on a hanger or worn by a model. When a customer estimates the fabric qualities based on such limited exposure to the fabric, it is possible for the actual fabric qualities to not be as they expected. In such a situation, the garment is frequently returned, causing inconvenience to the consumer and financial loss to the business.

The Need And Our Proposed Solution - Digital Interface That Communicates 'Touch And Feel' Qualities Of Fabrics

We identified a need for a digital interface solution that would bridge the offline and online clothes shopping experiences by communicating true fabric qualities without the need to touch the fabrics. We imagined a scenario where a consumer would interact with the fabric on the screen and create an expectation of how the fabric would feel when touched. If the interface was successful in communicating fabric qualities, their expectations would be aligned with the actual properties of the original fabric.

An additional challenge was to create a solution that could be easily accessible, widely distributed and inexpensive. While there existed different experimental interfaces that communicated textile qualities with the use of force feedback, vibrations or electric current, they were either not suitable for the wider market (e.g. too fragile or expensive) or only suitable for a small subset of textiles and qualities. An example of an inexpensive and effective solution would be an app running on a publicly available touchscreen device (i.e. iPad). Additionally there was a need for the recording rig and software to capture physical fabrics, turn them into digital representations and distribute them to the devices with the app.

In this thesis we have not focused on the technical aspects of development of the app and recording setup, but instead we described the research on how digitised fabrics could be communicated in a realistic way.

1.2 Perspective

Human Computer Interaction And Multidisciplinary Perspective

It would have been possible to approach this problem from the perspective of various areas of science and research. We believed that for a holistic understanding of the problem space we had to investigate the contributions of the following branches of science: Psychology (to understand why and how people perceive fabrics), Computer Science (to design a model of a fabric, and how it can be simulated on a screen), Art and Design (to explore the ways a piece of textile can be used to communicate qualities), Ethnography (to observe and catalogue the differences between groups of people in how they interact with textiles), Educational Science (to create solutions to the problem that are easiest to learn and provide the least mental effort), Textile Science (to understand the connection between physical and structural qualities of fabric), E-commerce (to focus on textile value and trust perception given the limited presentation techniques), and finally, Hardware and Systems Development (to build a system of physical devices and software that could mimic the behaviour of various fabrics).

We decided to look at the problem from a Human Computer Interaction (HCI) perspective, which could be considered a combination of all the above approaches and methods, taking the most appropriate research tools from other branches of science. Each of the consecutive chapters starts with an extensive literature review, often branching out into the areas mentioned above to identify any methodology or contributions that could help us achieve our goal.

We looked at perception psychology to understand how visuals, movement and sound are processed. We also investigated motivation literature, to introduce elements of gamification to our studies to motivate our participants and hence gather good data.

Additionally we were inspired by manipulations often used in psychology, where participants at the time of taking part in the studies did not know exactly what we were measuring (otherwise they could have tried to purposefully perform well on a measured variable, and skew the results). Finally, literature from educational psychology helped to guide our approach in presenting and teaching the interfaces, as well as helping us to evaluate and optimise the cognitive load that users experienced.

Computer science literature guided most of our methods and experimental designs, as well as providing user-centred prototyping approach, where we built studies and prototypes in their simplest possible form first and then added new features in iterations. While building the hardware and software experimental apparatus (and recording rig that was created as a part of this thesis), we tried to find the simplest and most accessible solutions, often replacing hardware elements with software and expensive solutions with cheap alternatives.

The ethnographic toolkit was used in observing participant studies and whenever we had to analyse the differences between experts and non-experts handling fabrics. We looked at e-commerce literature to understand how decisions are made and what elements of fabric perception take part in making a purchasing decision. Finally, we looked at some design and art literature to have a better understanding of how closing the feedback loop (the ability to quickly get customers' opinions about one's designs) can change the design process and the final product.

Overall this thesis took on a holistic approach, often seen in HCI, to gain a deep insight into the researched area and ensure that the outcomes have a wide application.

The Complete Research Journey

We started this research project with gaining an understanding of the profile of the end user and what is important to them, of the population that textile simulators would be built for, what is important for them, and we also defined our success criteria. We decided that a textile simulator would be seen as successful if it could communicate to non-experts the same textile qualities as a real physical piece of fabric would. Further, to have an understanding of how non-experts extract qualities from fabrics, we asked non-expert participants to evaluate fabric qualities and we observed them as they touched physical fabrics. Thanks to the understanding of how people wanted to and could touch fabrics, we designed our experimental apparatus in such a way that it was instantly familiar and usable. Finally, we conducted our studies based on all the previous work and used the results of these studies to interactively improve our interface solution.

A User-Centred Approach Rather Than Technology-Centred Approach

Studies evaluating our touch-screen textile simulator interfaces aimed at recreating and understanding not only the researched interface, but also different aspects of use when non-experts interacted with fabrics. We ran pilots of all studies and collaborated with other researchers, thus relying on the users and collective human judgement rather than our own opinions. We believe that with this approach we created a blueprint for how research of this type should be conducted, and this also allowed us to contribute towards building an understanding of fabric simulator interfaces.

In this thesis we chose to investigate textile simulators that follow a holistic approach (look at wide fabric interaction experience), are perceptual and natural (build upon human experience of interacting with fabrics) and are accessible (are available and affordable to people who wish to interact with fabrics).

1.3 Research Questions

How To Evaluate Performance Of A Textile Simulator?

We needed to have a simple and functional method of evaluating whether one textile interface performs better than another. We needed to know how we can evaluate the quality of a textile interface. Given that a successful simulator is one that communicates textile qualities accurately and realistically (creates the same subjective ratings when a user interacts with the interface as when they interact with a physical fabric), what should be the qualities we aim for it to communicate? How should we measure subjective ratings of textiles, to capture the subjective opinions of textile non-experts?

How Can A Textile Simulator Recreate A Real Fabric Handling Experience?

We needed our textile simulator's interface to recreate an experience of handling physical fabrics. To create such an interface, we first had to fully understand that experience of handling physical fabrics. We needed to know what were the ways people evaluated physical fabrics and what actions people performed in the process. Did everyone evaluate fabrics the same way and what evaluation methods were most common? Could the most common ways to interact with a physical fabrics be used to create a digital solution mimicking the experience of physical fabric handling?

How Does Our Interface Compare To The Currently Existing Solutions In Terms Of Performance?

We aimed to design a textile simulator and investigate if it could mimic the physical handling experience and communicate subjective textile qualities. What would be the main principles and metaphors of this interface? What elements of the interface would make it more acceptable and usable for the users (e.g. interaction, visuals, sound)? How would the performance of this interface compare against other ways to present fabrics digitally?

How Accurate In Communicating Fabric Qualities Could The Textile Simulator Be?

Could the textile simulator interface communicate textile qualities accurately? What elements of the interface (e.g. interaction, visuals, sound) made it more accurate in communicating fabric qualities? Were some fabric qualities communicated more accurately than others and what were the differences in accuracy between different fabric types?

1.4 Scope

Fabrics Used For Making Clothes

In this thesis we were only concerned with fabrics that could be used for making garments and fabrics that non-experts had experience of handling. While there has been research reported that investigated very narrow sub-sections of textiles, such as car seat upholstery research described by Giboreau, Navarro, Faye, and Dumortier (2001), we decided to not limit our research to such narrow scope.

We investigated only fabrics before they were turned into garments (without stitches, buttons and garment elements), to limit the sources of noise and personal preference of participants.

Non-Experts Not Trained In Evaluating Fabrics

The textile interfaces that we investigated were aimed at non-experts with no formal knowledge of how fabrics could be investigated and evaluated in an expert context. We decided to make sure that all the tested prototypes and evaluation methods (rating scales and tasks) were understandable and relevant to non-experts. We recruited all of our participants from amongst non-experts to ensure that all of our data and findings were relevant for this group. All studies were conducted with participants' consent and according to the ethical regulations of Heriot-Watt University.

Interfaces For Off-The-Shelf Devices Available To Public

We only used publically available and inexpensive hardware and software components to create our platform for textile simulation. We did not consider force feedback, 3D simulations, Virtual Reality, Multi-point vibration and other experimental technologies to be within the scope of this thesis. The reasons for excluding these technologies were their cost, availability, and the lack of ease with which they could be programmed and adjusted.

We aimed for our textile simulator to work on Apple's iPhone and iPad touchscreen devices, because they had the state of art sensors we required and were available to the general public at the point in time when we started building our apparatus.

Chapter 2 – Textile Descriptive Words

Goal:
Combine expert and non-expert textile descriptive words into a set of 8 dimensions to be used as rating scales

Contribution:
A set of 8 dimensions that non-experts use to describe textile qualities. Each dimension is described with a representative term and an icon

Study 1:
Which expert words do non-experts Know?

Study 2:
What words non-experts Use in unconstraint speech when handling fabrics?

Study 3:
Group the most Known and Used words by meaning

Chapter 3 – On-Fabric Gestures

Goal:
Investigate on-fabric gestures that non-experts perform while they investigate textile qualities

Contribution:
A dictionary of on-fabric gestures, including their sub-types and modifiers

Study 4:
Observation of gestures that non-experts perform when asked to evaluate fabric qualities

Chapter 4 – iShoogle Textile Simulator

Goal:
Design a multi-gesture touch-screen fabric simulator iShoogle. Create a recording rig for recording video and sound content for iShoogle. Enable distribution of iShoogle content via the Internet

Development:
iShoogle Interface - Stop Motion Animations of fabric deformations are triggered by on-screen gestures corresponding to these deformations

Development:
Sound interactivity designed and added to iShoogle simulator. Playback attributes of sound respond to user's actions

Contribution:
iShoogle interface interprets user's on-screen gestures (inspired by on-fabric gestures) and plays stop-motion animations of corresponding fabric deformations. Pairing of gestures and deformations provides the effect of direct manipulation of video

Chapter 5 – Evaluating iShoogle Interface

Goal:
Evaluate the performance and acceptance of iShoogle's visual and audio elements

Contribution:
iShoogle is not slower and does not decrease performance when compared to an alternative slider interface

Contribution:
Interactive sound controlled by the gesture's type, speed and direction is considered more realistic and suitable to represent fabrics

Study 5:
Comparing iShoogle with an alternative interface in terms of performance and speed. Participants use various gestures or sliders to deform on-screen fabrics and identify hidden fabric imperfections

Study 6:
Comparison of two sound extensions of iShoogle: Interactive Sound (gesture-controlled playback) and Non-Interactive Sound (constant playback). In a pairwise comparison study participants decide which one is more "Realistic/Suitable"

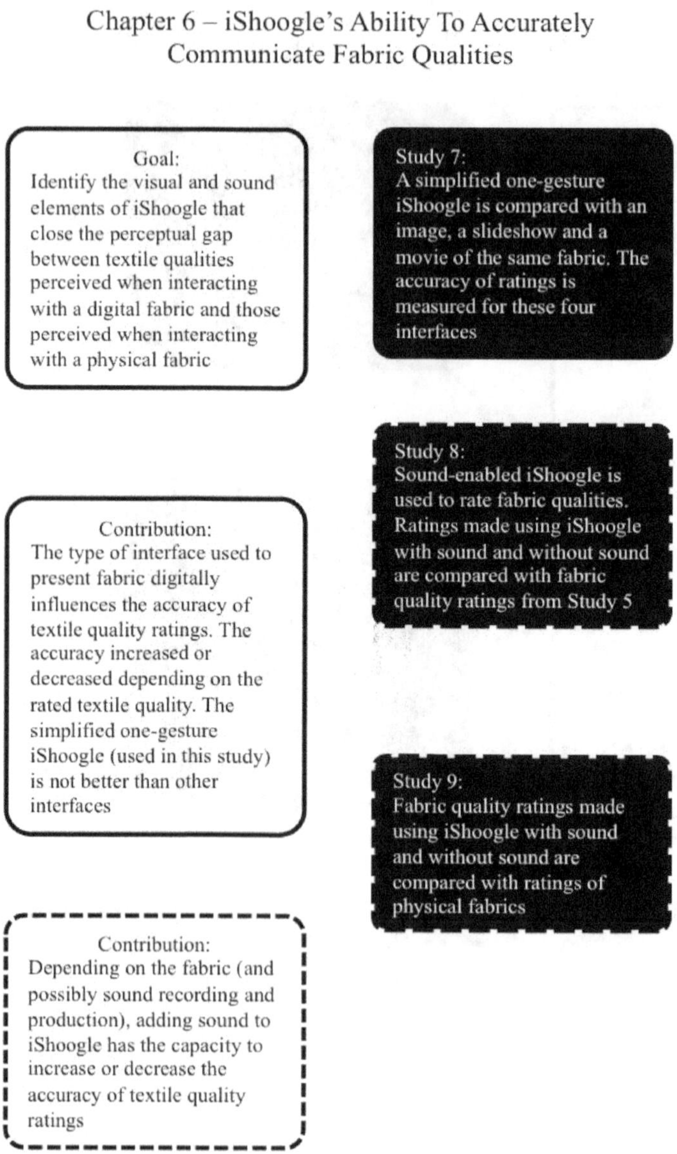

Chapter 6 – iShoogle's Ability To Accurately Communicate Fabric Qualities

Goal:
Identify the visual and sound elements of iShoogle that close the perceptual gap between textile qualities perceived when interacting with a digital fabric and those perceived when interacting with a physical fabric

Study 7:
A simplified one-gesture iShoogle is compared with an image, a slideshow and a movie of the same fabric. The accuracy of ratings is measured for these four interfaces

Study 8:
Sound-enabled iShoogle is used to rate fabric qualities. Ratings made using iShoogle with sound and without sound are compared with fabric quality ratings from Study 5

Contribution:
The type of interface used to present fabric digitally influences the accuracy of textile quality ratings. The accuracy increased or decreased depending on the rated textile quality. The simplified one-gesture iShoogle (used in this study) is not better than other interfaces

Study 9:
Fabric quality ratings made using iShoogle with sound and without sound are compared with ratings of physical fabrics

Contribution:
Depending on the fabric (and possibly sound recording and production), adding sound to iShoogle has the capacity to increase or decrease the accuracy of textile quality ratings

Figure 1 – Organisation of this thesis.

1.5 Thesis Outline

Research Described Within This Thesis

We represented the structure of this thesis (chapters, studies and main contributions) in a form of a graph in Figure 1.

Prior to designing textile interfaces, we needed an apparatus to evaluate their performance. (We followed the iterative Test-Driven development principle described by Janzen and Saiedian (2005), which dictates that a tool to measure success of a solution should be developed before that solution). The performance of an interface was measured by the difference between the fabric quality ratings of the simulated digitised fabric and the original swatch. Both measurements were derived from fabric qualities questionnaire administered in each condition. In Chapter 2 we show how we created that questionnaire for evaluating fabrics, by conducting a series of studies identifying and sorting words that non-experts use to describe fabrics.

To imitate the experience of handling a fabric within a textile simulator, we needed to understand why and how people interacted with physical fabrics. In Chapter 3 we report how we recorded videos of participants' hands as they evaluated fabric qualities and annotated these videos with our on-fabric hand gesture annotation scheme. The frequencies of on-fabric gestures informed the design of on-screen gestures for our touchscreen interfaces.

In Chapter 4 we have described the design of our textile simulator interface iShoogle. We have also described how video content for iShoogle should be recorded in high fidelity and low fidelity setup. We also outline possiblities of expanding iShoogle with sound and how sound samples should be recorded. In Chapter 5 we have evaluated the performance and acceptability of all the visual and sound elements of the iShoogle interface.

Finally in Chapter 6 we have assessed the ability of the iShoogle textile simulator to communicate textile qualities accurately. In a series of studies we explored the impact of different visual and sound adjustments to the iShoogle interface on its ability to accurately communicate fabric qualities.

Structure Of The Chapters

We decided against having a large unified literature review chapter at the beginning of this thesis in favour of a starting each chapter with a smaller and more targeted literature review section. We believe that this structure improves the readability and clarity of our thesis, since different chapters often tackled questions routed in different areas. Literature review section of one chapter was rarely relevant to other chapters.

When we begun research presented in this thesis we did not predetermine the complete path that this thesis would follow. Frequently the outcomes of a chapter would inspire the goals of the next chapter. We decided on our research journey, one step at a time, depending on where the data lead us. With each next step in our investigation we reassessed what literature area would be most appropriate to review next.

Because of this non-predetermined route that this thesis followed it would be confusing to the reader if the literature relevant to the whole thesis were presented as one large literature review chapter at the beginning of this thesis. Instead we decided to write a small literature review section at the beginning of each chapter.

Chapter 2 – Textile Descriptive Words

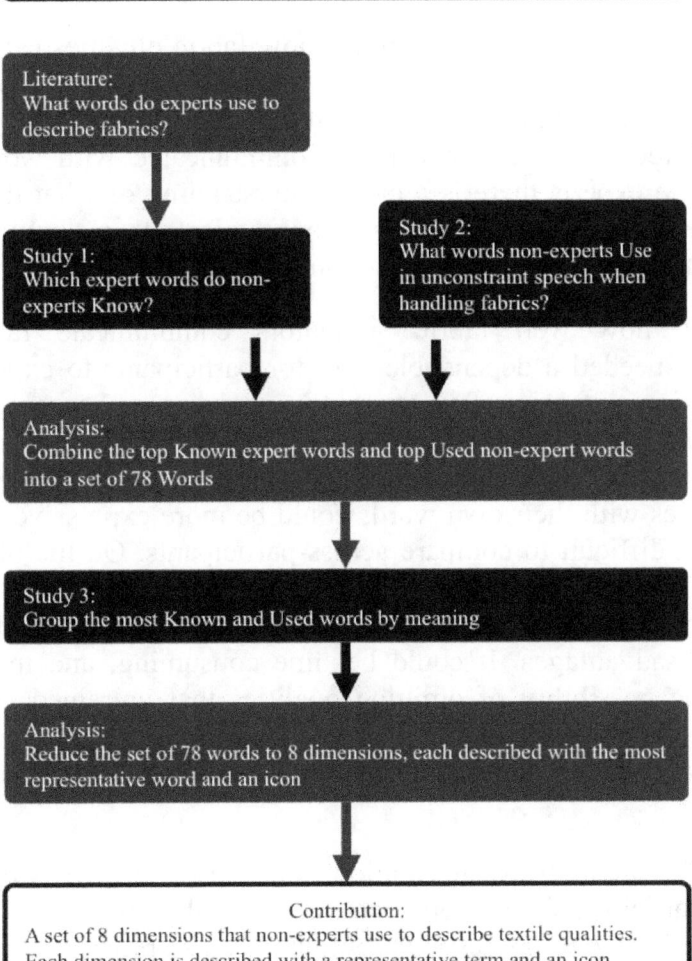

2. Words Describing Textile Qualities

2.1 Introduction

2.1.1 Context

The goal of this thesis was to establish how fabric qualities can be communicated through digital means and to create interfaces enabling such communication. In the research described here we only considered qualities that can be communicated with words. Among textile experts there is a clear understanding of what these qualities are and how to evaluate and communicate them, however this may not be the case among most non-expert consumers.

To evaluate how well fabric simulators communicate fabric qualities, we needed a dependable way for participants to express their perception of fabrics. Two straightforward approaches were to allow participants to use their own words, or teach participants an expert language of fabric qualities. Letting participants describe fabric qualities with their own words could be more expressive and accurate, but difficult to compare across participants. On the other hand, teaching participants an expert language could provide an easy way to compare across participants, but was hypothesised to also have disadvantages. It could be time consuming, and might introduce the possibility of omitting qualities that untrained non-expert participants pay attention to in everyday interaction with fabrics, as a result of failure to learn the complete set of expert words.

We opted for an in-between solution: we used a mix of expert words and participants' descriptions of fabrics in their own words to create a set of fabric qualities that could be used as rating scales in further studies. As a result of using this approach, participants' ratings were comparable with each other; rating scales did not have to be explained or taught; and rating scales also communicated the fabric qualities that non-expert people pay attention to when evaluating fabrics.

In this chapter we describe a set of studies where we identified expert and non-expert words describing textile qualities, combined them into a large set, and then reduced it into a smaller set of broader terms. The small set of terms was then used as a language of communication about fabric qualities among non-expert consumers to evaluate effectiveness of textile simulators.

2.1.2 Chapter Goals And Motivation For Goals

> GOAL 2.1 – Determine A Set Of Textile-Descriptive Words Understood, Used And Agreed Upon By Non-Experts.

In this chapter we investigated the words that non-experts used to describe textile qualities. Our goal was to create one large word set by combining words that experts and non-experts use to describe fabrics. This word set had to be usable by non-experts, who often have a common understanding of a word, in the context of textiles that emerged from everyday use of language and experience of handling fabrics. Additionally these everyday, non-expert meanings of words could vary from dictionary definitions (which use not fabric specific context), thus we could not use pre-existing general-purpose thesaurus data to identify words of similar meanings.

The criteria for finding suitable textile-descriptive words were as follows: words had to be *known* to non-experts, actively *used* by non-experts, and non-experts had to *agree* about the meaning of these words.

> GOAL 2.2 – Cluster The Large Number Of Textile-Descriptive Words (Goal 1) Into Groups Of Terms Synonymous In The Context Of Textiles.

Next step towards creating a common non-expert language for communicating textile qualities was to cluster the words identified in Goal 1 into groups of synonymous words. Ideally, each group of words would be represented by one term that described a top-level fabric quality. The purpose of such grouping was to create a manageable small set of terms for use in further studies.

We would consider such a grouping to be a success if it is *agreed* upon amongst a majority of participants.

> GOAL 2.3 – Determine A Small Set Of Textile Quality Scales To Be Used By Non-Experts In Evaluation Of Textile Simulators.

The primary goal of this chapter is to create a set of scales for evaluating textiles that could be used as an apparatus in the investigation of textile qualities. Each term will be represented by a word and an textile quality icon, so that it can be used as a rating scale in evaluation of fabrics by non-experts.

We would consider our set of rating scales a success if non-experts could *use* it to describe physical fabrics consistently.

2.1.3 Contributions And Acknowledgements

Unless otherwise specified, all intellectual input into this thesis comes from the author. The literature review of expert vocabulary was performed by Douglas Atkinson and is available in Appendix I; the study evaluating the familiarity of expert words and the on-site part of the word sorting study was performed with Thomas Methven and partially published by Methven et al. (2011). The word generation study was run in collaboration with the Digital Sensoria project. The collaborative work of all researchers who contributed to this research was described by P. M. Orzechowski et al. (2011).

2.2 Literature Review

2.2.1 Literature Review Introduction

The Scope Of The Literature Review

The scope of this chapter was the investigation of qualities perceived while handling fabrics and identifying words used by non-experts to describe those qualities. When people are touching a fabric they perceive a collection of attributes called 'a fabric hand'. The American Association of Textile Chemists and Colourists defined fabric hand as 'the tactile sensations or impressions which arise when fabrics are touched, squeezed, rubbed, or otherwise handled' and is further described by American Association of Textile Chemists and Colorists (1993) as 'those components, qualities, attributes, dimensions, properties, or impressions which make the sensation of touching one fabric different from that of touching another'.

In order to investigate qualities that constitute fabric hand, researchers analysed the way people described, compared, ranked, or rated fabrics according to researcher-defined qualities described by Brandt et al. (1998). Researchers in fabric perception agreed to use textile quality terms, usually labelled with a single English word, as the anchors of rating scales for evaluating fabrics. On the other hand when within-the-industry panels of expert textile handlers evaluated fabric qualities, there were differences in how non-experts would describe the same qualities as analysed by Soufflet, Calonnier, and Dacremont (2004).

Literature Review Criteria

To the best of the author's knowledge, there was no publicly available research that would provide the answers required to achieve our research goals. Research related to textile qualities was concentrated on expert evaluation of fabrics: either with panels of trained fabric handlers (experts) as described by Soufflet et al. (2004), or with hardware devices measuring a particular quality of a fabric as established by Kawabata and Niwa (1991). Recently, there were also attempts at comparing how these expert methods translate into consumer perception. As we investigated relevant publications, we focussed the search on the following topics:

- Differences between experts and non-experts in terms of fabric qualities they perceive and describe. We were interested in how the perception of fabric changes with increasing experience, especially in terms of the vocabulary that one can actively use to describe fabrics. We were mainly concerned with the applicability of these words as axes upon which fabrics can be rated by non-experts,
- Methods of handling fabrics that are applicable to non-expert observers. These involved investigations of the exact method of touching the sample, the size of the sample, and differences between touching the fabric with and without seeing it,
- Ways of grouping and clustering large sets of words into smaller, more manageable terms. These were necessary for reducing all the words that non-expert observers have

used into a smaller number of textile concepts that can be used for rating fabrics.

2.2.2 The Effect Of Pattern Construction On The Tactile Feeling Evaluated Through Sensory Analysis.

Sensory Panel – Experts Evaluating Fabric

Bensaid, Osselin, Schacher, and Adolphe (2006) described an alternative to machine evaluation of fabrics used in the industry: a panel of experts trained in evaluating fabric with their sense of touch. This paper discusses the differences between such a panel of experts, and non-experts, handling fabrics.

According to the authors, it became an industry standard to measure fabric qualities with the help of a 'sensory panel' – a group of expert fabric handlers trained in evaluating a set of specific textile attributes. During the evaluation process, each of the members of such a panel would describe an evaluated fabric without seeing it, just by its tactile qualities. Panel members rate the fabrics on 15 scales representing different qualities, and their results are analysed statistically. Each member of the sensory panel would be extensively trained and the consistency of their ratings is confirmed in between fabrics with the use of neutral samples. Environmental conditions (heat, moisture) are controlled for and panel members are retrained in between measurements by being exposed to fabrics that fall on the extremes of each rating scale. This methodology has been appropriated from the food industry and is considered a valid alternative to mechanical measurements.

According to Bensaid et al. (2006) humans perceived fabrics via feedback from many senses, considering information about touch, vision, sound, smell, temperature, vibration and resistance. While some of those perceptions could be measured with instruments, perceiving what experts call the fabric's hand was problematic. Fabric hand was defined in this paper as the quality of fabric or yarn assessed by the reaction obtained from the sense of touch.

In addition, when humans were assessing a fabric, they not only perceived its qualities, but also other attributes concerning hedonistic (e.g. pleasant), emotional (e.g. lovely), and cognitive (e.g. loud) sensations. In the work of a 'sensory panel' such perceptions (not directly connected with fabric qualities) were usually not measured, but they could be of importance when considering a customer's perception of a finished garment.

The study described by Bensaid et al. (2006) evaluated the effect that the pattern construction of the fabric (i.e. the way the fabric is woven) had on the tactile qualities as perceived by the sensory panel. The results showed that changing the structure leads to statistically significant differences in perception of most qualities (falling, thick, heavy, rigid, slippery, soft, granulous, pilous, grooved, responsive, crumple-like). These results suggested that fabrics with a different woven structure have different sensory qualities.

From the work of Bensaid et al. (2006) we used a method for extracting textile descriptive words from non-expert participants. Authors of this study introduced a handling procedure where evaluators sit at the table and touch fabrics while communicating perceived qualities by rating fabrics on scales described with words. Another useful element was the authors' distinction of perceived fabric attributes into quality descriptive (e.g. soft, hard, crisp) and non-quality descriptive (e.g. words describing feelings, temporary states or comparisons such as: wonderful, ripped or fur-like) sets.

2.2.3 Sensing The Fabric: To Simulate Sensation Through Sensory Evaluation And In Response To Standard Acceptable Properties Of Specific Materials When Viewed As A Digital Image.

Evaluating An Interface By Comparing It With A Physical Object

Dillon et al. (2001) analysed the process of evaluating textile qualities by handling fabrics, identifying the possible sources of bias and inaccuracy. The authors provided an exhaustive list of reasons why invalid results might be obtained, and they suggested solutions to those pitfalls.

The authors assessed a digital interface (a force feedback mouse) by comparing qualities perceived while handling a physical swatch, and the same swatch, represented digitally. They used a number of rating scales (from 1 to 15) of qualities found in the literature such as work of Civille and Dus (1990), and other qualities that they considered relevant.

The authors devised a method of handling physical fabrics that would afford the perception of similar qualities as using the force feedback mouse. With the physical swatches taped down to the table, participants touched the fabric with all five fingers of their right hand, and moved their hand in four cardinal directions. Physical on-fabric movement was designed to look and feel the same as operating the mouse.

Possible Pitfalls While Evaluating Fabrics

The authors identified the following issues that affected the evaluation process:

- light reflection can affect perceived roughness and graininess,
- blindfolded evaluation produces a stronger tactile feeling, but evaluation without a blindfold produces a better experience,
- colour of the fabrics appeared to have impact on quality ratings,
- a time break between different evaluations is required to avoid confusion and to prevent participants from remembering previous results,
- patterns (printed or woven) enhance the perception of texture,
- visual perception can distort a subjective property, especially when a participant has no experience with this fabric,
- different directions of movement can produce different perceptions of fabric (corduroy, velvet) which needs to be incorporated into the interface,
- some fabrics have different degrees of stretchiness in different directions.

From this paper we incorporated: the method of evaluating a digital interface by comparing the ratings of a physical and digital representation of the same fabric; the idea of arranging physical interactions with a swatch in a way that resembles the tested digital interaction; the exhaustive list of considerations, including light and breaks between ratings.

2.2.4 Factors Underlying Fabric Perception.

Moody, Morgan, Dillon, Baber, and Wing (2001) tackled two problems of interest to our research: how to design a study where non-expert participants describe important fabric qualities with their own words, and how to cluster such words into meaningful groups that can be used for describing fabrics.

In the study, participants were given 3 familiar fabrics at a time and asked to indicate the one that did not fit in with the other two. Once the odd fabric was selected, participants were asked to describe what made the fabric they had picked different from the others. For that purpose they were asked to use adjectives describing fabric qualities. This study was designed to generate words describing distinguishing fabric qualities.

When participants finished describing fabric triads, a panel of researchers sorted each participant's answers into word groups. These word groups were used in the second part of the study, during which the same participant indicated which fabrics could be suitably described by which word groups. Through this process, researchers acquired knowledge about the appropriateness of descriptive terms. Clusters from all participants were analysed using Principal Component Analysis. This method allows for reducing a large number of groupings into a small number of factors.

The second study described in this paper was run in a very similar manner. However, the word clusters were not created by the researchers, but by four participants during a brainstorming session. With this adjustment, the authors aimed to remove their personal bias and use the wisdom of the crowd to extract word groupings.

During their analysis the authors considered two main categories of descriptive words: the surface texture words (describing textile qualities) and the emotional/cognitive/mood words (describing feeling and reactions towards those qualities). The PCA clustering provided different results depending on whether the surface texture and emotional words were analysed separately or together. According to Moody et al. (2001), integrating those two categories would provide unified results in the context of fabric consumers, while separation between those two categories would provide better results in the context of objective fabric qualities.

From this paper we incorporated a number of methodological approaches. One was the idea of running a playful study in which the participants' task is to describe fabrics with their own words. We also used the separation of words into surface texture and emotional/cognitive/mood words. We decided to concentrate only on surface texture words, recognising that focusing on a single group would lead to more consistent results. In terms of a method for separating words into surface and emotional words, we combined two solutions used by Moody et al. (2001). To separate the word types we used brainstorming in a panel of four people (as in their second study), but these people were always the same and were always researchers (as in their first study).

2.2.5 Development Of An Interdisciplinary Method For The Study Of Fabric Perception.

The purpose of the in-depth analysis by Brandt et al. (1998) was to develop a new systematic approach to measure how non-expert consumers perceive fabrics in real world contexts. In most previous research, terms were generated a priori by the researchers to describe, compare, rank or rate six to ten fabrics. While the authors recognised using predefined words as an accepted method to describe fabric qualities, they aimed to base their own technique on familiarity and meaningfulness of terms used to describe fabrics, and suggest that this method needs to:

- be open ended to explore the issues of variability of textiles and consumers,
- be open to many solutions, rather than claim that one method fits all possible scenarios,
- balance the issues of scientific control and real world applicability,
- use a user-friendly terminology that draws on phrases used by the consumers themselves.

The following findings were relevant to our research:

The terms that participants used to describe fabrics depended on whether participants were blindfolded or not. If they could only feel the swatches, they used words like soft, stretchy, smooth, lightweight and stiff, but when they could also see the swatches they used words like soft, thick, smooth and silky. While some words were used in both conditions (e.g. Soft), others appeared more frequently in only one condition, often being specific to the modality (e.g. Stiff for blindfolded and Thick for non-blindfolded conditions). The authors suggested that restricting the way in which participants can interact with fabrics introduces the danger of acquiring results that are irrelevant in non-laboratory settings. They concluded that in researching behaviour and perception of people in a shopping environment, research methods emulating that environment should be used.

The authors also investigated whether fabrics changed their perceived qualities as they were being handled during the study and becoming worn out. Objective measurements with a hardware friction tester showed that at first new fabric changed their roughness because of handling, but once handled enough times, the roughness measurement stabilized. The authors advised to apply some initial handling onto the samples before running a study, so that they would not appear brand new anymore and the initial changes in roughness would have already occurred. Thanks to that process, the first and the last participants would be handling a fabric of the same objective roughness and it would be possible that other textile qualities also remained unchanged after the initial wear and tear.

Final notes suggested that the optimal size of the fabric swatch should be no larger than 15 x 25 cm to enable handling with one or two hands, but not obstruct the participant's movements or the researcher's view. Additionally, all participants should be asked to rinse their hands in the same way prior to the study, to control for hand softness and sensitivity.

2.2.6 A Comparison Between Industrial Experts' And Novices' Haptic Perceptual Organization: A Tool To Identify Descriptors Of The Handle Of Fabrics.

Soufflet et al. (2004) investigated the differences in how non-experts and experts perceive fabrics. In the several studies they performed, these two types of people were asked to group fabrics, and explain their decisions about grouping fabrics. The findings suggest that grouping data were independent of the expertise of participants, but experts were better at verbalising the reasons behind their choices. In other words, experts and non-experts perceive the same differentiating qualities in fabrics, but experts can describe them more accurately.

Analysis of words differentiating groups of fabric allowed the researchers to identify the axes along which participants were arranging fabrics. The Multidimensional scaling (MDS) analysis indicated that experts were rating fabrics using finer, more precisely defined scales than non-experts. For example while everyone used the dimensions of soft-harsh, thin-thick, supple-stiff, only experts used an additional axis based on the term 'nervous,' which was a finer version of one of the other scales. The findings of this study confirmed the theory by Solomon (1997) that experts and novices perceive the world the same way, and do not use different axes to describe it; however, the experts can break down their axes into finer, more descriptive sub-axes.

On the basis of this paper, we decided to only work with non-expert participants, but to make sure that we created a dictionary of textile descriptive words that they commonly understand and use.

2.2.7 Most Popular Words That Experts Use To Describe Fabric

Douglas Atkinson in (Private communication with Douglas Atkinson, January 2010 in Appendix I) assembled the most popular expert terms that describe fabric qualities.

Partially published in the collaborative work by P. M. Orzechowski et al. (2011), Douglas Atkinson reviewed literature on the topic of expert terms describing fabric qualities. He reviewed a number of publications written by textile handling experts, and searched for the most frequently used terms. These terms were often words not encountered in everyday language, possibly not known to non-experts. One of the reasons for this could be the fact that for experts, the words have very specific and defined meaning. Additionally, a significant number of the reviewed papers used terms translated from other languages, hence there are words which were difficult to translate into English. For example the word Nervous (French word Nerveux also translated as Jittery, Fluttering, Flyaway) described the tendency of fabric to come back to its initial state after being crunched up into a ball.

From the set of 114 words identified in the literature, we selected the most popular 69 words to be used as a baseline of expert word set. These words are popular within expert literature and are popularly used to describe textile qualities.

2.2.8 Literature Review Summary

Most of the goals of this literature review were achieved, either by finding the answers in the literature, or by identifying a design of a study that would answer those questions. We designed our studies following the literature described above and the main contributions were:

- We will concentrate on non-experts, since they are our target group and they do not to differ substantially from experts in terms of perceiving fabrics. Following the above research we will pay special attention to ensuring that they understand all the words used for describing textile qualities, because communicating perception appears to be the main difference between experts and non-experts,
- The expert word set provided a baseline of most popular words used in textile industry. These words are likely unknown to the non-experts and a study is required to evaluate which members of this set are known to non-experts,

- We would design a playful study that will collect words that non-experts actively use in everyday communication. Words should be gathered without discriminating those that communicate emotional responses or temporary qualities of fabrics,
- Separation of words describing fabric qualities from those that describe judgement or feelings should be done by a panel (to achieve consistency) of researchers (to achieve good quality of ratings),
- The best way to cluster words into groups and high-level terms would be to analyse a sufficient amount of data from word sorting performed by non-experts. The task needs to be well described and understood by participants and the process of grouping needs to be simple with an unobtrusive interface.

In the next part of this chapter we will describe the design of the study that enabled us to gather words that non-experts use to describe differences between fabrics. We will also describe the design of a sorting study that will enable us to cluster quality descriptive words into high-level terms.

2.3 Organisation Of This Chapter

Based on the lessons from the literature we ran three studies, the first Study 1 aimed to identify expert words known by non-experts, Study 2 aimed to reduce the word set and finally aimed at creating and expanding a word set, and finally Study 3 attempted to cluster the word set into a smaller set of concepts.

Words Used By Non-Expert Participants To Communicate Fabric Qualities

During the first set of studies, described later on in this chapter, we asked participants to evaluate the familiarity of words used by textile experts. Participants were given a deck of cards with expert words written on them, and asked to sort the cards into three piles: words that they used, words that they knew but did not use, and words that they did not know. From these sorting data we could evaluate the expert set, and remove the words that were not familiar to non-expert users, and hence would not be good words for ratings axes.

In order to explore the words that non-expert observers use to communicate fabrics, we designed a study where participants described fabrics with their own words in a game-like setup. During this study participants were handling 11 different fabrics each and were asked to say words that describe each fabric. Analysing all of the spoken words gave us insight into which words were familiar and frequently used, as well as which words participants agreed about. For example, it was possible to say how often a given fabric was described with a particular word (e.g. Soft), and hence we could assess whether that quality was present in the fabric. From that data we could easily say which fabric descriptive words were generally agreed upon, which in turn would make them good candidates for becoming anchors of the ratings axes.

The final element of creating a set of words was to combine the findings from the studies we ran. First, we considered all the popular words used in the word generation study, and excluded those that were not suitable for describing objective fabric qualities. For this purpose we used a method described by Bensaid et al. (2006), where a panel of four researchers evaluated each word according to clearly set criteria, and extracted unsuitable words (subjective, temporary, hedonic). The outcome of this part of the research was a set of textile descriptive words that were well known and used by non-expert observers.

Clustering Words Into High Level Textile Quality Terms

The next important stage described later on in this chapter was to combine all the descriptive words into a small group of terms that could be used as rating axes in testing interface prototypes. We decided to perform a word sorting study with the large set of words acquired from previous studies. We asked participants to cluster words of similar meaning and point to a word that was most representative in each cluster. After analysing the similarity information of words (that describe the frequency of them appearing together in one group), we could separate all the words into a small set of groups. In addition, based on the information about representativeness of each word, we were able to label each of those groups with a single most representative word. Because of this process we acquired a set of eight textile quality terms, each representing a set of words and described by a one-word label.

We ran Study 3 in three different environments: on-site (in a lab setting), in local libraries and on a crowd-sourcing platform. In the last one, we encountered the problem of online cheaters. It became clear that some participants took part in the study to receive the payment, but did not perform the sorting task with full honesty and in a meaningful way. We devised a set of heuristics to identify those cheaters and observed an increase in the quality of data when they were removed.

Connection To Other Studies In This Thesis

During the word discovery Study 2 where participants handled fabrics and described them with their own words during, we also captured the video footage of the participants' hands. Further on in this thesis we analysed the gestures that participants performed on the fabric as they tried to discover new fabric qualities. This analysis of gestures for clarity was called Study 4. We believe that it was necessary to combine two above mentioned studies, because we believed that gestures performed by participants with the purpose of discovering fabric qualities were also the gestures that a user could use to discover fabric qualities in a textile simulator.

2.4 Study 1 – Evaluating The Expert Word Set And Its Familiarity

2.4.1 Study Design

Texture Descriptive Words Used By Experts

Experts in the textile industry use a range of terms (e.g. Stretchy, Mossy) to refer to a very specific aspect of a fabric. However, these often have a wide and unclear meaning for non-experts. Non-experts could differ widely in their explanations of what expert words mean in the context of textiles. It follows from this that, asking non-experts to rate fabrics on expert scales would provide noisy data, due to a possible lack of common understanding of the expert terms.

We decided to evaluate to what extent expert terms are well known and familiar to non-experts. To evaluate this, we used the 69 most popular expert terms from the literature (Private communications with Douglas Atkinson from January 2010 quoted in Appendix I) that describe fabric qualities, and asked non-expert observers whether they looked familiar. Using these data, we were able to estimate which words were indeed known to non-expert observers.

At this point we had to evaluate how familiar non-expert users were with these expert words, and to identify the most popular and most frequently used words for our further research. The expert set evaluation study was run in collaboration with Tom Methven.

Study Design Of Refining The Expert Set

To evaluate which words from the initial set were relevant to non-expert users, we designed a card sorting exercise Study 1. During this study participants were asked if they knew and used the expert words we identified during the literature review. Each word was printed on an individual cardboard flash card. Each participant was given the complete set of 69 flash cards with all the expert words (see Table 1), and was asked to separate words into three stacks as seen in Figure 2:

- (used) words they **know and actively use** (in the context of textiles)
- (unused) words they **know but do not use** (in the context of textiles)
- (unknown) words they **do not know** (in the context of textiles)

Participants were instructed that the study was concerned with the meanings of words only in the context of textiles. Participants were not timed and were informed to take as much time as they required. Study was complete when participants had placed each flash card on one of the stacks.

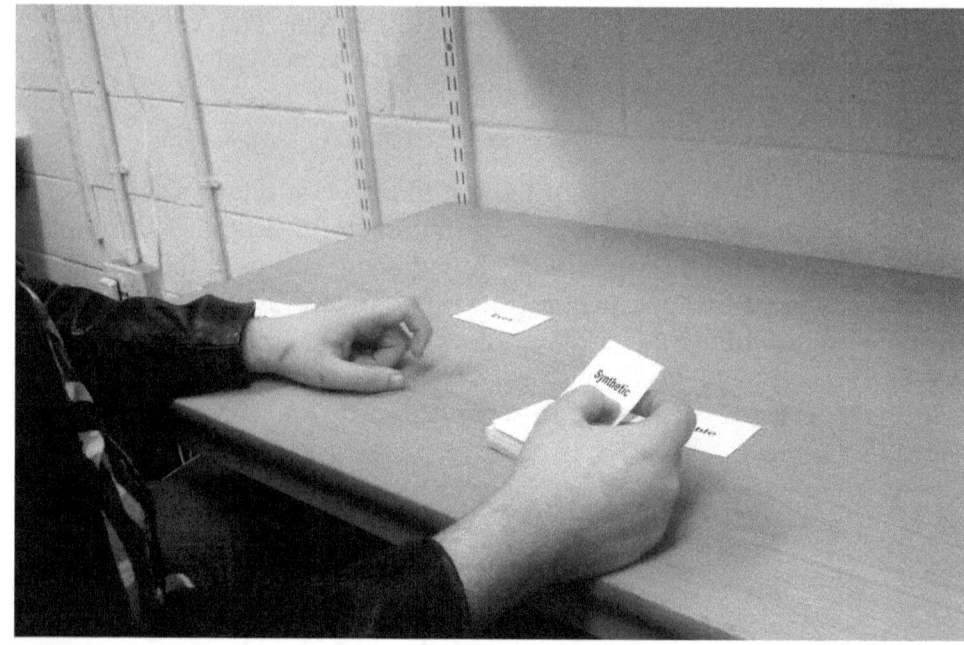

Figure 2 – Participant arranges cards with 69 professional words into three stacks, corresponding to words being Used, Unused or Unknown in relation to fabrics in Study 1.

Once the data were gathered, individual words were given a score: a positive score for used and negative score for unknown. The sum of points for each word constituted a cumulative **Know score** describing how well known a word is. We decided that all answers would be combined into the Know score using the following formula: +1pt (used), 0pt (unused) and -1pt (unknown).

2.4.2 Study Results Of Refining The Expert Set

Most participants took part in Study 1 right after Study 2. The reason why we considered such an arrangement of studies to be beneficial was that after 20 minutes of naming fabric with their own words, participants were familiar with their own active dictionary, which made recognizing words easier for participants and possibly closer to their actual knowledge of the textile-descriptive words.

A total of 30 participants took part in the study (13 male, average age 21), sorting all 69 expert words, and no data was missing. We calculated the Know score for each expert word with expected results between +30pt (everyone said they used that word) and -30pt (everyone said they did not know that word). The actual results for words ranged between +30pt and -22pt.

For readability purposes in our later analysis, the Know score was normalised to range between -100 pt. (unused/unknown) and +100 pt. (used/known) and it is that format that is shown in the Know column of Table 1 and Table 4.

Expert Word	Know Score	Expert Word	Know Score	Expert Word	Know Score
Smooth	100	Rigid	63	Supple	17
Soft	100	Hard	57	Crumpling	13
Thick	100	Synthetic	57	Crushable	7
Fluffy	97	Tight	57	Hot	7
Light	97	Clingy	53	Snagging	7
Stretchy	97	Non-Stretchy	53	Irregular	3
Rough	93	Spongy	53	Dry	0
Delicate	90	Flowing	50	Harsh	0
Bumpy	87	Slippery	50	Floating	-3
Elastic	87	Loose	47	Malleable	-3
Heavy	87	Springy	47	Pliable	-13
Thin	87	Crisp	43	Resilience	-13
Flexible	83	Grainy	43	Sheer	-13
Shiny	83	Sleek	40	Granulous	-20
Tough	83	Ribbed	37	Starchy	-27
Coarse	77	Solid	37	Full	-33
Fuzzy	73	Greasy	30	Downy	-37
Hairy	73	Dense	27	Sparse	-37
Stiff	73	Even	23	Mossy	-43
Firm	70	Limp	23	Falling	-53
Lumpy	70	Cold	17	Boardy	-60
Sticky	70	Matte	17	Raspy	-67
Fine	63	Raised	17	Relief	-73

Table 1 – All the expert words used in the word recognition task in Study 1 and their Know Scores.

2.4.3 Discussion And Conclusion

The study investigators decided to interpret any word with a score lower than zero to be on average unknown and unused by non-experts. As a result, 17 words scoring zero or less points were removed from the set, narrowing down the expert set to 52 words.

In the next step we needed to combine the 52 known and used expert words with the non-expert words used by participants during the fabric handling study.

2.5 Study 2 – Words Used By Non-Expert Participants To Communicate Fabric Qualities

2.5.1 Introduction And Objectives

Introduction

During the literature review, it became apparent that some of the expert words were neither known nor used by non-experts. Hence, to achieve our goal of creating a universal set of words, we decided to merge the vocabulary that experts and non-experts use. It appeared that non-experts used everyday words to communicate fabric qualities; therefore, our first step was to gather a set of words actively used and agreed upon.

In Study 2, participants were given a fabric swatch and asked to describe it with as many meaningful textile-related words as they could. The whole study was designed to extract as many communicative words as possible. Participants were led to believe that they were taking a part in a game, where the objective was to describe the handled fabric with the largest number words in a very limited amount of time. Although they were not given any additional payment for performing well, they appeared to be highly motivated and eager to achieve good scores.

The collection of all the distinct words that a given participant had used during the study was called their active dictionary and represented a dictionary of words that they knew and used.

2.5.2 Study Design - Creating A Word Set

Study Design

To extract a set of words that non-experts naturally use to communicate fabric qualities, we designed a simple fabric handling study. We asked participants to describe the fabrics with their own words and analysed those words. Elements of this study were designed in collaboration with members of Digital Sensoria project, and described by P. M. Orzechowski et al. (2011).

Task And Fabric Samples

During this study, participants were each given 11 swatches of different fabrics and were asked to evaluate fabric qualities by touching swatches with hands. We devised a game where participants were asked to name as many quality-descriptive words as possible within a limited time. We asked participants to say out loud words that they considered descriptive of the fabric they were handling. We encouraged participants to handle fabrics, so that the words they spoke communicated the qualities they perceived through touching and handling the fabrics.

We wanted participants to use words that described a wide spectrum of different qualities, so we gave each participant 11 random fabric samples from a set of 20 varied fabrics (as seen in Table 3). The samples were selected by a panel of four researchers (Pawel Orzechowski, Tom Methven, Douglas Atkinson and Bruna Petreca) from a larger set of about 100 fabrics. The criteria we used for the selection were: fabrics should be as different from each other as possible; fabrics should be familiar to non-experts; fabrics should be playful in texture and Hand to suit the playful design of the study. We aimed to provide the widest possible selection of wearable fabrics that would describe the space of wearable fabrics as well as possible given the limited amount of swatches we could use in the study. We ensured that the fabric swatches we used were large enough to be handled comfortably and to create a familiar shop-like experience (on average 30x30cm, with the largest being 40x40cm and the smallest being 20x23cm).

Room Setup And Video Recordings

Participants were seated individually in the experiment room, side-by-side with the experimenter. The experimenter's main task was to place fabric samples in front of the participant and take away the old ones. To enforce the gamification element and enhance motivation, the researcher sat nearby and wrote down in a notebook all the descriptive words spoken by the participant. In terms of the game mechanics the experimenter could be seen as a judge or a proxy of competitors. Participants were instructed that each swatch of fabric would be available to them for a maximum of 2 minutes, and they needed to say as many descriptive words about the swatch as they could within that time. Limiting the time was also aimed at engaging the participant in a competitive and challenging task.

All the spoken words were audio recorded, as well as written down by the experimenter sitting beside the participant. We also recorded participants with a video camera, and the sound from those recordings was used to clarify any ambiguous handwriting. There was no limit introduced on the type of words that the participants could say, and if they ran out of words for the currently handled fabric, they were allowed to request the next fabric. If some words were not clearly pronounced, the experiment asked for clarification before handing the next fabric to the participant.

Ethics

We have taken a number of steps to respect the privacy of our participants and comply with the ethical guidelines for conducing research. We only captured as much data and images as absolutely necessary for answering our research questions. The camera was positioned in a way that did not record participants' faces, but only their hands and voice. Participants were asked if they agreed to their hands and voice being recorded and were given the opportunity to refuse to be recorded without giving any reason.

Videos were stored on an external hard drive in a safe location and were deleted as soon as they were analysed and no longer necessary. We have taken those steps to ensure that the best practices for handling video recordings of participants were followed.

Participants

We ran this study with 12 students of the University College London (UCL) and 20 students of Heriot-Watt University (HW) in Edinburgh. 12 participants were male and the average age of all participants was 21 years old. The UCL students came from mixed courses, and HW students came from Computer Science and Psychology departments. Three students were excluded (two at UCL, one at HW), because they were non-native speakers and they struggled with English. This resulted in a final sample of 29.

2.5.3 Results - Words Used By Non-Expert Participants To Communicate Fabric Qualities

Most Words Were Unpopular

We analysed how many participants had each word in their active dictionary (knew and used it), not how many times each word was spoken. An average of 66 different words were actively used per person and the group of 29 participants together had 429 unique words in their active dictionaries. Most recorded words were unpopular, used by just one participant, but a small group of popular words was frequently known and used. Indeed, only the top 10 most popular words (2% of all words) were known and used by over a half of participants.

The least popular 75% of all the words spoken by the participants during the study were used by one person as seen on Figure 3. We removed from the word set any words used by only two people as we considered them to not be common enough to be used for communication between people.

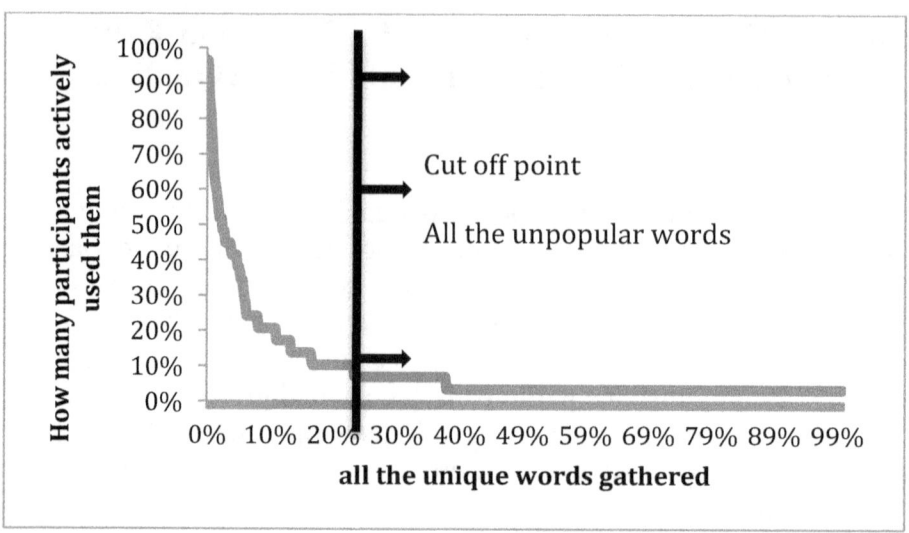

Figure 3 – Histogram of how many participants used each word. Words used by fewer than three participants were discarded.

2.5.4 Data Analysis

New Appropriate Words

The words that were used by only one or two participants listed in Appendix II were assumed to not be common or agreed upon and were removed from the word set as seen on Figure 3. To remove irrelevant and inappropriate words from the remaining set, we decided to discuss and vote for each word using a panel of four researchers, all of whose work was described by P. M. Orzechowski et al. (2011). The groups of words we excluded as not appropriate for communication were related to:

- hedonic (pleasure-related) (nice, horrible),
- temporary state (dirty, shaded),

- emotion (surprising, boring), ambiguous (girly, cool),
- opinion (cheap, useful)

While some words were unanimously accepted or rejected by the panel, we also accepted words accepted by two or more members of the four-person panel. The words discarded during this voting are presented in Table 2 and the words that were judged as acceptable for representing textile qualities are in Table 4.

Hedonic	Temporal	Emotion Opinion	Ambiguous	Other discarded
nice	patterned	cheap	colourful	strong
pleasant	old	odd	netted	see-through
comfortable	dirty	fake	protective	durable
rubbery	shaded	ugly	common	weak
attractive	dark	artificial	feminine	airy
horrible	frail	strange	animal	cold
pretty		different	bright	friction
appealing		expensive	girly	waterproof
dull		practical	hardwearing	bendy
fun		useful	meshy	fragile
good		varied	metallic	gentle
lovely		cuddly	plastic	opaque
ugh		easy	retro	foldable
		elegant	skin-like	matted
		fashionable	sparkly	tactile
		functional	wool	
		itchy		
		old-fashioned		
		sexy		
		interesting		
		boring		
		comforting		
		weird		
		cosy		

		random		
		surprising		
		interesting		
		boring		
		comforting		
		weird		
		cosy		
		random		
		surprising		

Table 2 – Words discarded as inappropriate and reasons to discard them.

The Word's Use Score - How Often Words Were Used

To accurately describe different attributes of each word, we calculated a number of scores. The first one was a **Use score**, a metric we devised describing how frequently a word is used. We calculated the use score of a word by finding the percentage of participants who used it at least once, hence have it in their active dictionary. For example, the word Warm has a Use score of 45% since it was used by 13 participants out of 29 (13/29 * 100%).

The Describe Score: The Frequency Of A Word Being Used For A Fabric

Communication requires a common, agreed understanding of words, and in order to investigate that, we analysed the co-occurrence of words and fabrics in our data. For example, we expected that if many participants described a rubbery fabric with a word Stretchy, then the word Stretchy described that fabric.

The measure of that co-occurrence, called a **Describe score** (one word – one fabric co-occurrence) was the percentage of participants who used a given word when talking about a given fabric. These scores can be found in Table 3 alongside the images and descriptions of fabrics. Example of how the Describe store was calculated is: Ripstop (fabric number 2) was shown to 15 participants and was described as Smooth by 14 of them – that means that Describe score of the Ripstop + Smooth pairing is 93% (14/15).

The Word's Agree Score – Consistency Of Use Across All Fabrics

The **Agree score** (or Agreement score) describes whether participants used a given word for the same purposes. The Agree score of a word is calculated by averaging that word's Describe scores across all fabrics described with it. For example, when fabrics considered Soft were considered Soft by everyone, then Soft would have a high Agree score. Since we wanted to find only the most communicative words, we were interested in only the most agreed upon words. We excluded fabrics that were paired with a word only occasionally (had very low Describe scores), to promote the most popular words. For calculating the Agree score we only used fabrics with Describe scores higher than 0.1.

For example, the word Hard had been used to describe 7 fabrics, with fabric numbers 1, 9, 20, 3, 7, 8, 18, each of these fabrics having a respective Describe score of 0.50, 0.32, 0.21, 0.10, 0.07, 0.07, 0.05 for the word Hard. This data can be interpreted as follows: fabric 1 was described as Hard by 50% of participants, fabric 9 by 32% participants, fabric 20 by 21% participants, etc. In this example, a calculated Agree score for the word Hard is 0.35 (because an average of 0.50, 0.34 and 0.21 is 0.35). Note that we only included the first three fabrics, because they had Describe scores over 0.1. In this example we would say that Hard had an Agree score of 35%.

Swatch ID, Picture and Description	Agree Score	
1 Stiff hard piece of white plastic mesh	hard	0.50
	rigid	0.36
	rough	0.36
	thick	0.36
	smooth	0.29
	tough	0.29
	bendable	0.14
	plain	0.14
	shiny	0.14
	soft	0.14
	stiff	0.14
	strong	0.14
	sturdy	0.14
2 apron – brown ripstop	smooth	0.93
	soft	0.53
	silky	0.33
	light	0.27
	strong	0.27
	synthetic	0.20
	thin	0.20
	artificial	0.13
	cold	0.13
	grainy	0.13
	patterned	0.13
	plasticky	0.13
	shiny	0.13
3	rough	0.62
	see-through	0.24
	crunchy	0.19

	light	0.19
	nice	0.19
	pleasant	0.19
	scratchy	0.19
	soft	0.19
	coarse	0.14
	flexible	0.14
	thin	0.14
	weak	0.14
tutu - black net	airy	0.10
	brittle	0.10
	comfortable	0.10
	friction	0.10
	hard	0.10
	loose	0.10
	meshy	0.10
	netted	0.10
	strong	0.10
	tough	0.10
4	smooth	0.65
	plasticky	0.29
	sticky	
		0.29
	flexible	0.24
		0.24
	soft	
	rubbery	0.18
	see-through	0.18
	thin	0.18
transparent foil	cool	0.12
	elastic	0.12
	nice	0.12

	pleasant	0.12
	protective	0.12
	shiny	0.12
	strong	0.12
	tough	0.12
	transparent	0.12
	waterproof	0.12
5. squares sofa - brown, dark blue with patterns	smooth	0.44
	rough	0.38
	soft	0.38
	textured	0.31
	thick	0.31
	bumpy	0.19
	stretchy	0.19
	strong	0.19
	varied	0.19
	velvety	0.19
	expensive	0.13
	fluffy	0.13
	pleasant	0.13
6. waves, black flower - warm felt with pieces of the same fabric sewn on	soft	0.50
	rough	0.33
	warm	0.33
	interesting	0.25
	smooth	0.25
	bumpy	0.17
	coarse	0.17
	different	0.17
	flexible	0.17
	flowing	0.17
	layered	0.17
	nice	0.17

	patterned	0.17
	strong	0.17
	stylish	0.17
	thick	0.17
7 scarf golden glitter - net like brown stringy scarf	soft	0.50
	light	0.31
	rough	0.25
	thin	0.25
	stretchy	0.19
	stringy	0.19
	airy	0.13
	flexible	0.13
	smooth	0.13
	sparkly	0.13
	weak	0.13
	weird	0.13
8 leather squares - fake leather fabric	rough	0.35
	smooth	0.35
	shiny	0.24
	soft	0.24
	sticky	0.24
	fake	0.18
	flexible	0.18
	appealing	0.12
	bumpy	0.12
	cheap	0.12
	durable	0.12
	expensive	0.12
	rubbery	0.12
	stretchy	0.12
	strong	0.12
	stylish	0.12
	textured	0.12

		thin	0.12
		tough	0.12
		ugly	0.12
9		rough	0.68
		hard	0.32
		coarse	0.26
		thick	0.26
		soft	0.21
		strong	0.21
		durable	0.16
		rigid	0.16
		tough	0.16
		ugh	0.16
		boring	0.11
		cheap	0.11
		dirty	0.11
		insulating	0.11
		lumpy	0.11
		old	0.11
		stiff	0.11
		warm	0.11
carpet - crème brown thick carpet		woven	0.11
10		rough	0.50
		bumpy	0.33
		stretchy	0.33
		light	0.28
		flexible	0.22
		soft	0.22
		nice	0.17
		cold	0.11
		colourful	0.11
		lumpy	0.11

stripy textured - orange white and blue striped thin fabric with ironed pattern	rigid	0.11
	smooth	0.11
	textured	0.11
	thin	0.11
11 spider web white thin fabric - layered thin white threads	rough	0.29
	smooth	0.29
	delicate	0.24
	hairy	0.24
	soft	0.18
	strong	0.18
	durable	0.12
	fine	0.12
	light	0.12
	see-through	0.12
	springy	0.12
	strange	0.12
	thin	0.12
	tough	0.12
	weird	0.12
12 blue fur - thick blue synthetic fur-like fabric	soft	0.69
	furry	0.50
	thick	0.44
	fluffy	0.31
	strong	0.31
	warm	0.31
	rough	0.19
	smooth	0.19
	animal	0.13
	hairy	0.13
	pleasant	0.13
	stringy	0.13
13	shiny	0.53

silver fish scale - sports clothes performance fabric, silver, reflective	rough	0.47
	soft	0.47
	smooth	0.29
	flexible	0.24
	reflective	0.18
	strong	0.18
	thin	0.18
	cool	0.12
	light	0.12
	nice	0.12
	patterned	0.12
	silky	0.12
	thick	0.12
	tough	0.12
14 white silky soft thin - very thin and flowing transparent-ish fabric	soft	0.72
	light	0.56
	silky	0.33
	delicate	0.28
	see-through	0.28
	smooth	0.28
	rough	0.22
	flexible	0.17
	floaty	0.17
	thin	0.17
	transparent	0.17
	airy	0.11
	elegant	0.11
	gentle	0.11
	gritty	0.11
	nice	0.11
	stretchy	0.11
	weak	0.11

15 ![silver leggings image] silver leggings stretchy - disco reflective stretchy fabric	stretchy	0.75
	shiny	0.63
	smooth	0.63
	soft	0.31
	rough	0.25
	rubbery	0.25
	elastic	0.19
	flexible	0.19
	sticky	0.19
	artificial	0.13
	grainy	0.13
	light	0.13
	reflective	0.13
	springy	0.13
	strong	0.13
	synthetic	0.13
	thin	0.13
	tough	0.13
16 ![brown sofa image] brown sofa covering - dull uniformly brown medium thick	rough	0.54
	bumpy	0.31
	coarse	0.23
	soft	0.23
	warm	0.23
	dull	0.15
	durable	0.15
	grainy	0.15
	natural	0.15
	old	0.15
	thick	0.15
	tough	0.15
17	soft	0.47
	rough	0.27

IKEA table cover - white ribbed fabric	strong	0.27
	textured	0.27
	thick	0.27
	durable	0.20
	smooth	0.20
	bumpy	0.13
	comfortable	0.13
	natural	0.13
	nice	0.13
	ribbed	0.13
	rigid	0.13
	tough	0.13
	uneven	0.13
18 pink scarf - cashmere thin delicate scarf	soft	0.69
	stretchy	0.44
	warm	0.31
	nice	0.25
	delicate	0.19
	feminine	0.19
	smooth	0.19
	woolly	0.19
	girly	0.13
	light	0.13
	synthetic	0.13
19	strong	0.29
	tough	0.29
	hard	0.21
	rough	0.21
	soft	0.21
	coarse	0.14
	durable	0.14
	grainy	0.14

	heavy	0.14
	robust	0.14
	smooth	0.14
jeans - slightly stretchy blue jeans		

Table 3 – Fabrics used in studies and the agree scores of words used to describe them.

2.5.5 Discussion

The goal of this part of the thesis was to create a set of fabric descriptive words used by non-experts. The results suggested that the majority of used words were unique to individuals who used them and there were also words that were not agreed upon. We analysed the words mentioned by participants in this study to identify the most suitable word set. In the process of identifying words, we applied the following heuristics:

- We removed words used by fewer than two participants
- We removed words considered irrelevant or expressing emotion and judgement. A panel of four researchers voted on and discussed the words before excluding them
- From the remaining set we chose the words with the highest Use and Agree scores, which means that they were popular among participants and often appeared to describe the same quality in fabrics.

2.5.6 Conclusion - The Final Word Set Of Accepted Words

As a result of above study we accepted 29 non-expert words into the final word set, as seen in the right-most section of Table 4. Interestingly, 5 of these 29 accepted words were actively used by participants even through participants said they did not use them in Study 1 as described in Section 2.6.1.

From all the 429 words mentioned by non-expert participants, we used the above described method to narrow down our selection to 29 words which were accepted for being suitable, most popular and most agreed upon.

2.6 Combining Non-Expert And Expert Word Sets

2.6.1 Combining New And Old Words

Combining Two Word Sets

The goal of the first part of this chapter was to create a set fabric descriptive words that are accessible to non-experts. We decided to create such a set of words by combining the non-expert and expert words into one group that we could use for our further research. In this final set we would use only the most popular and agreed upon non-expert words and the most well-known expert words.

	KNOW	USE	AGREE
	Word is recognised as known and used in recognition study 1	Word is used by participants in fabric description study 2 (% people)	Agreement to use this word to describe fabrics (% agreement)
ACCEPTED EXPERT WORDS			
54 expert words that were known and used by non-expert participants.			
word	know	use	agree
Smooth	100	83	30
Soft	100	97	39
Thick	100	59	26
Fluffy	97	38	22
Light	97	66	26
Stretchy	97	72	30
Rough	93	86	35
Delicate	90	34	23
Bumpy	87	45	21
Elastic	87	17	15
Heavy	87	21	14
Thin	87	52	16
Flexible	83	41	19
Shiny	83	62	27
Tough	83	48	16
Coarse	77	28	19
Fuzzy	73	7	0
Hairy	73	24	18
Stiff	73	21	12
Firm	70	24	0
Lumpy	70	14	11

Sticky	70	14	24
Fine	63	45	12
Rigid	63	14	19
Hard	57	55	34
Synthetic	57	24	14
Tight	57	10	0
Clingy	53	0	0
Non-Stretchy	53	72	30
Spongy	53	0	0
Flowing	50	10	17
Slippery	50	10	0
Loose	47	10	0
Springy	47	10	12
Crisp	43	3	0
Grainy	43	3	14
Sleek	40	0	0
Ribbed	37	10	13
Solid	37	10	0
Greasy	30	0	6
Dense	27	3	7
Even	23	3	6
Limp	23	0	6
Cold	17	17	9
Matte	17	7	6
Raised	17	0	6
Supple	17	0	6
Crumpling	13	0	7
Crushable	7	0	7
Hot	7	0	6
Snagging	7	0	6
Irregular	3	0	6
Dry	0	7	7

| Harsh | 0 | 10 | 6 |

DISCARDED EXPERT WORDS

15 expert words that were neither known nor used by non-expert

word	know	use	agree
Floating*	-3	0	0
Malleable*	-3	20	11
Pliable	-13	10	0
Resilience	-13	0	0
Sheer	-13	0	0
Granulous	-20	0	14
Starchy	-27	0	0
Full	-33	0	0
Downy	-37	0	0
Sparse	-37	0	13
Mossy	-43	0	0
Falling	-53	0	18
Boardy	-60	0	0
Raspy	-67	0	0
Relief	-73	0	0

ACCEPTED NON-EXPERT WORDS

29 non-expert words used by non-expert participants in the word discovery study.

word	-**	use	agree
Warm	-	45	26
Stringy	-	21	16
Floating	-	14	17
Creasable	-	7	0
Crinkly	-	7	11
Glossy	-	7	0
Grooved	-	7	0
Matte	-	7	11

Ridged	-	7	0
Textured	-	48	20
Furry	-	38	50
Scratchy	-	24	19
Crunchy	-	21	19
Malleable	-	21	11
Natural	-	21	14
Cool	-	17	12
Even	-	7	0
Plain	-	17	13
Gritty	-	10	11
Harsh	-	10	0
Pliable	-	10	0
Sturdy	-	10	13
Bendable	-	7	14
Breezy	-	7	0
Brittle	-	7	0
Dry	-	7	0
Noisy	-	7	0
Sandy	-	7	0
Tangly	-	7	0

*Floating and Malleable were later re-added as a result of non-expert

Table 4 – Know, Use and Agree scores of words.

Combined Word Set Of 78 Words

The two studies described earlier led to the creation of a set of words that were used and known by non-experts. We combined two sources of words described above:

- from the expert set of 69 words, we accepted the 54 (including 2 re-added) words that were self-reported to be the most used and known,

- from all the 429 words commonly spoken by non-expert participants, we accepted the 29 (24 new ones) words that were suitable, most popular, agreed upon, and not present in the expert set.

Interestingly, two words that were discarded as unknown from the expert set were also identified as being actively used during the word discovery study. In other words, these terms have met criteria to be removed in the recognition study and the criteria to be added in word discovery study. We gave the word discovery study precedence, because we considered active dictionaries (words used while handling fabric) to be more important than passive dictionaries (words recognised while not handling a fabric).

The final word set consisted of 78 words which are detailed in Table 4.

Heuristic For Choosing The Most Appropriate Expert Words: Know Score Or Use Score

We aimed to create a set of words that were in non-experts' active dictionary (words that they used in everyday life to describe fabrics). We had two possible criteria that we could use for selecting the most appropriate expert words: the Know score, acquired during Study 1 and the Use score, acquired for all of the words in Study 2.

We considered using the Know scores to decide which expert words would be accepted to the final word set, since we only wanted to accept words known and understood by non-experts. Interestingly, those expert words that had high Know scores, often also had high Use scores. A positive correlation between Know scores and Use scores amongst non-expert words suggests that even though we used Know scores as our acceptance condition, a similar set of words could have been selected if we used a Use score.

The analysis described below verified the positive correlation between Know and Use scores. Such a positive correlation would strengthen the argument for using a high Know score as a criterion for selecting the most appropriate words for the final word set.

Correlation Between Know Score And Use Scores

We expected that if a word was actively used while describing fabrics, it would also be identified as a 'known and used' word while not handling fabric. This effect would manifest itself as a similarity between Use score (whether participants actively used a word) and the Know score (whether participants recognised a word in a card sorting study). It would demonstrate consistency and would increase validity of both measures.

Indeed, there was a significant positive correlation of 0.71 ($p<.001$) between Use and Know scores of all expert words, meaning that the words in active dictionaries of participants were on average the same words that scored high in the recognition task. This indicates that there is a connection between recognizing a word and using it actively, hence it was a valid approach to combine expert and non-expert word sets into one.

In Figure 4 below we present the most popular expert words together with their Know and Use scores. This graph visualizes the tendency of frequently used words to also be known, in line with the highly positive correlation of the words' Know and Use scores. Additionally the occasional differences between Use and Know scores indicate that some of the expert words were not used even when they were known. We also annotated the Agree scores onto the Figure 4. However because of the threshold we selected for

Agree scores, the Agree score is often missing for those expert words that were used only by a small number of participants (see Table 4).

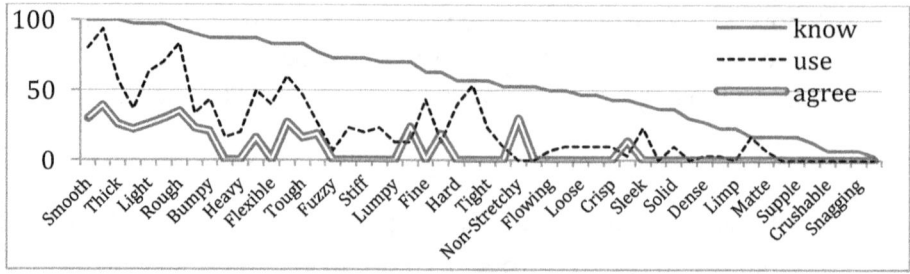

Figure 4 – Comparison of Know, Use and Agree scores of expert words, ordered by the Know score.

For completeness we listed the top 100 words used by the participants with their Use and Agree Scores on graphs Figure 5 and Figure 6.

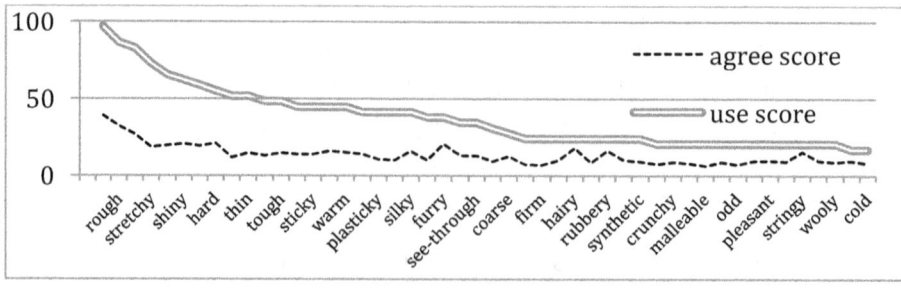

Figure 5 – Agree and Use scores of all spoken (expert and non-expert) words. Words with top 50 Use scores.

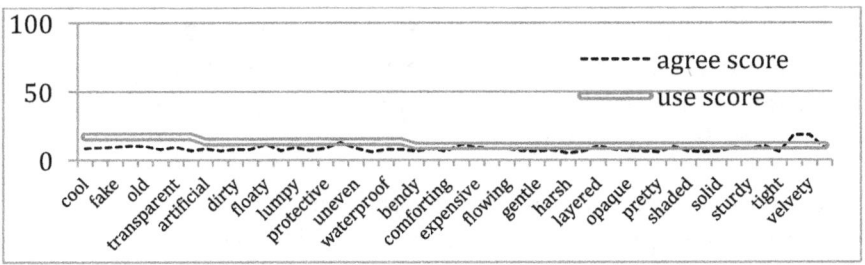

Figure 6 – Agree and Use scores of all spoken (expert and non-expert) words. Words with 51st to 100th of highest Use scores.

2.7 Study 3 – Clustering The Final Word Set

2.7.1 Grouping Task Introduction

Why We Needed To Cluster Data

At this stage, we had created our new improved word set of 78 words that could be used for describing fabrics. In further research we planned to use those words as rating scales for evaluating fabric interfaces, but the word set was too large. It would be impractical to rate fabrics on 78 scales (one for each word), especially since many words were possibly very closely related by meaning.

We planned to use the textile descriptive words as labels on rating scales and we considered the set of 78 rating scales to be too large. Such a large questionnaire with 78 items would be impractical for several reasons. Firstly, participants would take a long time to rate a fabric on each of these scales; they would become fatigued and the quality of the data would suffer. Secondly, since we planned to conduct some of our studies entirely on mobile devices, it would be unusable to fit that many rating scales on a tablet screen at once, and we wanted to avoid complex multi page questionnaires. Finally, from a statistical point of view, we wanted to perform a small number of comparisons to avoid chance findings, especially given that we considered some of the 78 words to be synonymous, hence likely to produce similar ratings.

We expected to see patterns of interdependency between some of the 78 textile descriptive words, because of the similarities in meaning between some of them. Reducing the number of terms to only those that are not synonymous could untangle relationships between rating scales that would otherwise be parallel in meaning. In other words, if we could bundle closely connected scales without losing textile-descriptive data, we could describe the rating space of textile qualities in a more structured, simpler way. As a simplified example, whenever words such as Soft and Rough were rarely used together to describe the same fabrics, it did not indicate that they were opposites, but rather that they belonged to two separate dimensions in a rating space of textile qualities.

This process could be understood as looking at the textile rating scales from a more distant zoomed out perspective, or with a lower granularity that would enable the perceiving of higher-level patterns. With fewer rating scales, which are non-overlapping and distinct in their meanings, the textile qualities rating space would be simpler to describe. When the rating space of textile qualities is mapped with i.e. 10 separate scales, rather than around 80 interconnected scales, that space could be explored easier. In the context of our research, it would be advantageous to notice patterns in ratings for a particular fabric or of a particular quality.

For the above reasons we decided to limit the number of rating scales by identifying and combining groups of synonymous textile descriptive words into groups. Each group of synonymous words would be simplified to one scale and the group's most representative member would be used as a label of that scale. An overview of this concept and an example bundling of words is described on Figure 7.

It is worth mentioning that we did not use Multidimensional Scaling (MDS) method to achieve this goal, but rather we combined a similarity matrix of users' word grouping with participants' perceived representativeness of words. We analysed the dendrogram representation the similarity data to divide the textile descriptive words into a manageable set of around 10 groups. In each group, the word that was most frequently indicated as representative was used as a label representing scale identified by the words in that group.

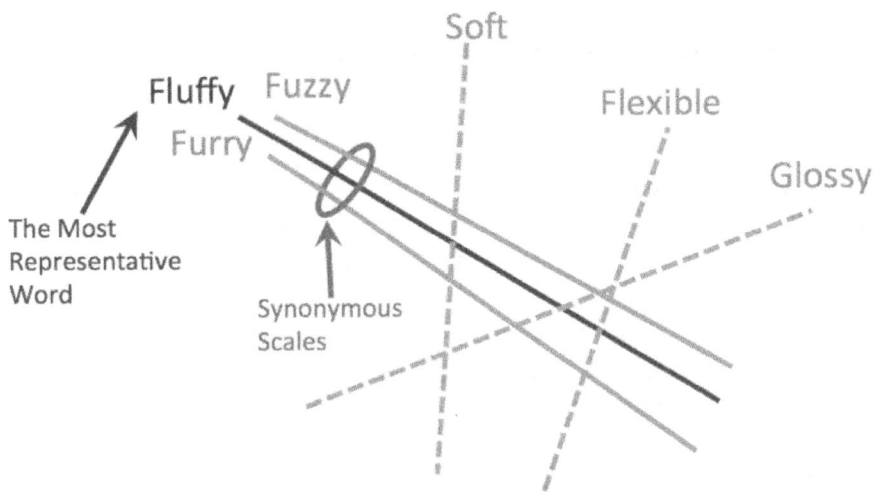

Figure 7 – Conceptual diagram of textile qualities rating space. This graph demonstrates a method of combining a number of synonymous scales describing textile qualities into one scale for simplicity. Above graph does not represent real data, but rather a concept of reducing number of dimensions.

Another solution would be to exactly define each word and train users in the usage of these words, but it would be time consuming and would make the set less relevant for non-experts who were not our participants (i.e. fabric consumers). Instead, the solution we chose was to meaningfully cluster words into a smaller number of groups and refer to each group with a meaningful term and label.

At this stage we needed a method to group together similar words (e.g. Ridged, Textured, Ribbed, Grooved) and to find a single group member that could be a meaningful umbrella term for all of them (e.g. Textured). For simplicity each word group would be labelled by the most representative of the words from that group.

2.7.2 Word Grouping Task - Study Design

Initial Design And Sources Of Participants

To remove our own bias from this grouping process, we decided to use crowd-sourcing techniques and to extrapolate knowledge from a large number of non-expert observers. During this study we asked participants to cluster words into groups of similar meaning and highlight the most representative word in each group. The word set they were asked to cluster was the set of 78 fabric-descriptive words derived during previous studies. Participants were always told to create as many or as few groups as they desired. We also asked participants to not leave any words on their own, without a group, but also to not make groups of 'left over' words that are odd and not well suited to any other groups. The reason for that was that the similarity data would be harder to analyse if some words would frequently be left ungrouped (hence the requirement for no single words) and if words were grouped with other heuristics than their similarity (hence the requirement for no groups of words that were connected by no easy and obvious similarity to other words).

We ran a large sorting study in a variety of locations, both online and offline. We recruited three groups of participants:

- 23 students in the lab, using paper flashcards for sorting (run by Thomas Methven),
- 41 local people recruited via Edinburgh libraries, using an online sorting interface,
- 94 users of the crowd-sourcing platform mTurk (mturk.com), using an online sorting interface.

Possible similarities and differences between those groups are discussed below, as we expected each recruitment method to have its own advantages and weaknesses. We specifically anticipated the challenging task of identifying 'cheaters' - people who completed the study without much care and just for the reward. It was important to identify and exclude those participants, because the data gathered from such dishonest participants was primarily noise.

On-Site Study Design

On-site participants were given a stack of 78 flashcards with words printed on them and were asked to sort those words onto clusters on the table in front of them as seen on Figure 8. They were instructed to group words by their meaning in relation to fabrics, to create as many or as few groups as they wanted, and to not leave ungrouped words. At the end they were given small paper tokens to place on the most representative word in each group.

Participants sat individually at a table large enough for them to lay out and manipulate all cards as seen in Figure 8. Some participants arranged flashcards into stacks, whilst others laid them out side by side into groups. After the participants were done, their results were encoded and the deck of flash cards was shuffled and reused for the next participant. To avoid making mistakes in encoding of results we photographed the table after the task was complete in such a way that all the words on cards were visible. Photographs were encoded and double checked by two researchers afterwards.

Figure 8 – Flashcards with words clustered into groups by a participant in a Lab setting in Study 3. Image below shows which words participant chose as most representative for each group.

Online Study Design

Online participants used a custom-made web browser sorting application. Inside the application, words were displayed on the screen, and participants grouped them by dragging and dropping words onto each other. Single words were displayed in grey, but once clustered together, groups of words were surrounded by a rectangle and all changed to a random colour as seen in Figure 9 and Figure 10.

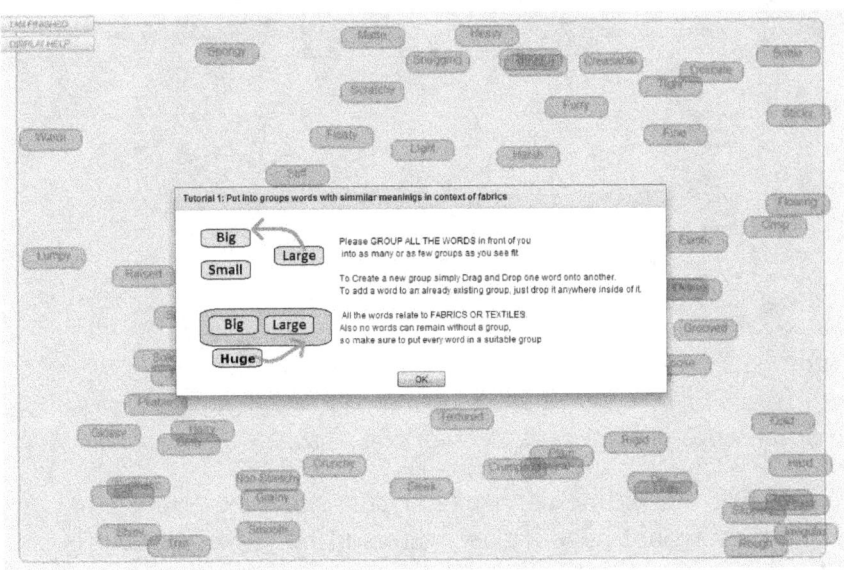

Figure 9 – Online word sorting interface – Setup. Participants were introduced to the sorting task with two simple examples (not related to fabrics).

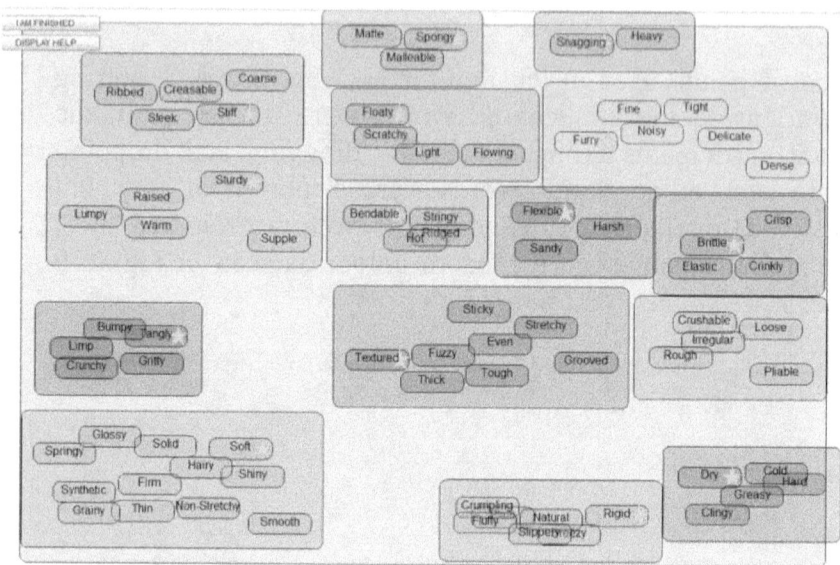

Figure 10 – Online word sorting interface – Result. Once participants joined all words into groups (by drag-and-dropping them onto each other), they were asked to star the most representative word within each group. Image for interface demonstration only (not a real user's sorting data).

We aimed to give our online users exactly the same experience and freedom that they would have if they were sorting paper flashcards. To enable that, our interface made it possible to join groups together, and to move words between groups. Once users indicated that their sorting was completed, they were asked to highlight the single most representative word in each group as seen in Figure 10. Participants were not allowed to leave any words on their own, ungrouped. When the task was finished, the application submitted the sorting data and time taken to complete the task to the server. Once this submission was confirmed, participants were given a unique reward code, which they could then exchange for the reward as described in Table 5.

2.7.3 Data Analysis – Similarity Data Representation

Data Analysis – Similarity Data

A total of 158 Participants took part in this study: 23 in the Lab setting, 41 in the Library setting and 94 via the Amazon mTurk crowd-sourcing platform. The detailed breakdown is presented in section 2.7.5. We did not record any details about the participants themselves (such as gender, age, education) because we were not able to check the validity of this data (for example using mTurk user information).

Both the on-site and online study setups were considered suitable for a word-sorting task. Participants found the interface and the task self-explanatory and we did not note any confusion or extensive requests for explanations.

From each participant we recorded the arrangement of words into groups and the one word per group chosen as the most suitable description of the whole group. We used MatLab software to represent the gathered data as a similarity matrix describing which words were together in a group. For each participant, a 78 x 78 matrix represented each possible pair of words with a 0 (not together) or a 1 (together) distance score representing each pair of words.

Average results of all participants were combined into a similarity matrix on Figure 11. The numbers in this matrix describe the frequency with which two words were placed together in participant data and can be interpreted as similarity of two words – the higher the number, the more similar the words. Numbers range from 100%, when every participant grouped two words together (e.g. Ribbed and Grooved), to 0%, when no one grouped the two words together (e.g. Ribbed and Pliable). For example, the Glossy-Shiny pair had a score of 71%, which means they were grouped together 71% of time, while Glossy-Thick had a score of 9% because they were grouped together only 9% of the time. For readability, numeric data were also represented with colours in the below graph.

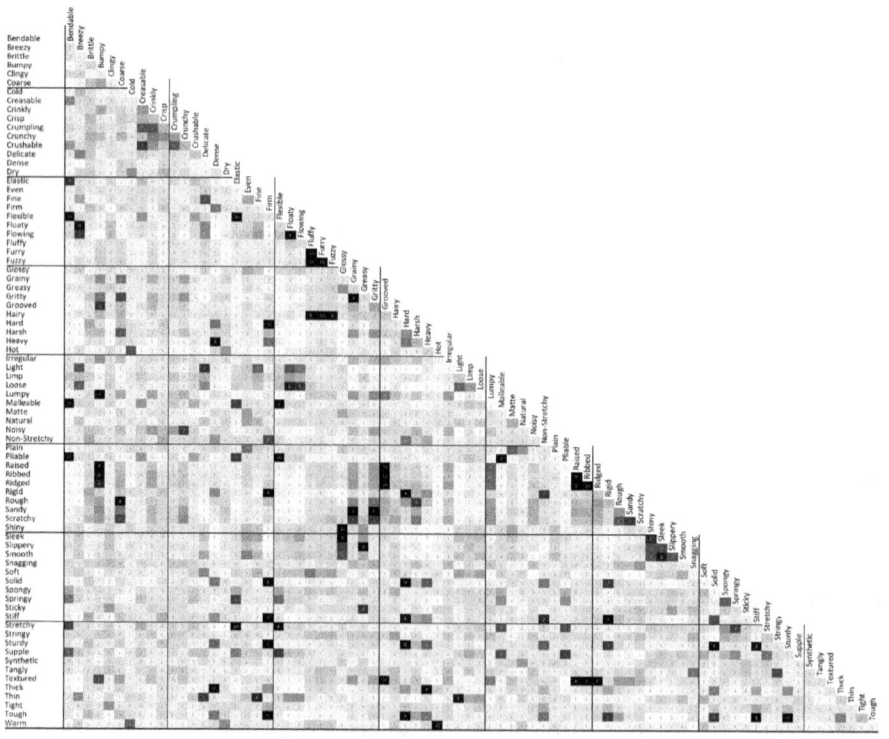

Figure 11 – Average distances similarity matrix - darker means more similar, numbers on intersections of words describe how many tens of participants grouped them together (out of 138).

2.7.4 Data Analysis - Grouping Task Results

Data Analysis – Dendrogram Graph And Separating Into Groups

Based on the average similarity matrix shown above, we can not only read the average distances between individual words, but also construct a dendrogram graph to represent the words in Figure 12. On such a graph, each word is represented as one leaf of a tree structure, and words are connected into branches that represent larger sub groups as we travel up the graph. In other words, each branch is a group of words that are closer to each other (have higher similarity score) than to words in other branches. We can visualize the distance between two words (when moving only along the branch-lines) as a representation of their average distance in participants' sorting. As such, words on one branch can be interpreted as groups of words with similar meanings, because they have small distances between each other. To create our dendrogram we used the MATLAB software with dendrogram function and the following settings: pdist (Pairwise distance between pairs of objects) was set to of 'cityblock' (City block metric) and linkage was set to 'average' (Unweighted average distance (UPGMA)). We used these particular settings, as they were most suitable for this type of sorting private communication with Khemraj Emrith and was also described by Padilla, Halley, and Chantler (2011).

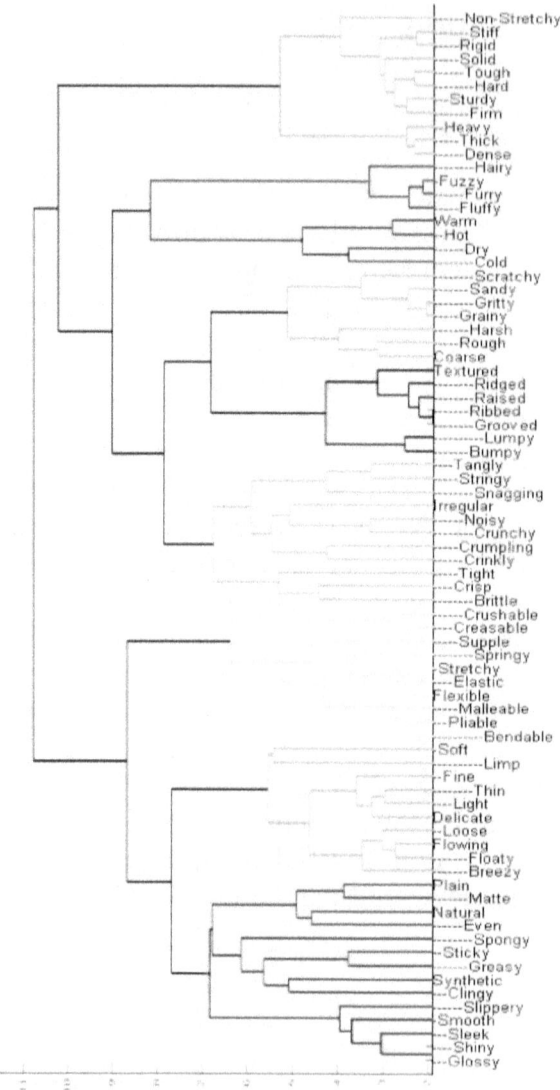

Figure 12 – Dendrogram of similarity matrix for word sorting results separated into 8 groups.

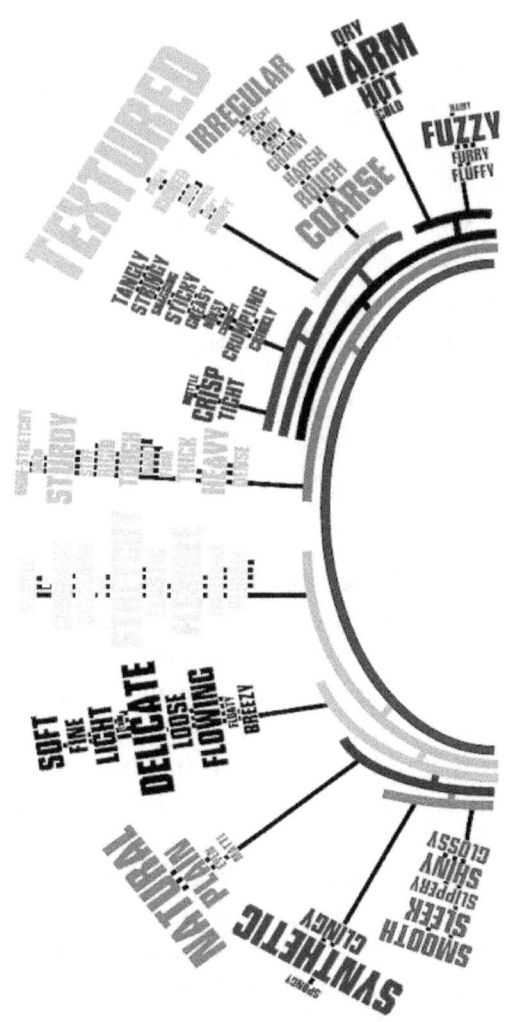

Figure 13 – Palette graph - another way to represent similarity data of the above dendrogram separated into 12 groups.

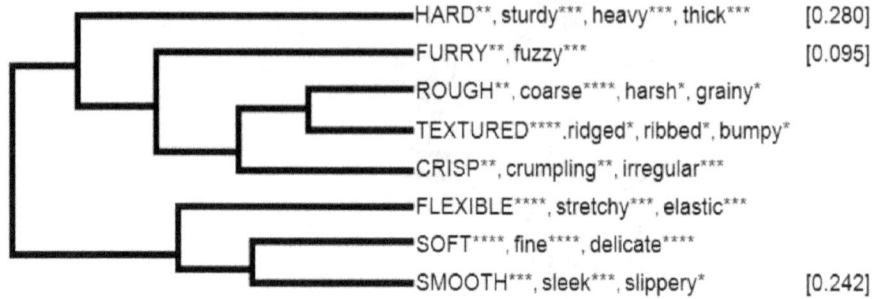

Figure 14 – Modified image used by P. M. Orzechowski et al. (2011) – a simplified dendrogram of word meaning similarity. Number of * indicated representativeness of the word.

In a dendrogram graph, since words in every branch were guaranteed to be more similar to each other than to words on other branches, it was possible to represent all words as a small number of groups (branches), each representing synonymous words. If we required 10 groups, we would cut the branches at the exact point on y axis where the tree has 10 branches. Additionally we modified the dendrogram generation code written by Khemraj Emrith, so that the x axis includes information about how representative each word was inside of its group. To annotate the representativeness of words, we used the information acquired when participants were highlighting the most representative words at the end of their grouping exercise. Representativeness data is shown as a distance from x-axis indicated with '-' symbols on the dendrogram (closer to the axis means more representative) in Figure 12. The dendrogram scripts used bottom-up aggregation and distance metric linkage mechanism. Another data visualisation technique was a palette graph where branches represent similarity and size represents how representative for its group each word was.

The process of using the dendrogram to extract small amount of groups from the set is described in Section 2.8.

2.7.5 Comparison Of Participant Groups And Finding Cheaters In Crowd Sourcing Studies

Participant Groups

We performed the sorting experiment with three different participant groups: at the laboratory of Heriot-Watt University, at Edinburgh Council libraries and over the mTurk crowd-sourcing platform. Table 5 describes how those setups differed in their environment, software/hardware, type of participants and motivation. Lab study and parts of the analysis were performed with Tom Methven and published by Methven et al. (2011) and by P. M. Orzechowski et al. (2012).

	Lab	Library	mTurk
Environment	Controlled laboratory setup, small room	Public library computers or participants' own computers	Participants' own computers
Software / Hardware	A set of paper flashcards with words printed on them	Custom-made interactive website for grouping words by drag-and-dropping them onto each other	
Recruitment	Internal department mailing list and posters around	Posters were mailed to local libraries and displayed there	Advertised on Amazon's Mechanical Turk (mTurk) crowd-

	the university	on noticeboards	sourcing platform
Participants	Students	Library users	Members of mTurk
Motivation / Payment	Book vouchers	Raffle of a cheap mp3 player	Small financial incentive
N of participants	23	41 (2% cheaters)	94 (10% cheaters)
Accuracy	Good – results appear to be consistent and meaningful	Good – results appear to be consistent and meaningful	Medium (needs cheater removal)
Time to setup	Good – requires only printing the flashcards and using mailing lists that are already in place	Bad – requires programming the interface and advertising in public spaces	Bad - requires programming the interface and arranging a payment method compatible with mTurk
Time to run	Bad – we managed to gather up to 8 participants a day	Medium – we managed to gather up to 15 participants a day	Good – We managed to gather up to 50 participants a day
Running Cost	Bad – traditionally	Medium – lower effort required	Good – the payment we

	vouchers are given to on-site participants	from participants makes smaller payment or raffle suitable	used was the minimum wage payment for the time spent doing the study.
Scalability	Bad – limited by the table space, number of decks, data encoding is time consuming	Medium – easy data gathering, but advertising is complicated, also because of trust issues and corporate culture in libraries	Good – it is very easy to put the study inside of the mTurk system. Steady flow of participants would not require any additional work to rerun the study.

Table 5 – Elements of word sorting setups: Lab, Library and mTurk with their advantages and disadvantages.

Cheaters

When we listed our study on mTurk, a large number of answers started appearing immediately. Most of the answers were participants who gave up (started the study and never completed it) probably because it was harder and longer than other m-Turk studies available at the time (mid 2010). There were over 300 attempts on starting to sort, but only 94 participants finished their sorting and submitted results. Another interesting trend was that some people took an unexpectedly short time to complete the study or their answers appeared to be very inconsistent. After eyeballing those results, we realized that these participants were most possibly dishonest, and that we needed to filter out those results.

At this point we suspected that some of our participants were cheaters - completing the task without much effort and care, only for the reward. It was not obvious how to validate which answers were cheated, because it is the nature of a sorting task that there is no one correct answer. We needed a heuristic to identify cheaters, and we realized that dishonest participants grouped together words that were never grouped together by honest participants. To capture that, we decided to calculate how far each participant's answer was from the average by comparing the participant's sorting matrix and the average similarity matrix. The result of this comparison was a number that described the distance of that participant's sorting results from the average sorting results. The higher this number, the more peculiar this person's grouping was, and hence the higher likelihood that that this person was a cheater.

Distance Score And Other Cheater Finding Heuristics

We called that mean distance between the person's and the average sorting result a **Distance score**. Whenever the Distance score was particularly high, such a person was flagged up as a potential cheater. This was not the only heuristic we used for highlighting cheaters, because we did not want to exclude participants who simply had a very different understanding of words. At the same time, we were searching for the most common understanding of the words, so we assumed that some overzealous cheater detection was acceptable.

Other cheating indicators were the unusual amount of time that participants took to complete the task, and the number of groups in their final sorting. Across our 158 participants, there was a 0.7

correlation between the Distance score and the number of groups that the person ended up with. At the same time, the correlation between the amount of time taken and the score was 0.35. This suggests that participants who grouped words into very small number of groups or did it very quickly, cheated.

For example, the 10 worse Distance scores among mTurk participants had an outstandingly low average number of groups (2.5 groups, while the study average was 12 groups) and time taken (8 minutes, while the study average was 15 minutes).

Whenever a participant had a high Distance score and an unusually low number of groups and time taken, they were considered a cheater and removed from the final dataset.

Comparing The Quality Of Data Across The Participant Groups

Online-studies are a faster and cheaper way to acquire experimental data when compared with on-site studies; however, they could present drawbacks in terms of data quality. To test that statement, we decided to compare the Distance scores of participants belonging to our three groups. We knew that the m-Turk group would contain some cheaters and in general would present a worse quality of data. We were also expecting very small differences between Lab and Library groups, which would have interesting implications for data gathering techniques (one used paper cards and the other an on-screen interface).

Our hypothesis was that the Lab group will be just as good as the Library group, and that the mTurk group will be worse than both of them. We performed a one-way between subjects ANOVA to compare the effect of the group on the Distance score for three groups: Lab, Library and mTurk. There was a significant effect of the group on Distance score results for three conditions [$F(2,158) = 6.372$, $p=.002$]. A planned contrast analysis revealed that participants in the mTurk group had higher Distance scores than participants in the other two groups [mTurk vs. Lib&Lab: $t(158) = -3.57$, $p < .001$], while there was no statistically significant difference between Library and Lab groups [Lib vs. Lab: $t(158) = .156$, $p=.694$]. This was in line with all of our hypotheses.

After Removing Cheaters The Differences Between Groups Disappear

In work described by Methven et al. (2011) we investigated methods of finding and excluding the cheaters. When the mTurk participants who finished the task in under 5 minutes or who scored very poorly on the Distance score were removed from the data set, then all three groups were comparable and there were no statistical difference between them as shown in Figure 15.

To test the impact of removing of highlighted potential cheaters on the quality of data, we removed 9 cheaters in mTurk group. We called this new group of participants mTurk-no-cheaters, as it consisted of those of the mTurk participants who were not suspected of cheating. We performed a one-way between subjects ANOVA to compare the effect of the group on the Distance score for three groups: Lab, Library and mTurk-no-cheaters. There was no significant effect of the group on Distance score for three conditions [$F(2,144) = 1.851$, $p=.16$]. This confirmed that removing cheaters from mTurk sample makes mTurk not significantly different from Library and Lab conditions.

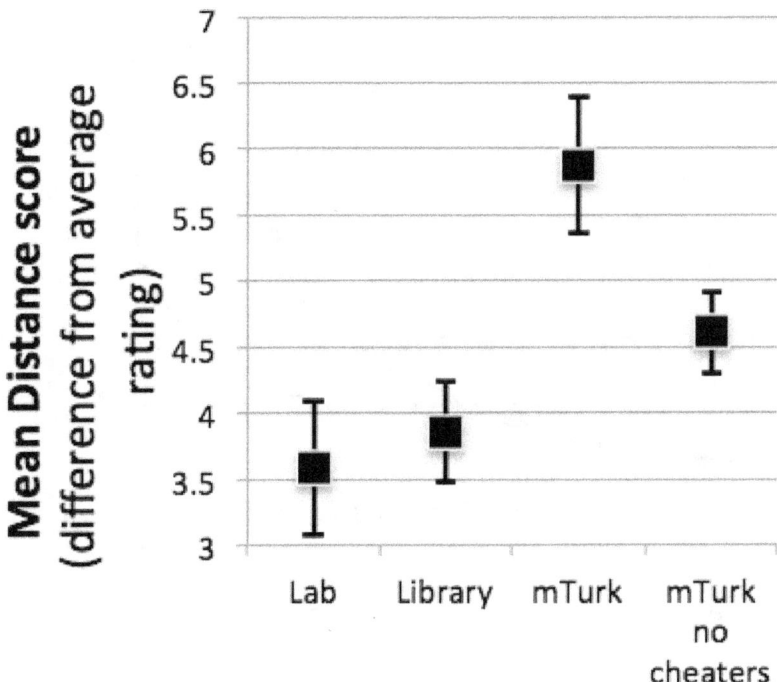

Figure 15 – Means and error bars of 3 groups of word sorting with and without cheaters – measure of distance from average.

The means and standard errors of Distance score are presented in Figure 15 and illustrated the results of the above analysis.

In Figure 16 the normalized Distance scores was shown for three groups side by side. On this graph we horizontally scaled each type of distance score across three measurement methods to the same width, for ease of comparison of the differences between the quality of results across the three groups. The three groups have a similar profile of results, getting progressively higher Distance scores, but the mTurk group has consistently worse results.

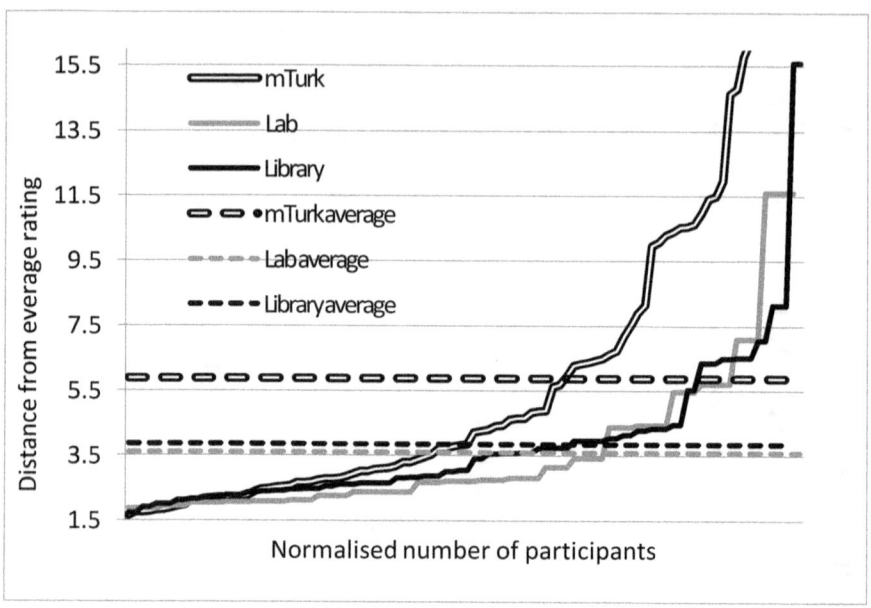

Figure 16 – Distance from average ratings across three setups in word sorting Study 3.

Differences Between Groups: MTurk – High Quantity, Low Quality

The results we acquired through the mTurk platform were of significantly worse quality than those acquired through the Libraries and Laboratory setup. It is possible that crowd-sourced participants were much less motivated to complete the study correctly. It is also possible that they did not understand the task, or did not pay as much attention to the instructions. On the other hand, we managed to acquire a 5 times larger number of participants, 5 times as quickly time. Crowd-sourcing would be a very attractive alternative to on-site studies if there was a way to improve the quality of data by removing the dishonest users. When we removed the cheaters from our data set, the quality of crowd-sourced data increased so much that their quality became statistically indistinguishable from other participants sources. We concluded that using crowdsourcing for obtaining sorting data is viable, but only if there are reliable measures to prevent or detect cheating.

One of the practical ways to remove cheaters in future studies would be to run a smaller scale lab-based study alongside the crowdsourced study. The purpose of the lab-based study would be to establish a correct, non-cheated set of results to compare crowdsourced results against, which would highlight which of the crowdsourced results could be considered valid and which were generated by cheaters.

Differences Between Groups: Lab (Physical) Vs. Library (Online)

As expected, the data from the Library and Laboratory setup were statistically similar despite the differences between recruitment methods and the interface described in Table 5. The fact that we can gather the same quality of data on a computer screen as in traditional table-top sorting means that we should be able to use those two methods interchangeably. Sorting words on a physical table has a number of drawbacks:

- it is not scalable, as it requires the presence of the researcher and the deck of cards,
- it can be only performed by a limited number of people concurrently (number of decks),
- it cannot be performed at participants' convenience (at the time and place that they choose) unless modified,
- it does not provide reliable mechanisms to put participants in study conditions, or to modify the study materials on demand,
- it traditionally requires higher payment.

While it would be an interesting research avenue to explore the impact of those factors separately onto the quality of data, it was outside of the scope of this thesis.

2.7.6 Grouping Task Online – Conclusion

As a result of the grouping tasks we structured the set of 78 words into eight groups of words with similar meanings. Additionally, each group is represented by one representative word term, which was found to be representative most frequently by participants.

We combined the word sorting data from all 3 groups (excluding the mTurk cheaters) and gave them the same relative weight. The decision to give all the words the same weight was driven by the fact that there was no statistical difference in the measurements of distance score between the laboratory, library and non-cheater-mTurk groups. We decided to use the filtered mTurk data rather than discarding them all on the basis that the cheater-identifying heuristic might have been imperfect. Thanks to a large number of data we were able to create meaningful groupings which are further discussed in this chapter.

Later on we will use the most representative word terms corresponding to those eight groups as rating scales for textile qualities. The process of refining the groups into representative words that were used as scales was described below.

2.8 Using Fabric Quality Terms To Communicate Textile Qualities

2.8.1 Words Communicating Qualities - Introduction

Reducing The Word Set Into A Small Number Of Scales

Ultimately, we needed a small set of words that could be used as rating scale labels in evaluation of fabric interfaces. Reducing the word set into a small number of labels was possible with the sorting data from studies described previously. First, it was necessary to decide upon a number of groups we wanted to separate our set of words into.

Initially, we clustered all words into 10 groups using the dendrogram information, but three of those groups were small, consisting only of four or five words. We decided to combine two of the small groups together (group: Cold, Dry, Hot, Warm, and group: Fluffy, Furry, Fuzzy, Hairy), and also to merge another small group (group: Glossy, Shiny, Sleek, Smooth, Slippery) with its nearest neighbour. After this procedure we obtained 8 groups of words of similar sizes, each representing a set of words describing synonymous qualities.

Next we found the most representative term in each group using the representativeness data from Study 3 described in Section 2.7.4. The most representative term words were: Crisp, Hard, Soft, Textured, Flexible, Furry, Rough and Smooth. In all further studies and throughout this thesis, we used those eight qualities as scales to evaluate external qualities of fabrics. We did not notice participants having trouble with understanding the concepts these words represent when we used that set of qualities in studies. In some studies we added an icon representing each of those words presented next to them, as in Figure 17.

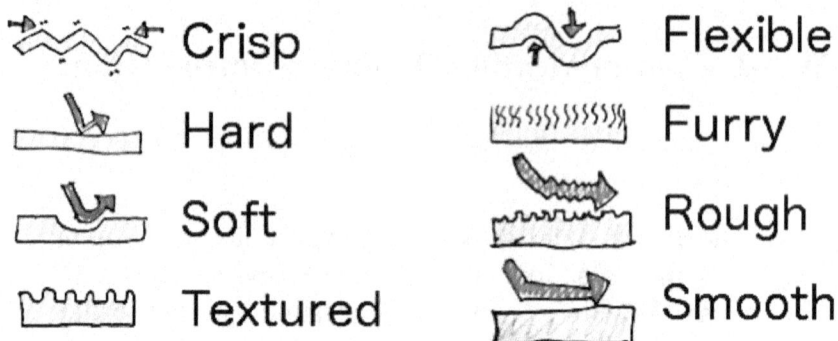

Figure 17 – The set of 8 textile quality words that were used in further studies.

2.8.2 Testing The Reliability Of The Set Of 8 Textile-Quality Terms By Using It To Rate Physical Fabrics

Testing The Reliability Of Textile Quality Rating Scales

We needed to test whether this set of eight qualities was commonly understood and could be used for communicating about fabrics. To evaluate this, we analysed the reliability of ratings of textile non-experts who rated physical fabric swatches. We considered unconstrained interaction with a physical fabric swatch to be a baseline of textile qualities perception – the most accurate way to extract the most qualities possible. If participants rated fabrics on the scales of eight textile qualities in a reliable way, than the scales can be considered usable for the purposes of rating fabrics.

Two Sources Of Rating Data

We collected data from non-expert participants rating physical swatches from two studies described in Chapter 0: Study 7 and Study 9. In those studies two different groups of participants (19 and 18 people respectively) were handling fabric swatches and rating them on our eight textile qualities scales. The same set of four popular fabrics was used in both studies: Buckram, Cotton, Latex and Ripstop (seen in Figure 35 in Section 5.4.2). The ratings of physical swatches happened at the end of both studies, however we believe that the study design had no impact on the ratings of physical fabrics.

These to studies evaluated different aspects of digital textile simulators, and required . In the Study 7 participants evaluated different visual settings of the digital interface, in the Study 9 they evaluated different sound settings of that interface. In both examples we considered that baseline testing (rating the physical swatches) performed at the end of the study was unaffected by the content of the study conducted before, as mentioned by Wu et al. (2011). Since people interact with many fabrics everyday, they are likely to have formed opinions about common fabrics and familiar ways to evaluate fabric qualities. In general, a short interaction with a digital simulator was unlikely to change their baseline perception of a physical fabric. We had reasons to believe that participants perceived fabric qualities the same way before and after the studies.

Even though in both studies participants were rating fabrics on the same eight dimensions, in Study 7 participants used a scale between 1 and 100, while in Study 9 participants used a scale of 1 to 7. We transposed the first set of results to the 1-7 scale using the following formula: *seven point rating = round (hundred point rating / (100/14))* to get a similar distribution on the scale and represent the extreme ratings correctly. A histogram of distributions is presented in Figure 18.

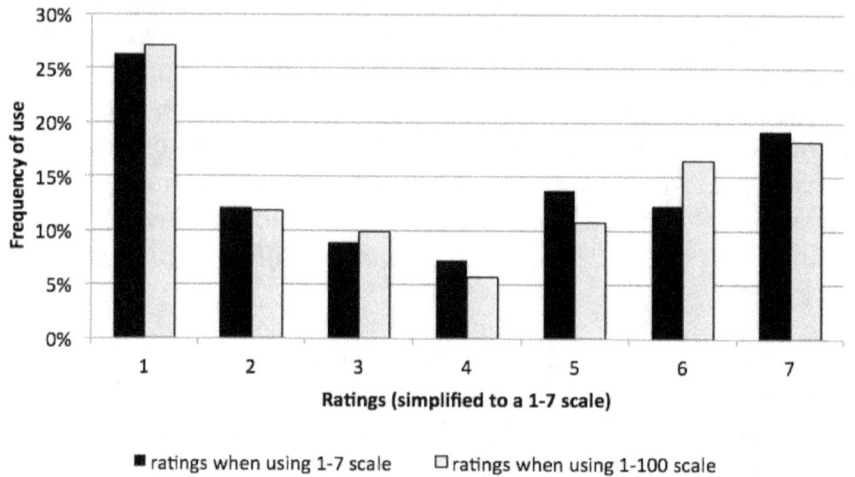

Figure 18 – A histogram of ratings of real fabrics when ratings were made on a 1-7 scale and a 1-100 scale. Eyeballing distribution indicated they were comparable.

Intraclass Correlation Coefficient

In order to measure the reliability of the scales we calculated two-way random intraclass correlations in SPSS. The values of the intraclass correlation coefficient indicated what amount of variance in using the rating scale could be explained. In Table 6 we described the results for all the scales, together with the 95% interval bounds. The coefficients for all the scales were above .975 and above their respective 95% confidence intervals, which indicated good reliability of the scales.

	Intraclass correlation, average measures	95% confidence intervals
Crisp	.978**	.930 - .998
Hard	.984**	.949 - .999
Soft	.985**	.952 - .999
Textured	.976**	.922 - .998
Flexible	.969**	.903 - .998
Furry	.993**	.977 - .999
Rough	.981**	.938 - .999
Smooth	.979**	.932 - .998

Table 6 – Intraclass correlation coefficients for eight rating scales calculated from 37 participants rating physical fabrics.

This result meant that the eight dimensions (and the terms we used to describe them) we used for rating physical qualities of fabrics were consistent, and that when one person rated something as Crisp, others rated it as Crisp as well. Thus, we could say that the eight dimensions we derived could be used consistently by non-experts to rate textile qualities.

2.9 Chapter Conclusion

Data Highlights

We asked participants to indicate the words they knew and used amongst a set of 69 words used by textile experts to describe fabric qualities. Words were allocated a score, depending on whether participants marked them as Known and Used, Known and Unused or Unknown. Seventeen words were discarded as unknown and unused and a set of 52 words was used in further studies.

Next, we gave 29 participants various textile samples and asked them to describe fabric qualities with their own words. From 429 unique words: most (320) were used by two or fewer participants and were discarded as unused; a further 76 were discarded because we considered them inappropriate (hedonic, temporal, emotional, ambitious, other). We described words in the remaining set with a Use score (how many people used that word) and an Agree score (how often the same word described the same fabric). We accepted the 29 words with the highest Use score as most used descriptive non-expert words, and used them in our further research.

Finally, the 52 words from the expert set with highest Know score and 29 words with the highest Use score from the non-expert set were combined into the final set of 78 words describing fabrics (some words appeared in both groups). Once 158 Participants sorted these words into groups by meaning, we used their groupings to create a similarity matrix. We chose to use the similarity data to identify 8 groups of synonymous words, each group labelled by its most representative word. The 8 words describing fabric qualities were: Crisp, Hard, Soft, Textured, Flexible, Furry, Rough, Smooth. We drew icons that represented each label word.

To validate whether the set of 8 label words could be used effectively to generate rating scales for fabric qualities, we analysed participants' ratings in all studies in this thesis where those scales were used. Analysis of intraclass correlations indicated that our 8 labels can be used to generate reliable rating scales for subjectively perceived textile qualities.

Strengths – Final Rating Scales Were Purposefully Designed For Final Users (Non-Experts)

The rating system we created was designed to be usable by non-experts. We involved the end users of our rating scales at three different points during the process of designing it: identifying known expert words; adding popular non-expert word; and sorting the words into a manageable set of textile descriptive terms. Thanks to their involvement non-experts could successfully use our scales to rate fabrics, as proven by the statistical measurements of the scales' validity.

One of the limitations of using an expert word set that we overcame was that non-experts might not have known the meanings of expert words. We also avoided the complexity that would be introduced by allowing participants to describe fabrics with their own words in an unconstrained manner. Such open descriptions would increase the time and effort needed to perform the studies described.

We believe that one of the greatest strengths of the research process described in this thesis was the decision to invest time and effort into creating a research apparatus early on. Thanks to having an appropriate and reliable apparatus we were able to conduct well-designed studies described later in this thesis.

Limitation – Comparing Subjective Ratings To Objective Measurements

Our studies described in this chapter did not evaluate the validity of the ratings themselves along our eight dimensions; for example, we cannot claim that when people rated something highly on a Crisp scale, it was indeed physically and objectively very Crisp. To gain this type of knowledge we would need to find other measures of our eight qualities (such as objective machine testing, or expert panel), but the scales we were using were designed for non-experts and used their perceptions described above in this chapter. In other words, measurement devices and experts would possibly be evaluating different qualities to those that non-experts evaluate, even if they happened to have the same labels for describing them. Instead, we confirmed above that when one person considered something very Crisp, other people considered it Crisp as well, which meant that these eight scalable dimensions could be used to communicate qualities of textiles to other people. In the following chapters we will use our eight scales to rate qualities of physical and simulated fabrics, and analyse how they change depending on experimental conditions.

Future Directions

The questions that the further work might explore:

Were words marked as Known understood in the same way by all participants (a short investigation of Agree scores suggested that it was the case)?

Did adding icons to the 8 words representing the rating scales make them easier to use and more accurate?

2.10 Chapter Contributions

In this chapter we described the process of creating and evaluating a set of terms to be used by non-experts to communicate textile qualities. To create those terms, we combined expert and non-expert words that non-expert participants used and understood. Later we clustered all words representing textile qualities into eight groups, each represented by a single term.

We believe that the apparatus designed with the help of the research described in this chapter is a state of the art tool for textile non-experts to describe perceived textile qualities.

CONTRIBUTION 2.1 – Set Of Textile-Descriptive Words Known And Used By Non-Experts.

We created a set of 78 words by combining words that experts and non-experts use to describe fabrics.

We evaluated this word set by ensuring that: all words are known to non-experts in a word recognition task: Study 1; the word set contains words actively used by the non-experts in a textile description scenario: Study 2; people agree about the meanings of these words (by analysing the Agree scores). Each word's Agree score was a metric we devised that indicated the consistency with which participants described different fabrics with that word.

CONTRIBUTION 2.2 - Clustering Of Textile-Descriptive Words (Contribution 1) Into Groups To Create Textile-Descriptive Terms.

We clustered the 78 words into groups of synonyms and quantified the similarities between them as in Figure 12. Our grouping structure can be used to break down the words into any different number of groups and to indicate the terms representing each of these groups. Each word group in such a breakdown could be represented by one term describing a top-level fabric quality.

To evaluate the correctness of our groupings we analysed data from 158 participants. After removing participants who we suspected of being dishonest, we arrived at consistent grouping data, which were then used to create a set of eight textile descriptive terms.

CONTRIBUTION 2.3 – A Small Set Of Textile-Descriptive Terms That Can Be Used As Rating Scales In Evaluation Of Textile Simulators

We created a set of eight top-level terms describing textile qualities. These quality terms are: Crisp, Hard, Soft, Textured, Flexible, Furry, Rough and Smooth as seen in Figure 17. Each term is represented by a word and an icon, so that it can be used to generate a rating scale for use in the evaluation of fabrics by non-experts.

To evaluate our set of eight textile descriptive terms we analysed data from two studies that used those terms in rating scales to describe four familiar fabrics. We found that overall non-experts agreed on the ratings of physical fabrics when using our eight terms, which implies that the terms were commonly understood and can be used for rating fabrics.

CONTRIBUTION 2.4 – Process Of Designing Research Apparatus (A Set Of Rating Scales In A Novel Area) By Combining How Expert And Non-Experts Communicate About That Area.

The design of the method for achieving Contributions 2.1, 2.2 and 2.3 described above was something we considered to be a novel contribution in itself. It could be used not only in the area of Human Computer Interaction but also in other areas that would require the creation of user-inspired language for evaluating attributes from a given domain. We documented the process of creating a set of rating scales with descriptive terms in an area where dictionaries of expert and non-experts differed in Appendix IV.

Chapter 3 – On-Fabric Gestures

Goal:
Investigate on-fabric gestures that non-experts perform while they investigate textile qualities

Literature:
Various gesture annotation schemes are combined into an initial on-fabric gesture annotation scheme. Initial scheme is piloted, refined and used to annotate gestures from Study 4

Study 4:
Observation of gestures that non-experts perform when asked to evaluate fabric qualities

Analysis:
Frequency and variants of on-fabric gestures are analyzed. The most popular gestures are combined into a gesture dictionary. This gesture dictionary is used as video annotation aid

Contribution:
A dictionary of on-fabric gestures, including their sub-types and modifiers

3. Gestures Used For Evaluating Fabric Qualities

3.1 Introduction

3.1.1 Context

Context - Thesis Goal

The goal of this thesis was to establish how people perceive fabric qualities and interact with fabrics, and then to use that knowledge to create better digital interfaces that communicate fabric qualities. In everyday life people interact with fabrics and evaluate their qualities using various modalities, such as vision, touch, and sound. From the research described in the previous chapter we knew what qualities people can describe in fabrics, however, it was unclear exactly what the process of evaluating a quality was before it got described with language. The word *evaluation* refers to the process of interaction with an object that leads to understanding of that object's qualities. The word *description* refers to the process of verbalising object's qualities. In this chapter we analysed videos of people handling and evaluating fabrics, focusing in particular on their hands. We wanted to understand user's actions in order to create better textile simulators.

3.1.2 Chapter Goals And Motivation For Goals

> GOAL 3.1 – Create A Schema For Describing On-Fabric Gestures, Detailing Their Characteristics And Popularity.

In this chapter we investigated how people interacted with fabrics with their hands as they attempted to evaluate those fabrics' properties. Our goal was to find a set of gesture labels (e.g. "Stroke") and their definitions that corresponded to movements performed by people touching fabric. Having such a set of labels and definitions would enable us to run studies that investigate on-fabric gestures - a person's movements as they touch fabrics.

To confirm the usability of our annotation scheme, we commenced a gesture discovery study and used it to research frequencies of individual gestures being performed. Knowledge of which gestures were most frequent was useful for understanding the affordance of fabric swatches, estimating people's intentions and in effect for designing better textile simulators.

> GOAL 3.2 – Design A Procedure For Exploring A Novel Gesture Space With The Purpose Of Creating A Gesture Scheme (Goal 3.1). This Process Can Be Reused In Other HCI Research.

The second goal of this chapter was to design a method for acquiring a set of gesture labels described above. Creating a classification of gestures (or other behaviours) in new and under-researched areas is a problem frequently tackled in HCI. We aimed to design and describe our research process so that it not only produces reliable results, but also could be modified and repeated by other researchers. The process consisted of: identifying the criteria for selecting appropriate literature, the choice of candidate methodology and candidate behaviour labels, pilot and experiment design, results analysis technique, discussion of findings, and analysing the strengths and weaknesses of our approach.

We aimed to describe the strengths and weaknesses of this procedure to make it possible to adapt and reproduce by other researchers and in different research areas.

> GOAL 3.3 – Devise A Graphical Representation Of The Scheme For On-Fabric Gestures (Goal 3.1) That Can Be Used For Annotating Video And In Further Research.

The third goal of this chapter was to create a graphical representation of the set of gesture labels, so that they might be easily understood. We searched for an appropriate graphical representation in the literature. Wherever we did not find applicable graphical representation of the on-fabric gestures, we devised our own. Our final goal was to devise a set of icons that could help to visually represent the gestures identified as part of Goal 3.1. The reason why we aimed for a single icon, and single word descriptions of gestures is so that we could use them as a tool in our further research, specifically for quick annotation of video and for reference.

3.1.3 Contributions And Acknowledgements

Unless otherwise specified, all intellectual input into this chapter came from the author. The fabric handling study was run in collaboration with the Digital Sensoria project. The collaborative work of all researchers who contributed to this research was described by P. M. Orzechowski et al. (2011).

3.2 Literature Review

3.2.1 Introduction

Literature Review Criteria

To the best of the author's knowledge there was no publicly available research providing direct answers to our research questions. We reviewed literature from neighbouring areas, and found studies that investigated hand movements. The criteria for selecting literature as relevant were:

- papers described hand movements or other human movement behaviour,
- the movements under investigation were related to interacting with textiles or other soft objects,
- studies aimed to create their own annotation scheme with a goal to devise gesture labels and their descriptions.

From this literature review we extracted relevant methods of recording movements, and later of annotating and clustering them. In those papers we also found word labels used to describe gestures (or movements) and descriptions given to those labels. Papers which did not satisfy these three requirements were briefly described if their methods or findings could contribute to any of our research questions.

What Gestures Were We Searching For?

We chose to define a gesture as "a motion of the body that contains information" as described by Kurtenbach and Hulteen (1990) (p. 311) where that information can be captured and interpreted by a human or computer observer. In the work of Cadoz (1994), they grouped gestures by their function into: semiotic (communicating information), ergotic (manipulating the physical world and creating artefacts), and epistemic (learning from the environment through tactile and haptic exploration). Historically Human Computer Interaction (HCI) research is mainly concerned with semiotic gestures as described by Mulder (1996) and by Rime (1991), because these type of interactions are most common in using human-computer interfaces. However we were most concerned with the crossover of ergotic and epistemic interactions during which user handled objects and attempted to extract knowledge about them.

Recreating manipulative and exploratory actions with the freedom known from a physical world would be desirable for creating a textile simulator. Interestingly, in their analysis of current trends in gestural interaction Buxton and Billinghurst (2011) pointed out the importance of direct manipulation and listed challenges that needed to be addressed. Direct manipulation is a type of interaction where action causes immediate reaction similar to interacting with a physical object. Users move objects on-screen and interact with them, which mimics real-life interactions with physical objects. The interface has to deal with situations when users expect features that are implausible or not included in the interface.

In this thesis we were initially concerned with understanding how people touch and deform fabrics when evaluating their qualities. We expected these to be the typical ergotic (deforming) and epistemic (evaluating) movements that people know from everyday life. At this stage we chose not to limit the observed gestures to only those that can be implemented on a touchscreen or any other technology. This is why we needed a very wide and open method of observing and annotating human movements.

We searched for literature exploring how naive observers interact with physical fabrics, but while we found a small number of papers, most of them were concerned with the qualities that observers are interested in, rather than with gestures that they perform. Below we describe studies that contributed to our research in one of the following ways:

- they analyse interaction with soft objects, either casually or to explore their qualities,
- they propose suitable labels to describe human movements applicable to our on-fabric scenario,
- they describe the process of creating such labels, detailing a method for observation, clustering, analysis, and annotation.

In this literature review we first describe previous research that informed our process the most. Next, we describe in Table 7 how findings from previous research helped to inform our study design. Finally, we describe how these papers informed our research methods.

3.2.2 Huggable Bear

In the work described by Knight (2008) researchers were interested in investigating the range of gestures that can be performed on a teddy bear robot companion. Their method is relevant, since they analysed human gestures on a textile object and used their own annotation scheme.

Their ultimate aim was to create a recognition algorithm for an array of touch sensors embedded within a robot bear and translate them into social signals. To achieve that goal, they video recorded participants playing with a non-robot bear while they acted out a role-play dialogue scenario. The annotation scheme created consisted of a diagram of the bear on which the touch area, direction, and strength were annotated with a pencil. The colours of pencils represented researcher interpretations of the social meaning of gestures. Five different colours were used for gestures categorised as: affectionate, manipulated, puppeteered, attention, playful.

A number of elements of this study informed our study design. Namely the recording method (video recording), task type (role-play), some of the gestures (Patting, Hugging, Scratching, Poking) and the idea to annotate strength and direction of gestures with lines of different colours.

3.2.3 Soft(N)

Schiphorst (2009) described their soft(n) project which explored playful interactions with a pillow-sized soft object and the gestures performed when this object was used as a medium to interact with other people. The detailed breakdown and description of gestures analysed in this project is a valuable resource for our research.

Soft(n) was an art installation consisting of pillow- and human-sized soft bean bags rigged with touch and movement sensors. To encourage more playful interaction and engagement, these pillows were also equipped with vibration, sound and LED feedback devices. Matrices of textile pressure sensors embedded in the bean bags recorded position, pressure, and change over time, which were then analysed as direction, time spent lingering, area touched etc. While the methodology of creating gesture labels or clustering the data is not described, this paper introduced a very clear and consistent way to describe gestures. For example, authors define a Tap as "a soft, short, small, touch, rendered with a single finger" while a Hold as "a lingering, soft, big, touch. A hold is encompassing" (p. 2436).

We appropriated the method of describing gestures with short, catchy and meaningful labels, while providing a key where labels are described with longer, exhaustive descriptions. We also used the idea of playful interaction, where participants are less self-conscious of their movements.

3.2.4 Smartkom

Steininger, Lindemann, and Paetzold (2001) described the process of creating an annotation scheme for gestures performed while touching and hovering over touchscreens.

This study provided a set of guidelines aiming to simplify annotation and analysis by maintaining low data complexity:

- Labels should be functional, rather than morphological. This does not mean that the analysis should be subjective or interpretative, but rather that researchers should concentrate on describing the whole action, rather than the elements of it. For example, labels should be used to annotate the movement of fingers pinching something, instead of describing angles in which fingers are bending,
- Labels should be easy to select and clearly understood. They should be well defined, with criteria that are easy to communicate and observe,
- Labels need to be easy and fast to use during annotation, even for annotators who are not experts,
- Labels should enable automatic processing and analysis, and at the same time they should be easy to read and accessible. Meaningful, but short tags should be used and modifiers

- should be grouped to simplify analysis (so that, for example, all the different pressure or direction modifiers can be compared between each other),
- Labels should be used to promote conformity within and between labellers. Free annotations are discouraged, because even though they could be more accurate, they promote subjectivity and noisy annotation.

From this paper we adopted the main workflow of creating an annotation scheme: two researchers labelled the video recordings, compared and discussed their annotations. Next, all similar annotations were clustered and described with a common label. We also incorporated the idea to use labels to describe movements and morphological modifiers (e.g. area of hand, or number of fingers) to describe variations of gestures

3.2.5 Combining Findings Into A Study Method

The existing literature did not provide a complete solution to annotate and analyse on-fabric gestures. We created a new gesture annotation scheme, informed by previous literature about the gesture-annotation labels and modifiers. We also found references to inform our study design, the methods of creating video recordings, the process of annotation and analysis of recorded gestures.

Table 7 describes the most relevant papers from the literature review, which has been broken down to list the gesture attributes that were used to distinguish between different movements, and the gesture labels that were used. Wherever possible we listed the methodology used for recording, annotation and analysis of gestures. If present, we also extracted the graphical representation of gesture labels.

Paper - Application	Gesture Attributes	Gestures Labels	Recording, Annotation and analysis method	Visual representation
Steininger et al. (2001) - To create new gesture recognisers a set of training data was acquired from people performing small tasks with a mock up interface.	**Purpose** (interaction, supportive, accidental, other), **Length** (long, short, shape specific), **Shape** (circle, point, free), **Contact** (contact, no-contact)	-	Video (face and side recorded in video, hands recorded in infrared) and Audio recordings (microphone array) Gestures were divided into Interactional, Supporting and Residual; described with screen contact area;	Pictures of people with context explanations (e.g. to distinguish long press from short press)
Shaari and Suleiman (2009) - Clarifying the design processes of clothing for people with disabilities required understanding of qualities people perceive and the handling method used	**Size** (small, large), **Pressure** (no, yes, deep), **Movement** (minor, yes, wide, large), **Active Part** (fingertips, hand)	-	Authors clustered the most popular gestures	-

to perceive them.				
Knight (2008) - Robot Bear companion design. Using a normal toy bear for investigation of gestures that people could possibly use to interact with a robot.	Intentions of gestures judged by their area and direction. Intentions: Affectionate, Manipulative, Attention, Puppeteering, Playful	Patting, Hugging, Moving, Supporting, Poking/Slapping, Scratching, Tickling	Roleplaying exercise where participants were reacting to imagined actions of the robot. Video recording. ANNOTATION: Map each touch-gesture to locations on bear, draw related region on sketch of bear with numerical label and category dependent colour	Touched areas of the fabric are highlighted, p 47
Schiphorst (2009) - To investigate playful gestures, participants were placed in a room with touch-sensor rigged pillows and encouraged to have a pillow fight.	Area, Direction, Time Length, Speed, Number of Fingers, Shape of Palm, Lingering vs. Traveling	Tap, Pat, Hold, Touch, Stroke, Glide, Jab, Knock, Slap, Press, Rub, Knead, Punch, Flick	Video and touch sensor data were gathered	Text labels with rich descriptions of movements
Scilingo, Lorussi, Mazzoldi, and De Rossi (2003)	Authors designed a glove and outfit rigged with pressure and stretch sensors to recognise movements and posture of the user. The analysis of signals from the prototype suggests that movements cannot be read from any one part of the body, but rather from the input of all sensors combined together. Following that methodology,			

113

	we decided to annotate the movement of both hands together, rather than, for example, individual fingers.	
Randell, Andersen, Moore, and Baurley (2005)	Authors used sensors build into textiles to observe gestures for interacting with one's own body. They used a variety of conductive fabrics and technologies to sense: embrace, squeeze, press, stroke. Not enough information is provided about how they derived those gesture labels.	
Moody et al. (2001) Dillon et al. (2001)	Authors described an investigation into perceived fabric qualities, and the gestures used to perceive them. They described gestures of Touch-stroke, Rotating cupped, multiple-finger (pinch) and two handed rotation.	

Table 7 – The most relevant papers from gesture literature.

3.2.6 Literature Review Summary

The main lessons learned from the literature review, were:

- The task design had to distract participant's attention from performing gestures – they needed to concentrate on something else as demonstrated by Knight (2008) and by Steininger et al. (2001),
- Video recordings seemed to be an accepted method for recording user's actions and could be combined with textile sensors as used by Steininger et al. (2001),
- After annotating the initial set of pilot participants, the video annotations would have to be clustered and the annotation scheme would need to be refined appropriately, as detailed by Steininger et al. (2001),

- Gesture labels and aspects of gestures annotated in previous literature form a base for the initial gesture annotation scheme in Section 3.4.3,
- Graphical presentation for annotation had to not only describe shape of the hand, but also strength, action, and change over time.

3.3 Organisation Of This Chapter

How To Use Findings From Literature

To continue our investigation of textile simulators, we required a set of not-overlapping labels to describe on-fabric gestures. Such gesture labels would describe movements as well as variants of those movements. This scheme needed to be precisely defined, appropriate to the fabric handling application, and based on literature and our research.

To create an annotation scheme we indiscriminately combined all of the gesture labels and modifiers found in the literature. This resulted in a large and detailed annotation scheme. The advantage of initially accepting all the labels was that with more detailed descriptions of gestures there was a smaller chance of missing an important part of human on-fabric movement. The main weaknesses to this approach was that we gathered a lot of unnecessary data and the annotation process was time consuming and tedious. We tackled this problem with a pilot study evaluating which of the many movement labels and modifiers were relevant to our scenario of fabric handling and extracting textile qualities.

In relation to devising a method for gesture research, we also inspected the recording and analysis methods that were used in analysed papers. The most frequently used gesture observation techniques were: video recording; on-site observation; interviewing;

digital movement recording; and self-description. We considered using a combination of these during our pilot studies and simplifying our method in further research.

What Was Our Study Design

To evaluate our gesture annotation scheme, we analysed video recordings of people handling physical fabrics in order to assess textile qualities. These recordings were acquired during Study 4. In these videos, we laid small fabric swatches in front of participants and asked them to estimate the qualities of these fabrics. Participants' on-fabric actions were analysed using our annotation scheme. The data were then analysed in two steps: in the pilot analysis we annotated the recordings from a small number of participants to create a concise final annotation scheme. In the main study we used that final annotation scheme to analyse all the participant recordings.

3.4 Study 4 – On-Fabric Gestures Performed While Evaluating Fabric Qualities

3.4.1 Introduction And Reasons For Running A Study

Why We Investigated Gestures

Since our goal was to design interactions for fabric simulators, we followed the paradigm of movement-based design outlined by Hummels, Overbeeke, and Klooster (2007). This paradigm states that by observing people's natural movements when they perform a task, we can deduce their intentions and habits. That knowledge can be then used to design digital interactions that are easy to pick up (intuitive), easy to learn (simple) and easy to understand (natural).

Final interface gestures designed for non-experts should fulfil all of the above requirements.

Process

To understand on-fabric gestures of lay people we designed a fabric handling study. The main goal was to acquire a large number of recordings of people handling fabrics in ways that allow them to evaluate the qualities of those fabrics. The task had to be designed in a way that encourages meaningful epistemic gestures (those evaluating qualities) and the recording mechanism had to record their complexity and differentiating features. Once those recordings were made, we began the process of annotating gestures and refining the annotation scheme. We tested the initial large annotation scheme on a small number of recordings, then refined that scheme and finally used it on all the data. That final annotation was illustrated as a table with graphical representation of each gesture. Below we describe our study design and the process of creating the pilot annotation scheme and simplifying it into what became our gesture labels dictionary.

3.4.2 Study Design

Study Design

We designed this study, further referred to as Study 4, to analyse on-fabric gestures of non-expert participants. This study was designed to be run alongside Study 2, which investigated participants' dictionaries and was described in the previous chapter.

 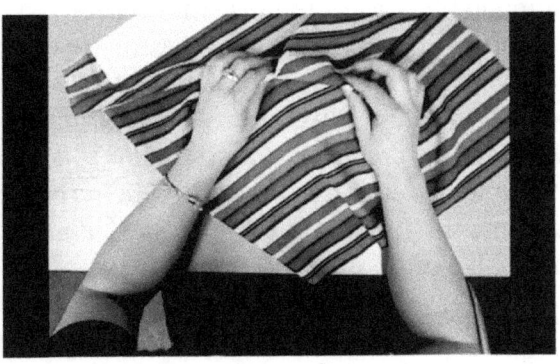

Figure 19 – Gesture recording video setup (left) and the view from the camera (right). This was the largest fabric sample we used (40x40cm) but most of other samples were smaller (on average 30x30cm).

Task And Fabric Samples

During this study, participants were each given 11 swatches of different fabrics and asked to evaluate each fabric's qualities with their hands. We ensured that participants would name many fabric qualities by devising a game where participants were asked to name as many quality-descriptive words as possible within a limited time. We asked them to say out loud the words that they would consider descriptive of the fabric they were handling. As participants were searching for words that described fabric swatches, they touched and handled the fabrics laying in front of them. Acquiring video recordings of that manual exploratory process was the exact purpose of this study.

We wanted participants to perform a variety of gestures relevant for evaluating a wide spectrum of different qualities, so we gave each participant 11 fabric samples from a set of 20 very different fabrics (listed in Table 3). Samples were selected by a panel of 4 researchers from a larger set of about 100 fabrics. We ensured that the fabric swatches we used were large enough to engage both hands and to create a familiar shop-like experience. We used swatches that were on average 30x30cm (biggest 40x40cm, smallest 20x23cm), that provided the area for interaction roughly consistent with the size of an iPad 2 screen (20x25cm).

Room Setup And Video Recordings

Participants were seated individually in the experiment room, side-by-side with the experimenter (the author of this thesis). The experimenter's main task was to place fabric samples in front of the participant and take away the old ones. To enforce the gamification element and enhance motivation, the researcher wrote down in a notebook all the descriptive words spoken by the participant. The experimenter could be seen as a judge or a proxy of competitors. Participants were instructed that each swatch of fabric would be available to them for a maximum of 2 minutes and they needed to say as many descriptive words about the swatch as they could within that time. Limiting the time was also aimed at engaging the participant in a competitive and challenging task.

As participants performed their task, we recorded their hands with a wall mounted camera pointing at their palms, positioned 40cm above the table (as see in Figure 19). Participants knew that their hand movements were recorded, but were not informed about the importance of it, or about the main objective of this study. If participants knew that their hand movements would be analysed, it might make their actions self-conscious, filtered, planned or controlled. It could introduce bias and undermine the validity of the recorded gestures, since we aimed to record natural, unconstrained and lay epistemic gestures. Thanks to that setup we gained insight into how participants use their hands to extract fabric qualities in a quick and efficient manner, and which were the most frequent hand actions used.

3.4.3 Pilot Annotation Design

An essential part of the study design was to decide on the annotation scheme. From six related studies described above in the literature review section, we aggregated all the gesture labels and classifiers to create a large annotation scheme. As a result of that process we assembled a set of 9 gestures labels: Rub, Pull, Crunch, Stroke, Fold, Sandwich, Wrinkle, Pat and Pinch. We also gathered 9 gesture features that could potentially describe each interaction and classify gestures: Repeated, Speed, Hand Area, Hand Shape, Hands, Movement Direction, Pressure, Hold in place with hands, and Amount of swatch (as in Table 8).

Since we accepted all the gesture labels and features from the related studies, we expected that many elements of our exploratory pilot annotation scheme would be redundant. This could happen either because of overlapping meanings of annotated features, or when gestures did not appear prominently in the video recordings, or were just not relevant to the fabric handling scenario. That was why we decided to first use this annotations scheme on the recordings from two participants and then cluster the results into a graphical annotation scheme. Another annotation scheme would then be created, consisting of only some of the initial 9 labels and 9 attributes. We anticipated that possibly some new relevant criteria and gestures could arise during the pilot annotation process. We anticipated that the design process would have to be reiterated and a simpler scheme devised of popular tags once we had the results of that initial annotation.

9 gesture labels used for pilot annotation	9 gesture attributes used for pilot annotation (for sources refer to the table above)
A – Rub - Schiphorst (2009){nl}B - Pull{nl}C – Crunch - Moody et al. (2001){nl}D - Stroke - Randell et al. (2005, Schiphorst (2009){nl}F - Fold{nl}H - Sandwich{nl}W - Wrinkle{nl}P - Pat - Knight (2008, Schiphorst (2009){nl}I – Pinch - Moody et al. (2001)	Repeated (once, many times){nl}Speed (none, slow, normal, fast){nl}Hand Area (finger, fingers, palm, hand){nl}Hand Shape (closed, half-closed, open, sticking finger){nl}Hands (one, both){nl}Movement Direction (opposite, towards, circular, changing, landing-at, turn){nl}Pressure (None, Light, Heavy), Hold in place with hand (Both, One, None),{nl}Amount of swatch (corner, rim, middle, whole{nl}{nl}For sources refer to Table 7

This is a graphical representation of the first pilot annotation scheme.
This drawing was used during as an aid in the annotation of first two participants.

Table 8 – Gesture labels and gesture attributes used in pilot annotation.

We used these gesture labels and gesture attributes to annotate the movements of the first two participants. Each time a participant moved their hands to manipulate a fabric in front of them, that movement would be annotated using one of the gesture labels and each of the relevant gesture attributes. An example annotation of stroking the middle of a fabric would be: D-once-fast-palm-open-one hand-opposite-light-one hold-middle.

3.5 Study Results

3.5.1 Observing Gestures – Piloting And Design Of Gesture Dictionary

Participants And Recordings

A total of 19 students from Heriot-Watt University (from Computer Science and Psychology departments, 12 male, average age 21) were invited to take part in this study. They were recruited through email groups of their respective departments and rewarded with £10 shop vouchers. Participants were introduced to the experimental task in a small room with a table and two chairs – one for the participant and one for the researcher. Participants were briefed about the purpose of the study and signed a consent form. They were then asked to use a moisturising antibacterial hand cream, which had two functions: sanitizing (to prevent spread of germs) and moisturizing (to make everyone's hands equally soft and sensitive). The researcher and the room were always the same and all participants took part in the experiment over two consecutive days. The task and recording equipment were set up as described in study design section.

Video was recorded with a webcam connected to a laptop with video recording software. Participants handled 11 fabrics each, and were always given two minutes to describe each fabric. Half of the time participants requested a next sample before the end of the two minutes, because they felt they named all the words about a fabric that came to their minds. On average, we recorded 21 minutes of footage per participant, adding up to 400 minutes of video for the whole study. A subtitle editing software Aegisub was used for annotating the gestures onto the video recordings.

Hands were clearly visible on the video recordings and lighting conditions were good. While we could clearly distinguish the types of gestures in the vast majority of interactions, it was often impossible to identify what part of the palm was in contact with the fabric (e.g. if the middle of the palm was resting against the swatch, or hovering above it, when fingers touched the fabric).

3.5.2 Pilot Annotation Procedures

Results Of Pilot Annotation Scheme

To evaluate the initial annotation scheme, we used it to annotate the video recordings of the first two participants. Across those two participants we annotated 95 interactions with use of our initial annotation scheme from Table 8. Examples of annotations can be found below:

- 'Rub-2hand-centre-closed' meant 'gesture A (Rub), with two hands, in the centre of the fabric with a closed palm'. This gesture looked like grabbing the middle of fabric with both hands and rubbing it,
- 'Stroke-2hand-2grab-small-slow-direction:opposite' meant "gesture D (Stroke), with 2 hands, both hands holding fabric, moving slowly, affecting small area of fabric with hands moving in opposite directions". This gesture looked like grabbing a fold of fabric with each hand and releasing it slowly, while stretching the fabric.

Understanding Gestures

It quickly became obvious that the descriptions of gestures needed to be more functional and less morphological. We needed to describe the action as envisaged by the user, rather than the directions and positions of fingers. For practical reasons we needed to decide which aspects of gestures are relevant (the fingers involved, their position, direction, etc.). For example when a participant stretched a fabric pinching it with both hands, we needed to decide how much detail of their hand-hold had to be annotated (e.g. two fingers vs. the whole fist). We aimed to capture more top-level gestures (i.e. grab and stretch), rather than to capture elements that constituted a gesture (a particular grip or arrangement of fingers). At times, participants' words were helpful in identifying performed gestures, because some participants described out loud what they were doing.

Clustering The Pilot Annotation Scheme

Once we annotated the video recordings of the first two participants with the pilot annotation scheme, we needed to analyse and simplify our method. To do that, we decided to organise the data and to find clusters in them. The annotations were arranged alphabetically, to examine which combinations of gesture labels and attributes were happening most often. Indeed, some label-attribute combinations appeared in the same or very similar arrangement most of the time. After identifying those interaction clusters, the annotator extracted all the fragments of video portraying those similar actions. The iMovie video package was used for separating and editing video recordings into one-gesture compilations. The result was the same video footage we recorded earlier, but instead of following the original order, the scenes could be rearranged so that similar gestures were presented one after another. After watching these same-gesture video compilations, the annotator identified what those particular interactions had in common, and labelled the portrayed gesture. Each of those compilations consisted of between 3 and 10 entries (gestures) in the annotation of the first two participants. The drawings produced in that process and names given to those interactions are shown in Table 8 and Figure 20.

Design Of Final Annotation Scheme

As planned, after using the pilot scheme for annotating the recordings of two participants, we reiterated the design process to devise a simpler scheme of annotation labels and attributes. We took the most common clusters identified above and organized them into a system. The main actions were: Stroke, Pull and Rub; however, they were performed in a number of permutations. The main variability seemed to be the number of hands actively used in a gesture and the area of fabric that was involved (edge or centre). Other common gestures were Crunch, Sandwich, Tap, Bend/Fold; however, they did not appear to differ between occurrences in terms of placement and number of hands. We also decided to use a modifier describing the shape of a palm (Finger, Fingers, Palm, Scratch). All this information is included in the final annotation scheme in Figure *21* (notice the direction and pressure). From this point onwards all the participant recordings were annotated with this final scheme. For simplicity of annotation we defined a gesture as a significant deformation of fabric recognisable by the annotator and purposeful on the side of the participant. We did not consider as gestures: combinations of multiple gestures (i.e. repetitive pull and bend gestures); movements too subtle or small to effectively recognise; movements which seemed chaotic or accidental.

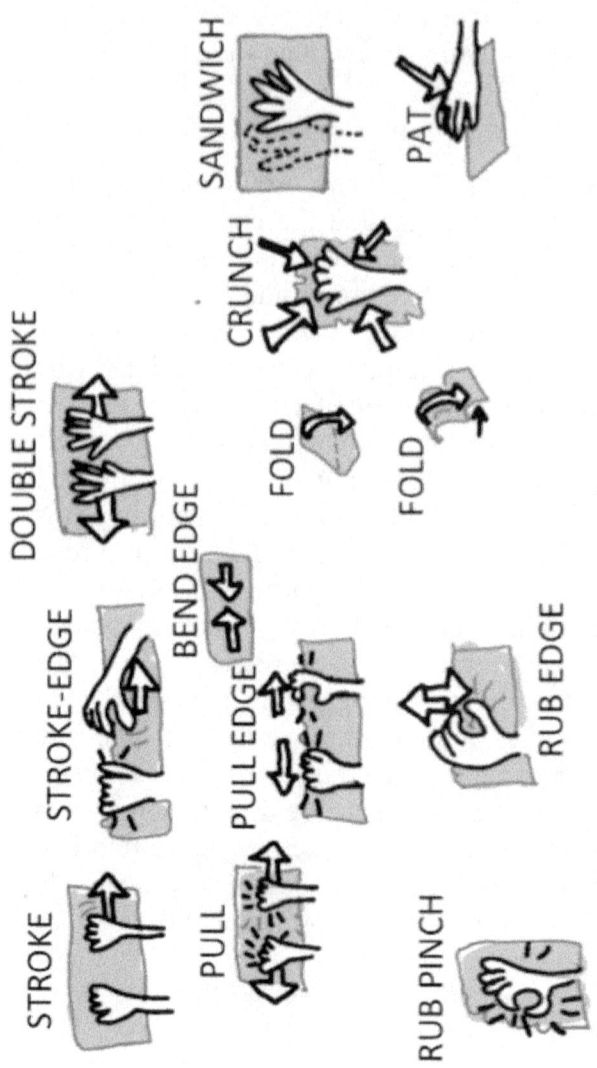

Figure 20 – Patterns that have emerged from the pilot scheme. First hand-drawn draft – handwriting was replaced and colours added for readability.

Annotation Issues

The process of initial annotation, video editing and gathering clusters from the 40 minutes of footage of the first two participants took around 100 hours. It was not feasible to continue at that pace, so we simplified the process of video annotation for the remaining video recordings:

- Annotation scheme was simplified into the final annotation scheme described above,
- Videos were no longer annotated or edited with use of software. Instead we noted them in a paper ledger where each row represented five seconds,
- Videos were analysed at 120% of their original speed to speed up and simplify the process. Whenever needed, the videos were rewound or slowed down.

Thanks to those adjustments to our process, the work on the remaining annotation took only three months. It was performed by one person only, the author of this thesis. Traditionally, annotation work is performed by a panel of at least two or three researchers to abstract the results from personal biases. The reasons why this particular set was annotated only by one person are:

- The annotating researcher was experienced in annotating gestures and it would be difficult to find another person with the same set of skills,
- This work was pioneering and it would be impossible to agree on annotation guidelines at this early stage, because the goal was to create such guidelines while annotating,
- Since this was highly explorative and high risk, no budget or staff resources were provided,
- Most of the intellectual input into this study had to come from the author of this thesis.

3.5.3 Final Gesture Dictionary

The final gesture dictionary that we used consisted of three main gestures (Stroke, Pull, Rub) and four simple gestures (Sandwich, Tap, Crunch, Bend) that did not use hand and position modifiers. The main gestures were annotated in four varieties each, depending on the number of active hands and the area of fabric that a given gesture was performed on, i.e. they were annotated as either 'one hand middle', 'one hand edge', 'two hands middle', or 'two hands edge'. Occasionally, a palm modifier had to be used to describe a specific quality of a gesture. The modifiers that we used were: Palm, Fingers, Finger, and Scratch. The identifying features of gestures and the key to read the diagram of gesture labels is described in Figure *21*.

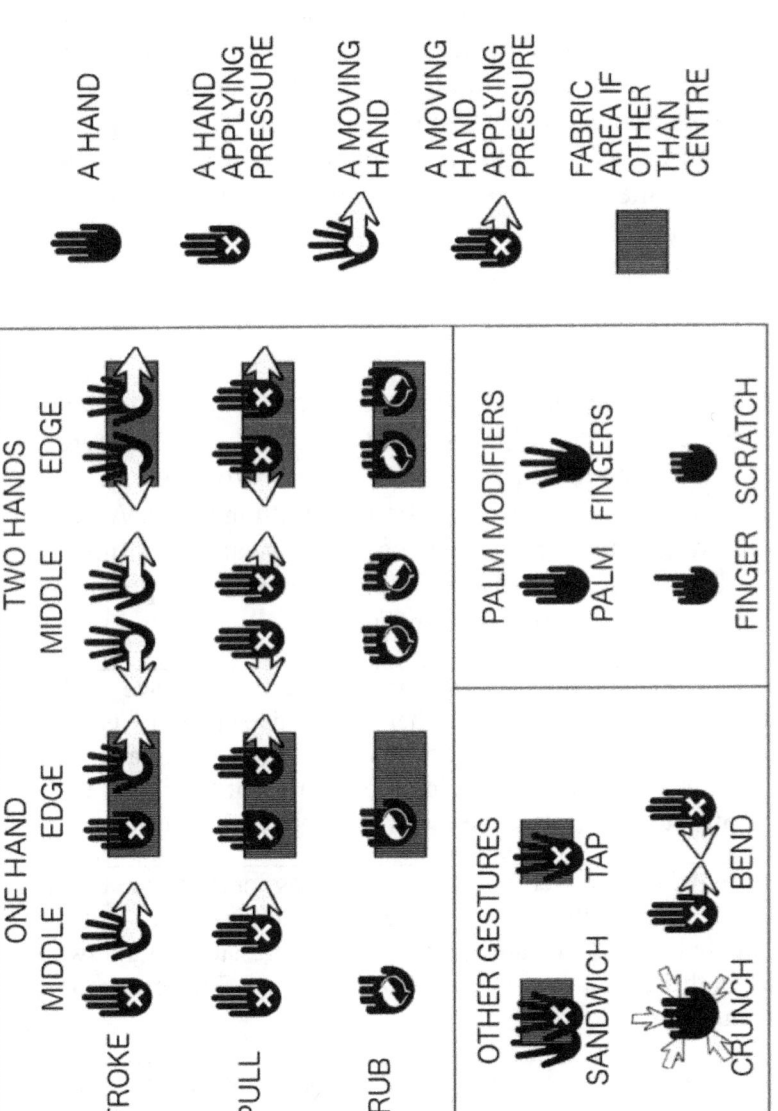

Figure 21 – Final on-fabric gesture dictionary.

The top part of the Figure *21* shows the three main gestures (Stroke, Pull, Rub) with their different variations. Variations depend on the number of active hands and position on the swatch. Below, the four other gestures (Sandwich, Tap, Crunch and Bend) are depicted alongside with palm modifiers (Palm, Fingers, Finger and Scratch). Our annotation scheme, aided by these visual representations has been successfully used to annotate video materials from our fabric handling investigation in Study 4.

How To Read Final Gesture Dictionary

We concentrated on three distinguishing features of on-fabric hand movements: applied pressure (pressing of the fabric is illustrated with a white X), movement direction (described with arrows), and performed action (in Crunch and Rub depicted with arrows). A grey rectangle on the diagrams represented the fabric swatch position in relation to its edge, wherever relevant. We presented descriptions of on-fabric gestures and their modifiers in Table 9

Stroke is a gesture performed by moving one hand on the surface of the fabric without pressing it strongly. The other (non-active) hand is used to hold the fabric in place. In a two handed version of Stroke both hands are moving away from each other, maintaining the position of the fabric with subtle pressure. Stroke often causes the fabric to ripple or flatten.
Pull is a gesture where an active hand is pressing or holding fabric strongly, while moving away from the other (non-active) hand. Pull is similar to Stroke, but both hands are applying strong pressure. In the two-handed version both hands move away from each other. Pull causes the fabric to stretch and expand.
Rub is a gesture of rubbing a piece of fabric between fingers. An element of a swatch is grabbed between two or more fingers that are then moved back and forth or in circles, while still pressing (scrunching) the fabric. Rub often does not cause the movement of a whole fabric swatch, so in a

one-hand version it does not require the use of non-active hand to hold the fabric in place. Two-handed rub is simply performing the same action with both hands.

Sandwich is a gesture of pressing a piece of fabric with both palms by placing one hand underneath the swatch and the other hand on top of the swatch and pressing both hands together. Hands might perform a movement similar to Rub, but both hands are involved. This movement is typically performed while the swatch is lifted off the table, to be able to put one hand underneath it.

Tap is a gesture of putting a hand on top of a fabric and pressing it against the table. The hand moves only on the axis of towards-away from the table.

Crunch is a gesture of grabbing a piece of fabric with an opened palm and closing that palm. It usually includes a series of consecutive moves of closing and opening the palm. It often starts like Tap and once the palm is closed, it might move into Rub.

Bend is a gesture of pressing both hands onto a table and moving them closer to each other. It causes the fabric to wrinkle, crease and bend. This gesture can be seen as the opposite version of two-handed pull, which would reverse the effect of bend, bringing it back to the fabric's resting state, laying flat at a table.

Palm is a modifier describing the use of a whole flat palm. It is assumed to be the default in the annotation scheme.

Fingers is a modifier describing the use of just the fingers without the inside of the palm,

Finger is a modifier describing the use of just one or two fingers, usually to perform a small version of a gesture.

Scratch is a modifier describing the use of fingernails, or crooked fingers to produce friction while touching the fabric.

Table 9 – Description of on-fabric gestures and their differentiaiting qualities

3.5.4 Observing Gestures – Differences Between Frequency Of Used Gestures

Using Final Gesture Dictionary

The complete 400 minutes of hand recordings were analysed using our final gesture dictionary. A total of 1168 gestures were annotated, with an average of 62 gestures by person (over the course of handling 11 swatches, on average taking a total of 21 minutes). During the annotation we stopped using the palm modifiers, because in about 50% of the cases it was impossible to annotate them accurately. Hand modifiers in those gestures where it was possible to annotate them correctly were omitted in the analysis. This problem could be solved by mounting another camera from the side of the table to provide another angle, which could make palm shape clearly visible. Another solution could be to run the study on a glass table with the camera from below. It was possible that during the annotation we have missed some gestures characterised by movements of the parts of the hand that were not visible in our camera recording setup (e.g. gestures performed underneath the fabric).

Popularity Of Gestures

The popularity of gestures was depicted on Figure 22. This diagram also shows the breakdown of how many hands were used, and whether the gesture was performed on the edge of the material. The four most popular gestures were Crunch, Pinch, Stroke and Rub, while the frequency of modifiers seemed to depend on a type of gesture. For example, most of the Rub gestures were recorded on the edge, but edges were not popular for Pinch or Stroke. A possible reason could be that most of the fabrics we selected deformed easily. When touched on the edge, the fabric would wrinkle and become hard to control, making it difficult to perform Pinch or Stroke on the very edge. Most gestures were performed with both hands active, apart from Stroke, which most of the time required one hand to hold the fabric in place. Interestingly, one fabric that provided strong friction against the table by itself, seemed to remove the need to hold the fabric in place during stroking.

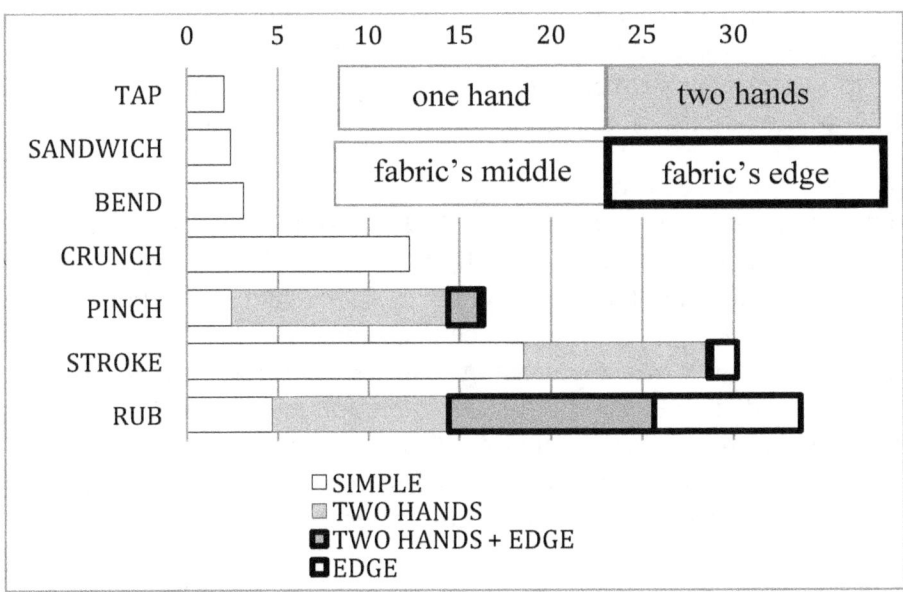

Figure 22 – Average total number of times each gesture was used by a participant during handling of 11 fabrics (over the average of 11 minutes).

3.5.5 Observing Gestures – Gesture Patterns Relevant To Interface Design And Space For Improvement Of The Annotation Scheme

Differences Between Gestures – Pressure Applied

Some gestures differed mainly by the pressure or grip that was applied, as depicted by 'X' icons in Figure *21*. Since the gestures were performed on a fabric moving freely on a table, at times it was necessary to use both hands to assist 'one hand' gestures either by pressing harder or grabbing the fabric altogether. For example, in order to perform a Stroke, it was necessary to hold the fabric in place with the other non-active hand that was not stroking.

Additionally, the gestures of Stroke and Pull differed only by the amount of pressure applied - in the Stroke gesture, the active hand slides over the fabric rippling it slightly, in the Pull gesture the active hand pulls the fabric stretching it. This had an important effect on the design of touchscreen gestures in the following chapters. It is also worth mentioning that the Bend and double Pull gestures are identical, except for the direction in which they are performed. Another possibly important distinction between gestures is the number of actively probing fingers/hands and the used area – Rub, Bend and Crunch share some similarities in this context.

3.5.6 Observing Gestures – Gesture And Word Co-occurrence

Issues With Gesture-Word Associations

In the data we searched for associations of specific gestures with specific words, focusing on patterns such as participants stretching the fabric and immediately saying "it is Stretchy". We planned to annotate both words and gestures on the video, with exact timing data when they were spoken and performed. It would create a very rich dataset and enable us to analyse co-occurrence between gestures and spoken words. This was not possible for the following reasons:

- The software we used for annotation was very out-dated, buggy, and difficult to customize, making it unusable for our purposes,
- It became clear that we did not have the time and resources for such an in depth annotation and analysis,
- Because participants were time constrained, they often performed a series of gestures and then spoke a number of words while still touching the fabric. This would likely complicate the analysis,
- We noticed a pattern where some participants always performed the same set of 3 to 5 gestures always in the same order just after receiving a fabric. For example they would consistently start their interaction with a new fabric with a set of Crunch, Rub, Stroke and Bend, and only after such an initial 'greeting' combination of gestures, would they start performing other gestures that differed between fabrics. We expected that this initial series of gestures served the purpose of evaluating the affordance of a given swatch and the gestures that followed were aimed at clarifying gesture qualities that were not clear from the initial 'greeting' gestures. Also the exact gestures and the length of the 'greeting' seemed to be very participant specific. Since these participants have spoken words during the initial gestures, but the 'greeting' gestures did not vary depending on the fabric, it is possible that the connections between gesture and word co-occurrence might be suffering from noise. In the example above, the first spoken word would always

coincide with the gesture Crunch, but possibly it was just the most obvious word that came to participant's mind, rather than a word in any way connected with the Crunch,
- Often participants performed the same gesture or spoke the same word many times within their two minute interaction with one fabric. This could mean that observing a textile quality might be a process comprising of many gestures. It might be the case that some qualities could only be obtained from a combination of gestures, not just a single gesture. The analysis of gesture-word co-occurrence where we take chains of gestures into account (rather than just single gestures) would be more complex.

For those reasons it was impossible to annotate accurately which gestures were associated with which words, without a subjective opinion from the annotating experimenter. Nevertheless, the results of the initial attempt on annotation of both words and gestures can be seen below. On the drawing Figure 23 are the notes from analysing 50 seconds of footage of one of the participants. This method has proved itself to take too long and be unfeasible, especially when we attempted to use the software annotation tool.

Figure 23 – An attempt on annotating 50 seconds of recording with both gestures and words.

Figure 23 represents one 50 seconds long video of one participant handling one fabric. On that video, we annotated spoken words alongside the performed gestures and searched for patterns. This method proved to be extremely time-consuming, as annotating 50 seconds of video on paper took about an hour, while when we attempted to use the software annotation tool (aegisub) this time almost doubled. Arguably aegisub was not designed for this type of annotation, however we did not have access to other tools and it was crucial to be able to record the data in a digital format to make it possible to analyse it easily. Words and gestures were already annotated digitally, however we only annotated their timestamps within 5 second intervals and we did not annotate words that were repeated within the same episode of fabric handling. Overall we estimated that to annotate digitally all the words and gestures with their time stamps would take a substantial amount of time (at one point we estimated additional 6 months of work). We decided against such a time commitment, since words-gesture co-occurrence was not the main scope of our research, and that time could be used to run a more constrained follow up experiment. Such a line of enquiry was not investigated within this thesis, however it could be continued as a part of future research. We were unable to perform analysis for the complete 400 minutes of video with the level of detail visible above because of time constraints and lack of access to annotation software.

Method Of Analysing Co-occurrence

Making firm conclusions about associations between specific gestures and specific words seemed to be infeasible. One of the reasons was the vast number of words and inability to acquire exact timings of all the words and gestures. Instead, in the final, complete annotation data we investigated the connection between two sets: all the gestures and all the words that were annotated in one fabric-handling episode. In other words, instead of searching for associations between single gestures and words, we analysed their co-occurrence within each 2 minute episode of handling a swatch. Even with that simplification, because of the large number of words, it was not possible to perform a comprehensive analysis of every word and gesture co-appearing together. This is why we decided to run only an exploratory analysis of just two selected words.

Gesture Differences Between Soft And Rough Fabrics

In an exploratory analysis of fabric-word co-occurrence, we investigated differences in gesture usage while handling fabrics often described with two different textile qualities. We decided to chose the qualities of Soft and Rough because after eyeballing our initial data and watching all the video recordings we had reasons to believe that people evaluated these two qualities in distinctly different ways. We felt it would be beneficial to analyse gesture-word co-occurrence for textile qualities that were perceived as different and handled in distinct ways. We did not consider Soft and Rough to be opposites, however we did consider these two words to have only a small overlap in meaning since no fabrics had Agree scores higher than 0.5 for both of these qualities at the same time.

First, we wanted to identify only fabrics that participants described with words Soft and Rough. Following the analysis from the previous chapter, where each word-fabric pairing had an Agreement score, we considered a fabric Soft or Rough if that fabric had over 0.5 agreement score for words Soft or Rough, respectively. Using that condition, we found six fabrics considered Soft (fabrics with numbers 5,9,10,15,17,22) and four fabrics considered Rough (fabrics with numbers 6,12,13,19).

Using multivariate analysis of variance (MANOVA) we compared how often the different gestures were performed when participants handled fabrics during the study. We found that participants used the same gestures with similar frequency when handling Soft and Rough fabrics (see Figure 24 for means). The average number of times that each gesture was performed was not significantly different for Soft and Rough fabrics (F(7,2)=1.45, p=.468). When looking at each gestures separately, we found that Crunch was used marginally significantly more often for Soft fabrics (M=16.3, SD=4.46) than Rough fabrics (M=8.2, SD=6.65) (F(1,8)=5.19, p=.052). A possible explanation would be that the gesture of Crunch helps to evaluate softness of the fabric or that soft fabrics afford the gesture of Crunch more easily.

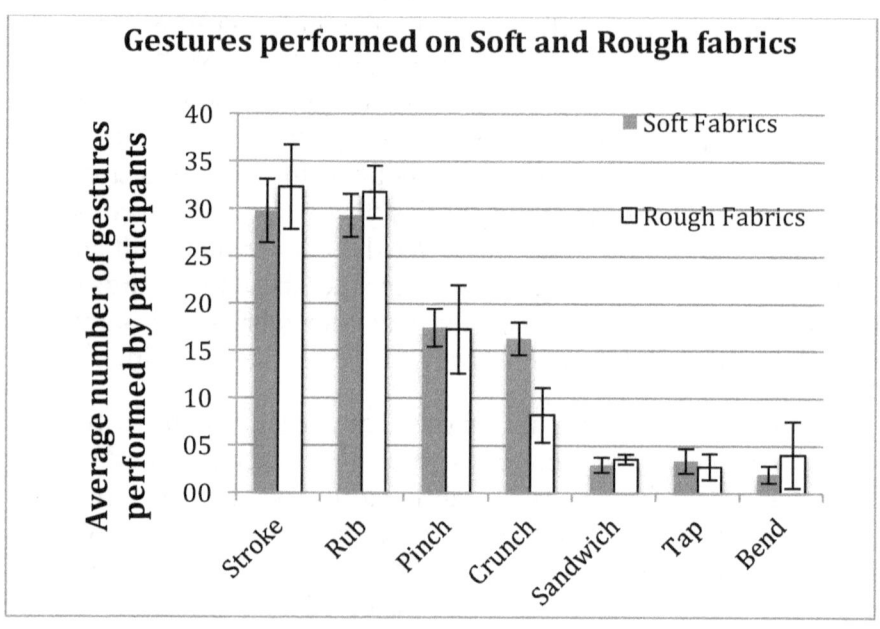

Figure 24 – Frequency of different gestures on Soft and Rough fabrics. The error bar on depicts Standard Error.

While this is an interesting finding, we did not find conclusive data for other qualities of gestures. We believe that it would be an exiting and promising avenue of research to explore the co-occurrence of fabric qualities and gestures. However, to truly explore this, we would need to run a separate study focused on extracting the differences between qualities and gestures in context of their co-occurrence. We used Soft and Rough for this analysis because these were two largest non-overlapping groups (fabrics considered very Rough were never considered very Soft), but given a more focused study design we believe that it could be possible to extract more quality-specific groups of fabrics (like Soft and Rough groups above) and identify new gestures that differentiate handling of these groups (like Crunch above),

Possible Future Work

In the future, it would be interesting to design a simple study that would investigate the association between a specific gesture and a specific word. For example, participants would have to evaluate one quality, and could be limited to only performing one gesture interaction of their choice. This would indicate whether they are more likely to Crunch the fabric when they are asked to evaluate Softness. Limiting to one interaction could work either by limiting their time to 1 second, or by explicitly instructing them to perform just one movement. This study was not performed due to time constraints.

3.6 Chapter Conclusion

Data Highlights

From the literature review we initially identified 9 gestures and 9 attributes that were used for describing on-fabric gestures. We used these gestures to annotate video footage of participants handling fabrics during our studies. After piloting the initial on-fabric gesture annotation scheme, we simplified it to 7 gestures with hand-position and fabric-area modifiers. The frequency of gestures was also analysed.

We recorded which fabric qualities participants examined (and said out loud) while performing gestures. While we hoped to pair gestures to the qualities that they helped to communicate, it was not possible due to a lot of noise in the data. The only significant correlation between gesture and fabric quality that we identified was that Soft fabrics were Crunched more frequently than Rough fabrics.

Strengths – Gesture Annotation Scheme Created From The Ground Up For The Application (On-Fabric Gestures)

The unique strength of the research methodology we used to create the gesture annotation scheme presented in this chapter was that we purpose-built it for one, concrete application (on on-fabric gestures). We found that it was impossible to describe on-fabric gestures with annotation schemes that were designed for other applications (touch-screens, in the air gesture interfaces, gesturing with smartphones, human to human communication, etc.). This is why we needed to design our own gesture annotation scheme.

Another strength of our work on the gesture annotation scheme was that we described our process in detail, so that it could be replicated. We believed that the same process of discovering a gesture annotation scheme as ours could be applied to gestures in different areas than that of handling textiles, which attempt to create a simulation of physical objects (i.e. e-commerce of upholstery, toys or jewellery). Our process has not yet been used for any other purpose than touching fabrics, hence the hypothesis that it could be re-created in another area has not been validated and is at present speculative.

We took on a new interaction area from the ground up, by using a combination of methodologies from different areas of HCI (spontaneous gesture research, human-robot interaction, in the air gestures, fabric simulators). This chapter is an example of the ability to expand HCI research to a completely new area (on-fabric and on-screen fabric interaction) and we believe that it has potential to inspire and empower the community of HCI researchers to do the same in their respective areas of interest.

Limitations – Limited Number Of Evaluated Fabrics And Only Fabrics Laying Flat On A Surface

Two main limitations of the work described in this chapter were the scale (number of fabrics) and the fact that application-specific decisions were made (focusing on the fabrics laying down flat). In our fabric handling study we selected 19 fabrics that covered wide range of types, qualities and textures. Even though our variety of fabric samples was relatively large, it is possible that we missed some types of fabrics and hence some gestures particularly relevant to those fabrics.

The other limitation was that we defined on-fabric interaction as interacting with fabrics laying down on a flat surface of a table. This decision was driven by the goals of this thesis i.e. by the need to use observed on-fabric gestures to design on-screen gestures for fabric simulators. However, in real life and shopping scenarios people often interact with fabrics that are hanging down, or lay bunched up/folded. Gestures performed in those different real-life scenarios would possibly be different from the ones we observed, but it was not possible to investigate them as well, given the time constraints of this thesis.

Future Directions

A number of interesting research avenues were not followed in this chapter, including the connection between gestures and textile qualities. Two aspects of that connection that could examined further were: the participant's intention (do non-experts use the same gestures when attempting to evaluate the same quality?) and the gesture's affordance (does performing a particular gesture provide knowledge of a particular set of qualities connected to that gesture?). While we performed a preliminary analysis (finding the correlation between Soft fabrics and Crunching gesture), these questions require separate purpose-designed studies.

To investigate the co-occurrence of fabric qualities and gestures we could design studies in which we restrict fabric qualities and possible gesture interactions. For example we could observe gestures of participants asked to describe only one quality of textiles (i.e. Soft) but their interaction with fabric samples is very limited (i.e. they have only limited amount of time to evaluate each sample). This could be a sorting study, where participants have 15 fabric samples and can touch each one only once and need to arrange them on the scale of Soft. We would expect to see that a particular gesture could appear more for a particular word (i.e. Stroke for Rough, or Crunch for Fluffy).

Another approach would be to limit interactions to only one pre-trained gesture (i.e. one hand Crunch) with a large set of visually similar fabrics, and to ask participants to say only three words that in their opinion best describe each fabric swatch. For the purposes of motivation and gamification participants could be told that another participant will use their descriptions to identify individual swatches from the set. We would expect to find that the same task of describing 20 swatches when conducted for different gestures (i.e. Crunch, Stroke, Pull) would generate different frequency of particular words. For example Flexible or Stretchy could appear more when participants were only allowed to Pull the fabric. Another experimental setup could involve triads where participants can interact with three fabrics only with one gesture and then need to point to the odd fabric in the set and describe one fabric quality that makes that odd fabric different from the other two.

3.7 Chapter Contributions

> CONTRIBUTION 3.1 – Labels Describing On-Fabric Gestures, Their Descriptions And Popularity.

In this chapter we created an annotation scheme for on-fabric gestures. The scheme describes movements that non-expert users perform when they handle a piece of fabric with the purpose of evaluating that fabric's qualities. The scheme is detailed in Figure *21* together with the distinguishing features of all the gesture labels. The scheme consists of seven gestures with their permutations: Pull, Stroke, Rub, Sandwich, Bend, Crunch and Tap.

We created and evaluated this annotation scheme by annotating 400 minutes of video of hands handling fabric from our fabric handling study. The scheme was created based on observation of handling unattached fabrics lying loosely flat on the table. The scheme can be revisited, expanded and modified for handling fabrics in other contexts, such as hanging on a rail, or pinned to a table. Because of the experimental scenario we used, the gestures described in the scheme correspond to unrestricted on-fabric gestures, but the knowledge we acquired can be used to understand user intentions and aid design of touchscreen textile simulators.

CONTRIBUTION 3.2 – Procedure For Creating A Gesture Annotation Scheme (CONTRIBUTION 1) That Could Be Reused In Different Application.

The second contribution of this chapter is a procedure for creating an annotation scheme that can be used to explore a new area of interaction. We used that method to achieve Contribution 3.1 by investigating ways that people touch fabrics, but it could be used in others' applications. We recommend combining findings from previous literature with observational studies to devise a prototype annotation scheme of gestures. Next we advise an iterative process of evaluation and re-design while observing target subjects.

We evaluated this process by following it in the investigation of on-fabric gestures. The findings and comments can be found in this chapter and in Appendix III. This process has not yet been applied and evaluated in another area, however we believed it could be beneficial to other researchers.

CONTRIBUTION 3.3 – Graphical Representation Of Annotation Scheme For On-Fabric Gestures (Contribution 1).

The third contribution of this chapter is a graphical representation of the annotation scheme describing on-fabric gestures. This chart, presented and described in Figure 17 could be used for easier and faster annotation of gestures, because the people annotating video would have a simple and well described reference sheet. The chart with on-fabric gestures could be useful because it depicts and explains how we have simplified gesture names by using edge and active hand modifiers. For example instead of creating a separate name for each version of the basic gestures (i.e. calling two handed Stroke a Ripple), we used simple names with modifiers (Stroke-

2Hand-Centre). Additionally icons were provided on the chart as a quick reference.

We evaluated the graphical chart by using it for annotation of the complete 400 minutes of recordings from our fabric handling study. It has been successfully used and enabled quick and efficient video annotation.

Chapter 4 – iShoogle Textile Simulator

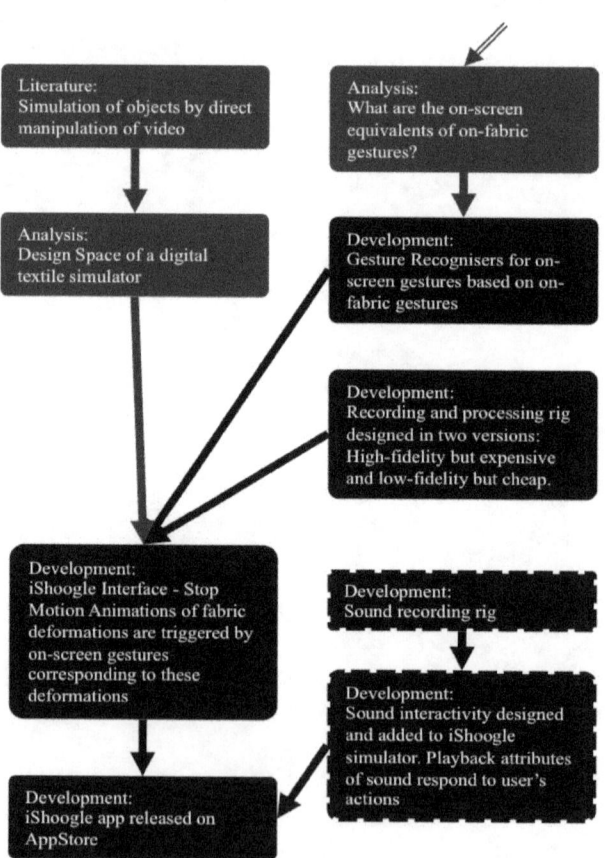

4. iShoogle – Multi-Gesture Textile Simulator Interface: Visuals, Interaction and Sound

4.1 Introduction

4.1.1 Context

Context Within The Thesis

This thesis reports on the investigation of interfaces that digitally communicate the qualities of fabrics. Such interfaces should enable non-experts to evaluate textile qualities described in Chapter 2. We identified gestures investigated in Chapter 3 as a promising foundation of a digital interface to interact with fabrics on the screen.

In this chapter we created a proof of concept touchscreen interface that used on-screen gestures based on the on-fabric gestures from Chapter 3. We explain how the iShoogle interface works and also describe how to record video content to be used in this interface. Also in this chapter we explain how sound could be used to extend the iShoogle interface and describe how sound such samples should be recorded.

The iShoogle interface described in this chapter was used in all further research described in this thesis. Videos of the iShoogle interface are available at the author's website http://www.macs.hw.ac.uk/texturelab/people/pawel-michal-orzechowski/

4.1.2 Chapter Goals And Motivation For Goals

> GOAL 4.1 – Create A Multi-Gesture Touch-Screen Interactive Fabric Simulator Using On-Screen Equivalents Of On-Fabric Gestures From Chapter 3

We needed to design and implement a gesture-based fabric simulator interface. In this chapter we describe the final design of iShoogle – an iPad touchscreen interface based on the gestures described in Chapter 3. We aimed to make the touch-screen fabric handling experience similar to the experience of touching a physical fabric sample. We describe the process of designing software that combines input (gestures) and output (visual and sound feedback) to provide direct and instantaneous reaction of the on-screen fabric to user's movements. This interface will be further evaluated and used throughout this thesis.

> GOAL 4.2 – Describe A Camera Setup For Capturing Video Recordings Of Fabric Deformations

We needed to design and describe a recording setup to capture video recordings of fabrics that then could be displayed on the iShoogle interface. Such recording had to be described in enough detail so that it could be replicated by other researchers or users of the iShoogle system. Additionally the setup had to take into consideration limitations of equipment and skill that could limit its practicality.

GOAL 4.3 – Extend iShoogle Interface With Sound: Interface Interactivity And Sound Recording Setup

We considered extending the iShoogle interface with sound feedback. Such an extension would play fabric deformation sounds in response to user's feedback, the same way as iShoogle played visual feedback. One of the goals of this chapter was to specify the algorithm that would translate user's actions into playback qualities of the sound (pitch, volume, etc.). Additionally a detailed description of the sound recording setup would be necessary to provide other researchers and iShoogle users with means to create content that could be used within the iShoogle interface.

4.1.3 Contributions And Acknowledgements

Unless otherwise specified, all the intellectual input into this thesis comes from the author. Douglas Atkinson took part in testing the prototypes of sound enabled iShoogle and in devising the microphone setup.

4.2 Literature Review

4.2.1 Introduction To The Literature Review

We conducted an extensive literature search about interface design for direct manipulation of objects on the screen. The challenges described by most researchers were: discoverability and learning, technical limitations, interfaces for controlling video playback, enabling multiple interactions, and a seamless way to switch between them.

For the purposes of this thesis, it was crucial to understand the balance of advantages and disadvantages between an interface with Graphical User Interface (GUI) widgets (visible on the screen elements, such as buttons or sliders) and a non-visible interface (where interaction was apparent only as a result of user's actions). We also looked at literature attempting to create the illusion of manipulating an on-screen object by user's actions with the visual, sound and haptic feedback.

We also investigated the limitations that were introduced when a multi-gesture interface required more cognitive load, due to the fact that the user needed to learn and remember all the available interactions. We looked at literature discussing affordances (natural tendencies) and conventions (learned tendencies), as well as Cognitive Load Theory (CLT) literature. Cierniak et al. (2009) outlined that CLT distinguishes between wasteful (Germane), invested (Extraneous) and active (Intrinsic) mental load. According to work described by Wong et al. (2009), animations and life-like presentation were beneficial when applied to manual tasks that involve human movement, and hence should be useful for fabric handling scenarios.

The design of the iShoogle interface is described in this chapter, but studies that we conducted to evaluate iShoogle are all described in the next chapter. Because of this close connection between the design and evaluation of iShoogle, both chapters share one literature review, reported in this chapter.

4.2.2 Video Browsing By Direct Manipulation.

Dragicevic et al. (2008) devised an interface for manipulating video recordings by dragging objects featured in the video directly on the computer screen. Instead of moving a timeline slider, a video could be navigated by moving objects along a visual trajectory that they followed on the recording. This technique was called Relative Flow Dragging and enabled manipulating movement of recorded objects using their position and movement flow, instead of timeline. For example, CCTV operators could analyse a car accident video by dragging cars to the point they collide, rather than by navigating video with the timeline slider.

In a low-directness interface (i.e. timeline slider) user's actions are separated in space and time from their feedback, introducing the following problems:

- Indirection of Flow (misalignment of movement trajectory). If the speed of the moving object changed on the recording, moving a slider at a steady speed would move the object at a changing speed, making it difficult to follow their trajectory.
- Incompatibility (inconsistent time and object of the movement): the slider was usually placed below the screen, creating a dissonance between manipulation and the resulting movement.
- Low integration of degrees of freedom (not all the movements were allowed and suitable for horizontal navigation): while sliders used a horizontal straight line, it was inappropriate for navigating a movement on non-straight and non-horizontal trajectories.

To make Relative Flow Dragging possible, a visual processing algorithm was used that extracted motion data from videos, by separating moving objects and mapping their spatial displacement on a timeline. Once videos were analysed this way, the video's playback could be controlled by dragging any movable object on the video, rather than by dragging the timeline widget.

The HCI challenges that needed further work were: manipulated content could sometimes move and deform in an arbitrarily disorganized manner; content only moves along a constrained and predefined path; when the object was dragged it also animated the rest of the visual scene, which could introduce distraction and confusion. Dragicevic et al. (2008) argued that these drawbacks of relative flow dragging were countered by the directness of manipulation, derived from how responsive and unobtrusive the system was, and how close the user input of the interface matched the output provided.

The suggested solution to the above problems was to perfectly match user's movements (input) to the inflicted motion of displayed objects (output), "matching the gestures space with the motions space". Thus Relative Flow Dragging was related to the following other methods of mapping a limited 2D gesture space to the range of visual motions:

- Curvilinear dragging - bending a timeline/interaction axis into a curve, to enable steering by following a non-straight line,
- Flow dragging - separately mapping movement and deformation of every point on a moving object, to allow separate curvilinear dragging trajectories. It was used to enable control over the moving object while it was deformed or changes direction,
- Relative dragging - when motion was induced from the background movements, the dragging trajectories were subtracted from that background motion.

Dragicevic et al. (2008) developed a movie browsing tool that analyses the video materials by searching for moving objects and their trajectories. With data referencing movement and position of objects, continuously on the timeline, it was possible to navigate video by dragging those objects. Because dragging was constrained by the actual trail of the recorded object, when a mouse was placed over a draggable object, the cursor changes into a hand icon, and a trajectory that could be followed was highlighted. For simplicity of dragging, the user did not need to follow the trajectory line exactly with their mouse, as the cursor position was approximated to the allowed path.

In the user study, participants had to navigate animations of objects moving on curved, looping trajectories (cars on an intersection, and insects flying in circles). The direct manipulation interface was compared with sliders (traditionally used for navigating video) in terms of speed and accuracy of finding one particular movie frame. The results suggested that relative flow dragging was faster and just as accurate as the traditional slider interface.

The limitations of this technique were: granularity (small manoeuvres were simplified to create a smoother path), arc continuity (the path cannot intersect with itself), and direction continuity (the interface does not support objects reversing and moving back along the same track).

From this paper we have incorporated a number of methodological and theoretical inputs. In line work outlined by Dragicevic et al. (2008), we tested interfaces by comparing them to an existing GUI equivalent, while also focusing on speed and accuracy of task performance. In terms of theory, we incorporated the concepts of gesture space and motion space into our interface design efforts. In order to tackle some of the problems encountered by the authors, our interface only incorporated gestures that had the potential to be direct and unobtrusive. We also required the interactions to closely match the performed gestures (input) and experienced visual or sound stimuli (output).

4.2.3 Draglocks: Handling Temporal Ambiguities In Direct Manipulation Video Navigation

Karrer, Wittenhagen, and Borchers (2012) modified their design previously described by Dragicevic et al. (2008) to enable manipulation of video with temporal ambiguity (movement pauses; parts of the video where the manipulated object was not moving). The paper aims to address problems presented by the direct manipulation of video in the following cases:

- object pauses its movement (model at a catwalk),
- the movements were recurring (hands of a clock),
- self intersecting trajectory (looping roller-coaster).

Karrer et al. (2012) tested a number of ways to annotate the speed at which the object was moving on the timeline curve. In a study performed on a touch tablet, participants were asked to find an event on a timeline, which happened just before, after or during a pause. Pauses had varying lengths. The findings suggested that the best solution would be to annotate pauses on the timeline with a different colour, or a loop that trails off and returns to the timeline after the pause.

From this paper we appropriated the experimental task of finding an element on a directly manipulated video, and the highlighted importance of training: exposure to the video material prior to the task.

4.2.4 Crossmodal Congruence: The Look, Feel And Sound Of Touchscreen Widgets

On-screen widgets' design (appearance and behaviour) can be visually based on their physical counterparts (for example a software button on a screen could be based on designs of physical buttons and switches). As new modalities get introduced to computers it would be desirable to base sound, vibration and haptic qualities of the digital elements on their physical blueprints. In the context of this thesis, it would mean that the fabrics to be presented digitally should be the source of video and sound recordings in the studies, since the digital interface should mimic the original physical fabric.

Hoggan, Kaaresoja, Laitinen, and Brewster (2008) compared different vibration and sound technologies with various ways to display and animate buttons. Their aim was to discover what would be an appropriate vibration stimuli associated with shape, size, shadow and responsiveness of GUI elements. The assumption was that participants would have a uniform expectation of how different digital buttons should feel, just as they have experience-based expectations of how physical objects would feel. Hoggan et al. (2008) defined the concept of congruence as the appropriateness or harmony between cross-modal widgets, where visual, haptic and sound feedback were complementing each other in creating a consistent and realistic virtual object. From the combined feedback of those three modalities, the users were able to deduce the implied physical qualities of on-screen objects.

Users were likely to use their knowledge of real physical buttons in estimating the qualities of GUI buttons, hence Hoggan et al. (2008) studied ten designs of physical hardware buttons to identify their distinguishing features. They then identified the following qualities of buttons and evaluated the feasibility of translating them into on-screen widgets: size, shape, colour, texture, weight, snap ratio, height, travel friction, surrounding.

In a pairwise comparison study, participants used varying visual designs of keypads to type in digits. In each trial, the displayed keypad had two vibration options and the user's task was to select the vibration feedback more suitable to the current visual button design. Vibration options varied by strength and technology (rotating and piezo), while buttons varied by the factors described above. The results suggested that a rotating vibration (and sound associated with them) was suitable for raised, round buttons, while the piezo vibrators (and the sound associated with them) were suitable for rectangular and small buttons.

The elements of this research we incorporated were: the initial stage of observing physical behaviour of objects to inform the digital design; separately evaluating the feasibility of translating each physical quality of artefact into a digital quality of an interface; the idea for a pairwise-comparison study presenting two interfaces and asking participants to point out the more congruent (Realistic/Suitable) one; holistic approach to cross-modal interfaces where modalities were complementing each other, rather than existing separately.

4.2.5 Integration Of Vision And Haptics During Tool Use

Takahashi, Diedrichsen, and Watt (2009) investigated how inconsistencies between visual and haptic feedback influenced the ability to estimate the size of virtual objects. In the physical world, whenever visual and haptic feedback of grasping an object were consistent with each other, it indicated that they both originated at the same object. A good example of this phenomenon is moving small objects with our hand while looking at them under a microscope: visual and haptic feedback are consistent with our movements, even though the scale has to be implied and we are using a tool to move the objects. When the object is handled directly or with a tool (i.e. pliers, tweezers), our brain is capable of maintaining manipulation accuracy with the tool because as we can calculate appropriate movements to counterbalance the tool's size and shape. However, especially in the virtual realm, there is often an offset (or even a delay) between user's actions and the movements of the object on the screen, because of the way interface or the hardware works. A good example of this phenomena is that most of the touchscreens interpret the touch point a few millimetres above the actual touch point sensed by the hardware. This offset is designed to counterbalance the human tendency to intend to point with the end of the finger (extension of the line running through the finger), but to actually touch sensors with the pad of the finger (where the fingerprint is located), hence creating a few millimetres of offset. Digital interfaces are designed to counterbalance our natural biases and interpret actions that users' mean to request, rather than those that they actually physically request as described by Henze, Rukzio, and Boll (2011).

In the described experiment, participants were asked to compare sizes of virtual objects by pinching them with two force feedback devices attached to their fingers. At the same time, the visual stimuli were provided with a stereoscope, allowing for an exact match between the object size perceived with haptic and visual feedback. The study investigated the impact that offsetting haptic stimuli from the visual stimuli had on perception accuracy in two conditions:

- when grasping the virtual object without a virtual tool (with virtual fingertips – points in the virtual space corresponding exactly to the moves of apparatus-connected fingertips of the participant),
- when grasping the virtual object with a virtual tool displayed on a screen (operated similarly to tongs attached to the abovementioned virtual fingertips).

The findings confirmed that the loss in accuracy caused by the visual offset when grasping an object was the same when the offset was applied to fingertips, or the ends of handling tool. The findings supported the theory that the brain could internalize geometry and dynamics of the tools it used and could take into account the spatial offset of visual and haptic signals only when it is necessary.

The findings of this paper influenced the design of simulated physics in our interface. Instead of enforcing exact alignment of user's fingers and movements of our simulated materials, we introduced a simulated flexible tool, acting like a rubber band between actual touch points and simulated virtual fingers deforming the fabric. This solution mediated between the movements of hands and the effect they had on the virtual fabric. Takahashi et al. (2009) suggested that users had taken account of a tool acting as a layer between their hand and the simulated fabric they interacted with. This level of abstraction created a smoother physics simulation, however the visual representation of the tool was removed from the final interface, providing a better aesthetic experience.

4.2.6 Potential Limitations Of The Multi-Touch Gesture Vocabulary: Differentiation, Adoption, Fatigue

Yee (2009) provided a comprehensive resource of criteria to consider while designing new gesture based interfaces. The authors identified the following criteria as crucial for acceptance of new gestures:

- interaction context (gestures were suitable, obvious, clear and intuitive for a given task),
- minimal effort (gestures were simple to perform),

- appropriate metaphors (logical relationship between the type of movement, interaction, and the object interacted with),
- minimum muscle stress (designed for repetitive use without muscle fatigue),
- accurately recognizable by software (with a minimum of false positives, and mistakes).

These criteria were especially relevant for continuous gestures, where the length of the gesture determines the extent of the action (zooming, dragging) and there was a single movement to object association (it was obvious what the user was resizing and dragging). This type of interaction benefited users by reducing their learning curve: attention was focused on direct interaction rather than on the interface.

Additionally, Yee (2009) expanded on the above list of criteria by adding:

- increased differentiation between gestures to minimize learning curve (provided better discoverability and made gestures understood and adopted easily),
- efficient cues hinting affordable gestures (in a subtle way and prompted by user's actions and errors),
- focused on finger movements (to avoid fatigue, gesture design should reflect the natural way in which human hands move and interact with the world).

Yee (2009) also suggested creating a consistent gesture ecosystem in which users were likely to discover interactions similar to those that they had already used. This could be achieved by using consistent semantic guidelines, such as always connecting the size of the gesture or number of fingers used with the magnitude of action. This comparability could be further enhanced with visual and audio cues using metaphors, indicators, and easy recovery options.

The knowledge and skills that users have from interacting with the physical world could be used to design a better interface: zones/areas could easily communicate groups, pointing was effortless and very accurate, elasticity and rebound increased the performance of dragging.

From this paper we appropriated many aspects of our interface design into our process. Examples include:

- interpreting the number of fingers used as the magnitude of gesture (the more fingers used, the higher the simulated pressure applied to the virtual fabric)
- adding the physical qualities (bounciness and friction) to the simulated fabrics to make gestures more similar to real life interaction with fabric,
- using on-screen hints which glow when gestures were performed, to hint available interactions,
- always using two directions for all gestures, for easier discoverability and to provide a consistent ecosystem of gestures.

4.2.7 Examining Working Memory Load And Congruency Effects On Affordances And Conventions

Still and Dark (2010) examined the impact of perceptual affordances and cultural conventions in a series of behavioural studies. They evaluated in which context the working memory and correct expected button-to-action mapping (congruency) have impact on performance. Participants were asked to perform simple tasks with arrow buttons that in some experimental conditions represented actions opposite to the expected ones.

Whenever the interface went against a perceptual or cultural expectation, its performance was hindered; however, whenever there was a high memory load, it further decreased performance only for the cultural expectations. Perceptual affordance (expectation driven by the fact that some actions were easier and more available) was not affected by high memory load, and hence was a very valuable resource for interface designers. Authors concluded that since conventions require an initial learning period, they should be combined with affordances whenever a new mode of interaction was designed.

4.2.8 Instructional Animations Could Be Superior To Statics When Learning Human Motor Skills

Wong et al. (2009) examined whether animated instructions were superior to static graphics instructions. Authors taught their participants to fold origami with those two methods and measured time, perceived mental load and error rate. The results confirmed their hypothesis that the animations would be superior for this particular task. The authors argued that this may be due to the fact that the working memory processor was facilitated by the mirror neuron system which in turn makes animations superior in explaining tasks that are connected with hand movement.

4.2.9 Explaining The Split Attention Effect: Was The Reduction Of Extraneous Load Accompanied By An Increase In Germane Cognitive Load

Cierniak, Scheiter, and Gerjets (2009) describes the split attention effect that occurs when verbal and pictorial information resources are physically separated, making it difficult to use those resources for learning. For example, when a picture and text that described an object within the learning materials were displayed separately, learners needed to hold information separately in the memory and mentally integrate both sources. An example of such placement on a map would be a name of an country written on the side of the map with a line leading to the area it describes, in comparison to the name of a country written directly on the area it describes. In the study, participants learned about the functions of kidneys with the use of either split-source materials (the key was displayed on the side of the image) or integrated materials (the key was annotated onto the image). The additional task of interpreting the key required using additional mental resources and increased the perceived difficulty of learning materials.

Cognitive Load Theory, which we describe in more depth in section 5.3.1, is one of frameworks for describing mental resources used during training and interacting with interfaces. Cierniak et al. (2009) used this theory in their work and they measured Overall Cognitive Load with a secondary task, while they used subjective ratings to distinguish between Intrinsic, Extraneous and Germane Cognitive Loads.

Participants who used split-source learning materials showed poorer learning and showed an increase in extraneous and germane loads. This meant that more effort was invested into understanding materials and interpreting the presentation of materials. There was a strong positive correlation between ratings of intrinsic and extraneous Cognitive Load This might suggest that these two types of Cognitive Load were understood by the participants as one concept, which was a weakness in the design of this study. There was no impact on the secondary task, possibly because the learning task was too easy and left enough mental resources to deal with the secondary task in a perfect manner.

This paper highlights the importance of constructing the question to measure different types of Cognitive Load and that the task participants performed had to be carefully designed.

4.2.10 Interactive Multimodal Learning Environments

A Multimodal Theory described by Moreno and Mayer (2007) is a theory competing with CLT in explaining mechanisms behind creating successful instructional materials and interfaces. It stems from the modality principle of instructional design support, where using a mix of verbal and non-verbal elements produces the best instructional materials. Another important feature of digital instructions is interactivity (responsiveness to user's actions). Moreno describes five types of interactivity: Dialoguing, Controlling, Manipulating, Searching and Navigating.

Additionally, the above described cognitive-affective theory of learning with media states that: humans have multiple channels to process different modalities; temporary memory is finite; learning takes effort; knowledge is built in the act of learning; engagement increases the amount of resources committed to learning; and with experience, schema acquisition becomes easier.

When demands on resources used for processing learning material exceed the available cognitive resources of the learner, a cognitive overload takes place. To fully understand and learn to avoid such an overload, processing was split into four types: extraneous processing happens when learning materials are analysed; representational holding (a specific case of extraneous processing) happens when information needs to be temporarily stored by learner to fully use learning materials; essential processing happens during manipulating new information in temporary memory; generative processing happens during generating schemas and storing knowledge in long term memory. Because the total amount of processing is limited, when extraneous processing is limited, there is more processing resources left to engage in essential and generative processing without causing cognitive overload.

Essentially Mayer's multimodal theory is an alternative to using CLT, however we opted for using CLT as a framework in this thesis due to the fact that other researchers who explored questions similar to ours (i.e. using instructional materials with gestural and controlled animation resources) also used CLT as in work reported by Wong et al. (2009) and by Mayer, Hegarty, Mayer, and Campbell (2005).

4.2.11 Probing The Mental Representation Of Gesture: Was Hand Waving Spatial?

Wagner, Nusbaum, and Goldin-Meadow (2004) have shown that gesturing reduced the mental load of explaining mathematical problems. Researchers varied the ability to gesture or not and the type of secondary memory task (remembering letters, or patterns). Findings suggested that gesturing increases performance in a memory task, possibly because it reduces mental load. Interestingly, when gestures were not consistent with words of explanation, they did not correlate with better memory performance. The authors concluded that gestures were propositional (meaning-centred), rather than spatial (movement-centred), and hence could be used to accompany and empower meaning-related tasks. An alternative explanation was that not gesturing introduced additional mental load, because participants had to remember not to gesture.

4.2.12 Altered Vision Near Hands

Abrams, Davoli, Du, Knapp, and Paull (2008) measured the performance in visual attention tasks when participants' hands were in varying positions (away from the screen; near the screen; near the screen, but obscured). The results suggested that people shifted their attention slower when their hands were next to the object that they were paying attention to. The authors interpret this as the tendency to closely evaluate objects nearby (that could be potentially manipulated), and briefly evaluate objects further away (that could be potentially dangerous).

The attention tasks were:

- visual search (finding one of two letters on the screen and pressing an appropriate button),
- inhibition of return (recognising a marker on the screen with a possibly confusing clue beforehand),
- attentional blink (recognising two elements within a sequence of characters, while recognising the second one was more complicated if it immediately follows the first one).

The results indicate that performing the task next to one's hands causes: slower finding of a target; longer time to disengage attention; lower accuracy of recognising second target if it followed soon after the first one.

The psychophysical method used in this paper inspired our experiments. The differences between perception of objects near the hands may indicate that people were paying more attention when interacting with simulated fabrics at one's fingertips, when compared to screen and mouse scenario. This would suggest the touchscreen textile simulators have an advantage over their mouse-and-screen counterparts.

4.2.13 Literature Review Summary

The main lessons learned from the literature review, were:

- It is possible to interact with pre-recorded video material by interacting with the movement of the recorded objects rather than by interacting with the timeline. This technique of direct manipulation was called Relative Flow Dragging outlined by Dragicevic et al. (2008),
- It is possible to solve ambiguities in direct manipulation (such as when a dragged object in the video passes by the same point) with visual clues and on-screen widgets as investigated by Karrer et al. (2012),
- Further visual clues (shadow, size, pressing delay) can hint on weight and physical properties of on-screen objects as detailed by Hoggan et al. (2008),
- When people move objects on the screen it is not necessary that the physical finger touch-points and places where animated objects depict touch points are exactly in the same place. The human brain can interpret distance and not lose accuracy (as when using tongs) in work outlined by Takahashi et al. (2009),
- A touch-screen gesture dictionary needs to address: discoverability, software recognition, metaphors, all described by Yee (2009),

- When gestures go against cultural and perceptual expectations their performance will be hindered, especially during difficult tasks as in a study described by Still and Dark (2010),
- In order to ensure good understanding of the interface and expectations of the gesture metaphors it is crucial to provide appropriate instructional materials. For hand movement related task, animated instructions are more appropriate: more beneficial according to Wong et al. (2009),
- When visual clues and instructions are not presented in a manner suitable for the interface and the task, it can impede the performance and learning while using that interface as investigated by Cierniak et al. (2009),
- Possibly performing actions with hands makes it easier to also perform other unrelated tasks at the same time as in work detailed by Wagner et al. (2004),
- When performing tasks while touching the screen, or with hands next to the screen, people tended to focus their attention more and for longer as in researched outlined by Abrams et al. (2008).

4.3 Organisation Of This Chapter

In this literature review, we investigated the state of research in the following areas: gesture driven interfaces; interfaces for handling objects in simulated or a virtual reality; cognitive load caused by using interfaces.

We described the design space of a digital texture simulator within which the iShoogle interface would exist. We describe the most important requirements and the trade-offs that were necessary with some potential alternative solutions.

Further, we described the decisions behind creating the iShoogle Interface, the design of video switching and navigation, our approach to stop motion animation and simulated dynamics of video playback that were designed as a simple emulation of fabric physics. We also describe the structure of gesture recognisers and tools that we used to process recorded fabric deformation videos, such as shoogleit.com.

Next we explain our implementation of the setup we used for recording fabric deformation videos. We created two recording setups, a time and resource expensive high fidelity recording setup and a cheap and simple low fidelity recording setup.

Finally, we describe extending iShoogle with sound feedback. In this section we describe the algorithm that translated user actions into the qualities of sound playback. We also detail how the fabric deformation sound samples were recorded.

4.4 Design Of The iShoogle Interface

4.4.1 Introduction

To meet the goals of this chapter we created an iShoogle: a novel textile simulator interface that makes it possible to Pinch, Stroke and Crunch fabrics on an iPad. The initial concept behind iShoogle was to enable interacting with fabrics on a touchscreen with use of the natural gestures investigated in chapter 3.

The biggest invention in the design of iShoogle was the ability to have one simulated textile object respond instantaneously to many gestures. This breakthrough was possible thanks to combining stop motion animation, a custom recording technique, gesture recogniser design and simulated physics. Below we describe creating the iShoogle textile simulator.

From the literature we knew that the perception of moving objects is different than the perception of static images and that seeing an object move and reflect light at certain angles might be a preferred way to look at objects people evaluate as described by Padilla (2008). According to Padilla, participants would find the most informative interaction for evaluating an object and would repeatedly perform it. For example, when evaluating the roughness of a piece of concrete, people tent to find the angle under which the light is reflected in a way to give the most informative reflection. Then participants moved the evaluated object slightly against the light always coming back to that optimal angle. We aimed to utilize people's tendency to move objects in the most beneficial way, which provided the most accurate perception of object's qualities (this could be called an affordance on physical objects). That was the reason we created an iShoogle interface by translating the natural on-fabric gestures (described in Chapter 3) as closely as possible onto touch-screen on-screen gestures. We developed a complex multi-gesture environment, simulating direct manipulation of fabrics via touch-screen tablet, aiming to create a visual, acoustic and interactive experience as close to touching real fabric as possible.

4.4.2 Design Space

What Is A Design Space

When looking for an optimal solution to a problem, we had to first understand all the dependencies of the system within which our solution would exist. It is rarely possible to satisfy all the requirements, hence trade-offs and compromises needed to be made. An optimal solution is not one which fulfils one or all of the requirements, but one which provides the best balance of key values. The famous description of design space described by Alexander (1964) used an example of requirements for a vacuum cleaner design. The vacuum cleaner would preferably be small, cheap, powerful and simple to repair, however it is not possible to achieve all of these traits at the same time. These four axes could be used to map the design space of a hoover where some of the axes stood in conflict with each other (small vs. powerful) while others could align (small and simple). Within such design space there was a possibility to create a number of valid designs that would satisfy different parts of the market. For example there could be a mass market for small, cheap, not-powerful household hoovers that did not have to be simple in repair, but also there could be a niche market for large, expensive and powerful industrial hoovers that needed to be simple to repair by in-house technicians. Mapping a design space of a problem allowed for visualisation of trade-offs and made it possible to consciously make sacrifices of features in favour of other valuable qualities of the design.

We designed iShoogle interface to stand in-between a physical fabric (or in some sense a person recording that fabric) and a person interacting with that fabric digitally. The system which supported these two agents and multitude of scenarios had to support simple, cheap and effective recording, editing, distribution, hardware to create and hardware to interact with the system. The interface itself had to be easy to learn, use and effectively communicate correct fabric qualities. There was a large amount of axis on which the design space of iShoogle could be described and below we describe how we charted that space.

Design Space Of A iShoogle Textile Simulator

To specify the design space of iShoogle we started by specifying our perceived constraints, and assumptions after reviewing relevant literature. As a foundation for our design space we chose an eight node design described by Whitworth and Ahmad (2014) (in section 2.3) which combines four requirements connected with taking opportunities (Functional, Extendable, Connected, Flexible) and four requirements connected with avoiding risks (Reliable, Private, Secure, Usable). On the picture Figure 25 which we appropriated and modified from figure 2.3 from the work published by Whitworth and Ahmad (2014), we detailed what these requirements mean in the context of iShoogle.

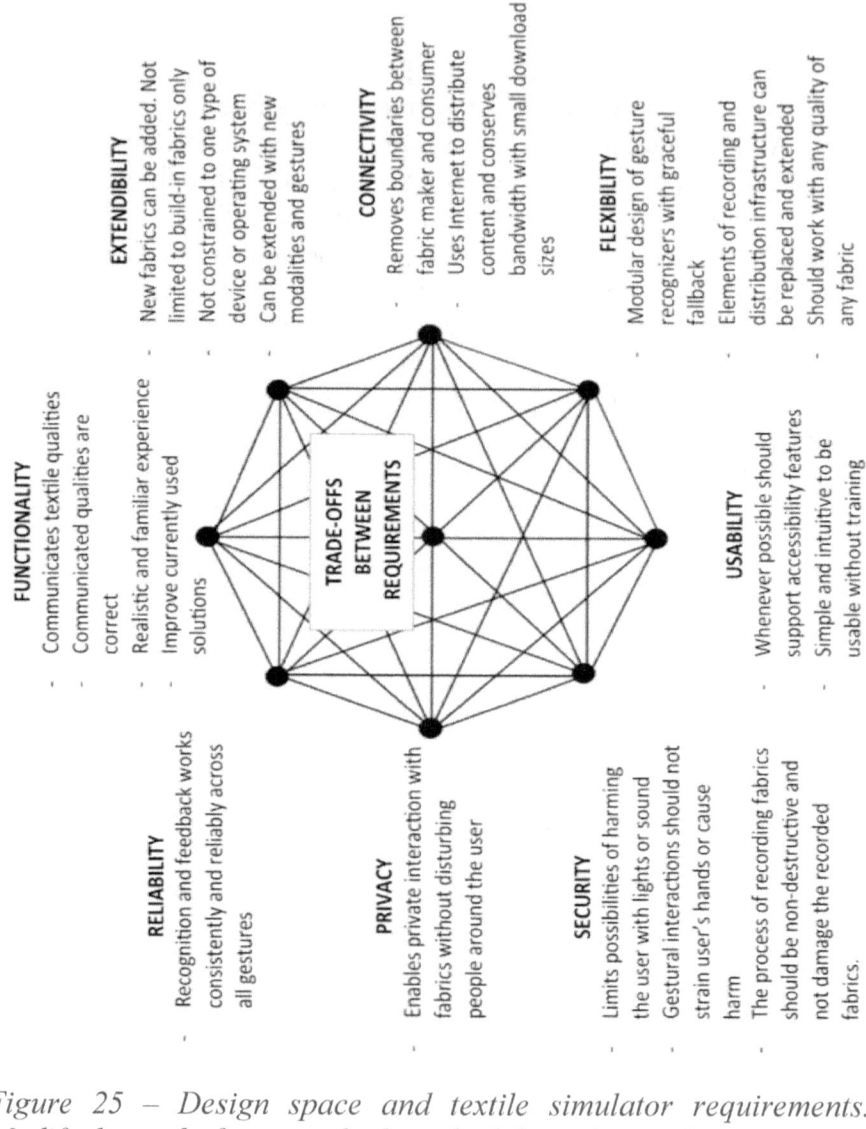

Figure 25 – Design space and textile simulator requirements. Modified graph from work described by Whitworth and Ahmad (2014) (in section 2.3).

Functional Requirements

- iShoogle should communicate fabric qualities of a swatch without that swatch being physically present. A non-expert user should be able to form an opinion about what the fabric qualities of the swatch they are interacting with digitally would be, if they held it in their hands,
- textile qualities communicated by iShoogle should be as close as possible to the textile qualities that a user would perceive if they were handling the original physical swatch,
- iShoogle should provide a realistic and familiar experience of handling a piece of fabric. Gestures and interactions, as well as visual and sound feedback should appear familiar and be understood by the user. Possibly iShoogle should not use metaphoric or symbolic interactions and feedback, but ones which are direct and resemble real life,
- iShoogle should be able to improve on a current standard of interacting with fabrics, i.e. books of swatches or clothes shops. iShoogle should display digitised fabrics that were pre-recorded (the original does not need to be present at the time and in the space of interaction), inexpensive to produce (making it possible to record and communicate a large amount of fabrics) and reproducible and durable (there is no additional cost or difficulty incurred by user or maker when iShoogle is reused repeatedly, the sample is not getting damaged).

Extendibility Requirements

- The set of fabrics that iShoogle can display should be extendable, rather than limited and pre-defined. Individual fabrics should be separated from the implementation, so that they can be added at a later date. Particular fabrics should be treated as content displayed in iShoogle, rather than

embedded part of the interface. Possibly iShoogle should be also usable for non-clothing textiles,
- iShoogle should not be device specific. Implementation of iShoogle should be available on any device with a touchscreen, irrespective of the software that it runs or its display, sensor and processing capabilities,
- iShoogle should enable being extended with additional modalities and gestures. Software and interaction design should leave space for implementation of additional gestures and other hardware sensors. Preferably iShoogle would gracefully fall back to most common denominator of features when used on devices that do not support specific sensors or specific gestures.

Connectivity Requirements

- iShoogle should remove boundaries between a fabric creator and the consumer who wants to experience the fabric and inform their purchasing decision. Use of off-the-shelf touchscreen devices and Internet technologies can make it simple and available to browse, access and interact with fabrics using iShoogle. Preferably iShoogle would be accompanied by a platform (app, website, cloud storage) that would enable the connectivity described above,
- Download sizes of iShoogle content should be small enough to enable interaction with iShoogle on request with minimum waiting time. Optimally shrinking movies download size would not decrease the quality of video or sound stimuli.

Flexibility Requirements

- The design of iShoogle interface should be modular to enable flexibility in exchanging its parts. In terms of

interface implementation, each gesture should be recognised separately and an inability to recognise a gesture on a particular device (e.g. most android tablets do not offer three-or-more finger gestures) should not make the whole interface unusable,
- The recording and distribution infrastructure should enable substituting its components with other ones to ensure flexibility of growth. Ideally, the movie and audio recording for iShoogle could be created with various applications and could be uploaded and downloaded via an API. Also playback of iShoogles should be possible not only with the official app, but also on social media and online retail outlets,
- Ideally iShoogle should be able to communicate any quality of any fabric. It should be possible to remove boundaries to communicating the hardest and most tactile fabric qualities (e.g. Soft, Stretchy) and representing fabrics that are difficult to capture visually (e.g. transparent and furry fabrics).

Usability Requirements

- iShoogle should be simple and intuitive enough to be usable by anyone with a touchscreen device. While there is no immediately obvious way to make it possible to use iShoogle with screen readers and external screen controllers, it should be possible to implement some way to interact with iShoogle in conditions of limited perception (sight or hearing difficulties) or problems with touch screen use. Adding sound feedback could be a step towards achieving this goal,
- There should be no need for extensive training before a new user could use the iShoogle. The interface should enable discovery of new features and gestures without a need to

know cultural or technological metaphors (i.e. double tap, hold and drag).

Reliability Requirements

- iShoogle interface should work consistently, without variability in performance between fabrics or gestures. All gestures should be equally responsive and recognised with the same confidence. Ideally a recovery mechanism should be put in place where gesture recognition fails, or a user changes a gesture in the middle of performing it. This could be a hierarchy of fall back gestures which gracefully recover from uncertainty introduced either by the user or by the gesture recogniser.

Privacy Requirements

- Mobile devices, that the iShoogle is primarily designed for, allow for greater privacy than shopping for clothes in a physical retail outlet. Optimally all the gestures should be simple enough to be contained within the user's personal space (i.e. no excessive whole-body gestures or need for loud voice commands) and feedback should not interrupt with people around the users (i.e. sound should also work on earphones, no need for strobe effects of device's build in LED light).

Security Requirements

- The iShoogle interface should be safe to use and not inflict any harm on the users, both physically and mentally. Content for iShoogle should not contain elements that could be triggering via visual or sound channels (i.e. strobe colour effects and rapidly changing colours, unexpected loud

sounds). Content should be safe for children and vulnerable people (video recordings should not contain violence or other inappropriate content).
- Gestural interactions should be safe for the user, even in conditions of repetitive usage. Unnatural or extreme usage of gestural interfaces can lead to a risk of RSI (repetitive strain injuries) and should be avoided.
- The fabric used to record iShoogle videos should not be destroyed in the process. Recording should not carry any risk to the sample, so that iShoogle could be used with expensive, historic or otherwise unique fabric samples. Optimally the recording procedure and training would be described in a way that minimised or removed risk of damaging the fabric sample.

Trade-offs Within The Design Space: Why iShoogle Used No Haptics And No 3D Simulation

Trade-offs are necessary when designing a solution within a design space. In their vacuum cleaner design example outlined by Alexander (1964), they described an example trade-offs of a smaller engine: design would loose suction power but become smaller in size and cost less. Below we describe the most important trade-offs in the design of iShoogle and we explain design decisions that shaped our design. Factors that shaped our decision making process were not only the requirements described above but also human factors and organisational constraints. Some of our decisions were taken because of technical expertise, time constraints and the need for academic validation of our designs.

Haptics, vibration or force feedback were not used in iShoogle. We decided to not use these technologies because there were no customer-ready devices on the market that featured them at the time of writing this thesis. Instead we replaced the need for haptics with touchscreen gesture interaction, supported by visual and sound feedback which were all supported by widely available and supported iPad and iPhone devices. Because of device constraints we were unable to communicate recorded haptic or vibration stimuli to the user, however even if the hardware did exist there would be a need to record the vibration information and make it interactive. Recording of haptic feedback would require creating a recording rig, new software to process the data, and a new data format to represent the data in the software. Introducing interactivity to the haptic feedback would present a set of challenges which we anticipated would be much more difficult and time consuming than adding interactivity to sound and videos. In this trade-off we limited functionality to achieve greater extendibility and flexibility.

Instead we decided to provide visual, audio and responsiveness feedback to user's actions. Later in this thesis we investigated if such simple and cheap replacement of haptic feedback was able to communicate fabric qualities to untrained users. Above trade-offs were illustrated on Figure 26.

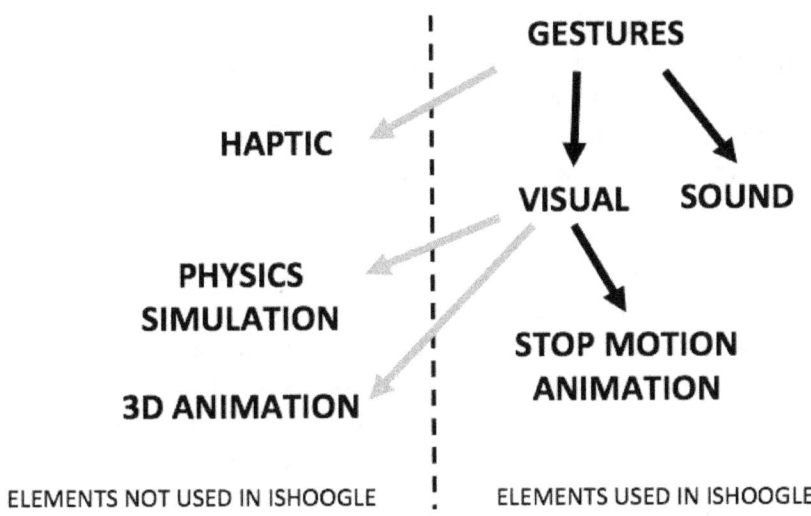

Figure 26 – To satisfy most important requirements haptics, physics simulation and 3D animations were not used and were replaced by gesture controlled stop motion animation and interactive sound.

3D simulations of the physics of a moving fabric were not used in iShoogle. The reason for that was that mobile devices did not have enough processing power to calculate realistic representations of 3D fabrics. Also (as with haptic feedback above) there was no cost-effective way to record fabric qualities with methods such as those described by Kawabata and Niwa (1991) that could then be fed into a 3D fabric simulator. We aimed to represent the textural richness of complex fabrics (e.g. handmade wool and tartan), rather than to create simplified simulations of a very narrow group of fabrics that would lend themselves to 3D representation as described by Magnenat-Thalmann et al. (2007). An alternative to calculating such 3D fabric behaviours in real time would be to pre-render fabric deformations, but that would be expensive pre-production and not present benefits over video recordings.

Instead of 3D simulations of fabrics we used gesture-controlled stop motion animations of fabrics where a spring-dumper system controlled the responsiveness of fabric videos. This provided a simple simulation of dynamics of the simulated fabrics, without the need for a substantially more complex recording rig and playback devices.

An important trade-off was that we did not show users real physical fabric samples, but rather simplified digital representation of those fabrics. Users could not easily perceive the richness of hand qualities of fabrics, however they could estimate what these qualities could be as described further in this thesis. Thanks to only using digital medium to communicate fabrics, we achieved a solution that is highly scalable and cheaper, but potentially less reliable at communicating the accurate fabric qualities.

We created our proof of concept implementation of iShoogle for iPad and iPhone devices running iOS because at the time of development these were the most advanced touch screen devices on the mass market. We also had programming expertise in the area which enabled us to create the interface in-house rather than outsourcing the build of the interface. Despite of the fact that at present iShoogle only exists on iOS devices, it would be possible to implement iShoogle on other platforms (e.g. Android).

Some trade-offs can be addressed by implementing two versions of the same solution. The final trade-off we considered was between the simplicity and speed of creating fabric videos and the quality of the video recording. We addressed this by designing two recording and editing setups: a high fidelity and low fidelity version, both described in this chapter. With such alternatives, users could choose the most suitable recording setup depending on their requirements.

4.4.3 Translating On-Fabric Gestures Onto On-Screen Gestures

On-Fabric Gestures Used By Textile Untrained People

In Chapter 3 we ran a study investigating on-fabric gestures that textile non-experts used to evaluate fabric qualities. Design of that study ensured that movements we observed were meaningful. While malleable fabrics could be deformed in countless ways, we were not interested in just any possible deformation that could be inflicted on a piece of fabric. Instead we searched for hand movements that deform fabric and cause feedback that could advance viewer's subjective knowledge of that fabric's qualities.

It is worth mentioning that at that point we did not measure whether the presented feedback indeed advanced user's knowledge of correct subjective fabric qualities. Users performed these deformations while being tasked to discover fabric qualities and they have self-reported perceiving fabric qualities (spoken the words that they believed described the handled fabrics).

An outcome from chapter 3 was the range of interactions that untrained participants used to deform fabrics. These findings were narrowed down to seven different gestures: Stroke, Pull, Rub, Sandwich, Tap, Crunch, and Bend as seen in Figure *21*. The gestures differed by the number of hands used to manipulate the fabric, the type and direction of movement and the pressure applied. The first task in finding on-screen equivalents of those on-fabric gestures was to identify how these distinguishing features mentioned above could be represented on a touchscreen.

Translating Gestures Onto Touchscreen Interface

Since touchscreen tablets are usually held in one hand, while the other hand is touching the screen, we aimed to translate the double handed gestures into their one handed equivalents, by recognizing movement of many concurrent fingers. The features distinguishing between gestures were the number of fingers and the orientation of movement. As described in Table 10 movement direction could also be a distinguishing feature, as in case of Stretch and Bend, where both of them were identical in every other aspect apart from of the direction of movement.

Because we needed to use low budget hardware, there was no possibility of sensing the force of pressure applied to the screen. To solve this problem, we decided to use the number of fingers positioned on a touchscreen next to each other as an indicator of how strongly the user would have to press the fabric. Other elements differentiating gestures were the part of the fabric used in a movement (edge vs. centre of the fabric sample), and small repetitive movements, such as rubbing. We did not implement different gestures when performed on the edge of the sample, because newly introduced off-the-edge gestures in the operating system of the iPad conflicted with gestures using the edge of the screen. We also chose not to implement accumulative, repetitive movements such as rubbing because of time constraints.

Concepts used	Meaning
Physical touch points	XY coordinates of each point where a finger was touching iPad screen. Fingers on the screen
Middle point of hand	Middle point between all the touch points. Middle of the palm.

Virtual touch points	Physical touch points were used to calculate digital, simulated touch points (virtual fingers, deforming the digital fabric)
Simulated dragging physics between physical and virtual touch-points	Virtual touch points and the middle of palm point were calculated using a simple spring simulation equation. This was an equivalent of each finger dragging a virtual finger behind it. This technique was used to achieve better smoothness of movement and to remove the limitations of the touch sensor and processing memory on the device. These limitations meant that it was not possible to calculate and animate the fabric in real time, without a delay. One alternative would be to attempt at any given point for the digital touch points to be identical to physical touch points, but this would mean that during fast movements animation would catch up with user's actions by jumping a number of frames and hence losing the smoothness of animation. Another solution would be to display every single frame of video that was supposed to be displayed, by placing each frame on a queue and displaying it once the processing of other images had caught up. This would simulate every virtual touch point, once it is possible. This way what the user would see on the screen during fast movements would be smooth, but would be consistently a fraction of a second delayed, hence giving an unrealistic impression of lag.

Feature of gesture (and gestures it differentiates)	Touchscreen solution
Direction of movement (Stretch vs. Bend)	Multiple times a second (depending on the available memory and screen sensor) we calculated the average distance between touch points and compared it with the value from the previous measurement. Elasticity was simulated to achieve smoothness.
Type of movement (Crunch vs. Stroke)	The number of touch points (fingers touching the screen), average distance between touch points and the change in the position of the middle point were used.
Number of Fingers/Hands (Pinch vs. Crunch)	Number of touch-points on the screen was counted
Small movement and Repetition (Rub vs. Stroke)	These were not implemented in the interface, since they would require a more long-term record (around 1 second) of recent finger positions. This would increase the complexity of the interface and hence was abandoned.
Applied Pressure (Stroke vs. Stretch)	When a number of fingers were positioned next to each other, they were treated as a pulling (two or more fingers) as opposed to stroking (one finger).
Area of the Swatch	New release of OS on iPad at the beginning of this

(Edge modified Gestures)	project introduced system-wide off-the-edge gestures, which made it impossible to use them within the interface. See Hardware Limitations section below.

Table 10 – Concepts used in on-screen gesture recognition.

Hardware Limitations

There were certain features missing from the iPad 2 devices which we used as a platform for our experiments and textile simulator. Hardware limitations of iPad 2 devices were:

- iPad 2 did not provide sensors for intensity/area of touch: pressure, proximity, skin conductivity (current flow), moisture or external camera, etc.,
- iPad 2 did not provide means of feedback about texture and physical touch qualities of the object on the screen: force feedback, vibrations, variable roughness of the screen, etc.,
- iPad 2 limited touch input by introducing system wide gestures, that would be recognised within a simulator and interrupt the simulator. Examples were sliding fingers from off the screen towards the middle of the screen and some 4 and 5 finger gestures,
- iPad 2 did not provide possibilities for extending the hardware possibilities either with hardware or software: iOS4 operating system used on iPad2 did not allow for extending functionality with plug in devices or changing the way touch input is interpreted by the touch sensors.

Mapping Between On-Fabric And On-Screen Gestures

On-fabric gestures were translated into their closest and most appropriate on-screen equivalents. Below we describe what were the final on-screen gestures, and which on-fabric gestures they originated from. We also describe whether each gesture was implemented in iShoogle and what the defining features of these on-screen gestures were.

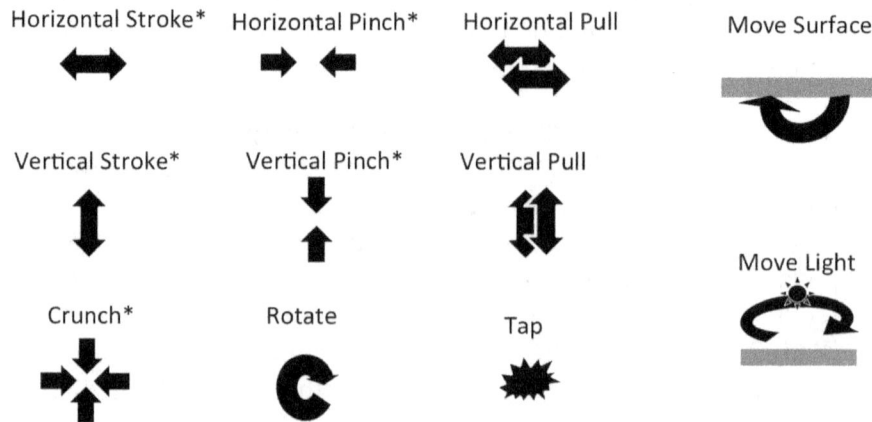

*Figure 27 – All the on-screen gestures derived from the on-fabric gestures identified in Chapter 3. All gestures were translated into touch-screen recognisable gestures, but only gestures with * were used in further studies.*

In Figure 27 we describe all the multi-touch gestures to control the textile simulator that were derived from the contribution of Chapter 3. The defining characteristics of these gestures were:

- Stroke: one finger moving along the horizontal or vertical axis (originally on-fabric Stroke)

- Pull: two or more fingers moving along the horizontal or vertical axis (originally on-fabric Pull)
- Pinch: two fingers changing the distance between them along the horizontal or vertical axis (originally on-fabric Pull, Crunch and two-hand Pull)
- Crunch: three or more fingers changing the average distance between them (originally on-fabric Crunch)
- Rotate: two or more fingers maintaining average distance, but rotating around their middle point (imitated: on-fabric Rub)
- Tap: one or more fingers touching the screen without movement (number of the fingers and length of touch correspond to the magnitude of the gesture) (originally on-fabric Tap, Sandwich)
- Move surface: the screen is moved and rotated in relation to the observer (originally not identified in the on-fabric set)
- Move light: the source of light as seen by screen-side camera (the brightest point in view) is changing position (originally not in identified in the on-fabric set)

The gestures we did not map and implement with their possible defining characteristics of gestures were:

- Rub: repetitive back and fourth movement of the touch points (not implemented because of the additional complexity of remembering the last few seconds of gesture history) (originally on-fabric Rub)
- Sandwich: pressing the fabric on both sides with two hands (not implemented because there was no touch sensors at the back of the device and because the touchscreen was designed to perceive touch points such as fingers, rather than areas of touch, such as whole palm) (originally on- fabric Sandwich)

Combining Gesture Recognisers

At this stage we had 7 on-screen gestures mimicking behaviours of people interacting with fabrics, and we were facing a challenge of combining them all into one interface. We aimed to keep all the interactions enabled at all times in all the interfaces, rather than switching between them. This decision led to the creation of an interface with no visual controls where the user was free to interact with fabric simulator in any way they pleased. A gesture recogniser had to instantly recognise any of the above gestures and trigger the appropriate visual feedback. It was essential to recognise the performed gesture immediately after the movement was started, to create the impression of directly manipulating the simulated fabric. A decision tree of how the software gesture recogniser decided which gesture should be triggered can be found in Figure 28.

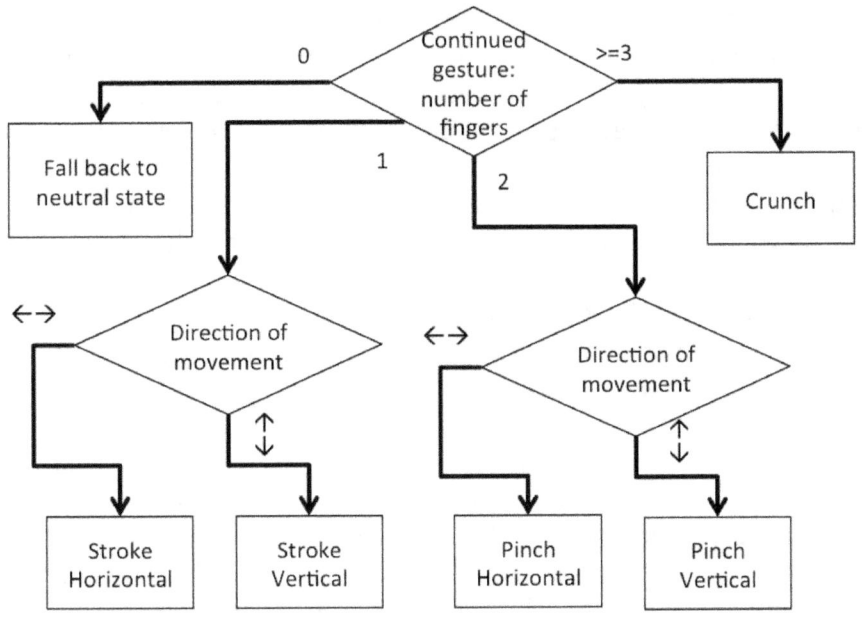

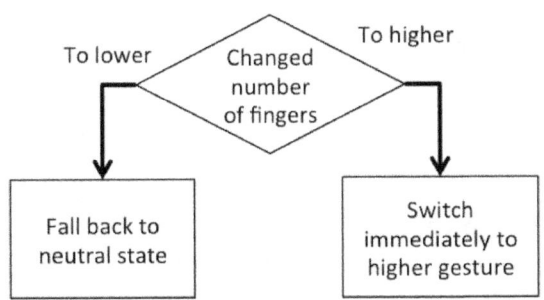

Figure 28 – Combining gesture recognisers - number of gestures and the direction of movement were the primary means of deciding the type of gesture triggered. When number of fingers changed during the gesture, the gesture was changed.

In the initial prototype we faced a problem of too high and too low recognition sensitivity, hence we decided to limit the above set of gestures and keep only those marked with the * in Figure 27. An example of sensitivity causing problems with gesture selection was the Rotate gesture being confused with the Pinch gesture. They both involved two fingers moving in relation to each other: during Pinch, fingers moved away-towards each other, while during the Rotate their distance remained roughly constant as they moved around a central point. In one of the prototypes that included both of these gestures, we discovered that the recogniser often recognised a different gesture than the one intended by the user. A different set of rules would have to be developed to decide when a gesture should be considered Pinch and when Rotate. However since this distinction turned out to not be trivial we decided to not implement Rotate, because it could render the gesture recognition no longer instantaneous (we could wait with displaying feedback until the gesture recogniser is certain which gesture is being performed) or no longer consistent (sometimes gestures would be interpreted incorrectly).

4.4.4 Interface Design And Creating Content

Combining Multiple Deformation Movies Into One Visual Element

The next design challenge was to provide a visual output whenever our textile simulator registered a gesture performed on a touchscreen. The simplest solution would be to present all the fabric-deformation movies separately, as independent movies, where each is triggered by just one gesture on a separate screen. However, as stated before, we wanted to avoid presenting separate interactions in separate windows. We aimed to visually present the response to any possible gesture within one and the same simulator window.

Each of the movies depicted a different deformation of one fabric, and we needed to combine them into one smooth digital experience, so that the user would not able to say when one movie finished and another started. Our solution was to record all the movies so that they each contained one movie frame which was identical across all the movies. For example, whether the movie depicted a Stretch or a Crunch, it always contained one frame in common with the other movies as in Figure 30. This way all the movies' timelines interjected at one point, and the playback of one would be smoothly changed into the playback of another movie, as long as it happened in that interjection point. On that frame, it was possible to switch between one movie and another in a way invisible to the viewer, without disruption of the playback.

Neutral State Of The Interface (The Common Frame)

We chose a moment when the fabric was laying flat on the table to be the source of the common frame which was displayed as the neutral state of the interface. We recorded each movie so that it contained the image of fabric laying flat on the table, making it possible to smoothly transition between them. In addition, when one gesture was performed, the interface would be locked on that gesture, and it was impossible to start performing another one without first going to the common frame. For example, the user could Pinch a fabric (causing it to wrinkle on the screen), and then immediately Crunch it (causing it to bunch), as long as the fabric was return to the flat state in between the gestures. The network of movie frames depicting various deformation is explained in Figure 29.

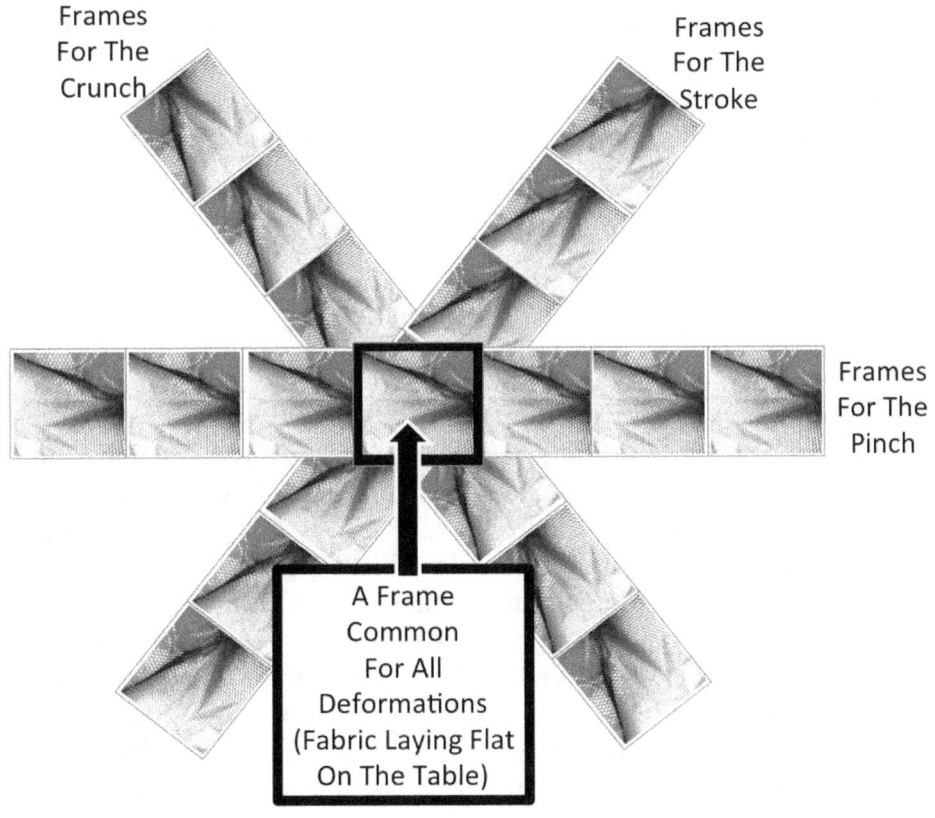

Figure 29 – Network of movie frames and a common frame.

All movies started with, ended with, or contained a frame where the fabric is laying flat on the table, which was identical for all movies. When not interacted with, the interface played back the most recently performed gesture-movie back to the common frame, simulating a fabric falling back flat onto a table. Switching between gestures was only possible at the common frame.

Animation Of The Fabric Falling Back Into Its Flat Resting Place: Simulated Dumper-Spring System Was Used To Control Playback

Another design challenge was the need for the movies to come back to the common frame in order to switch between the gestures. It would be troublesome and intrusive for the user to have to remember that they needed to flatten the fabric in between gestures. To solve this problem we introduced a simple physics simulation, where the simulated fabric would 'fall back' to its flat state whenever the user stopped interacting with the fabric. In other words, whenever the user was not touching the screen, the fabric deformation movie was played back to its beginning. The rewinding of the movie to the beginning was not linear - instead of playing all the frames with a constant speed, the speed simulated the physics of a falling object. This was a simple simulation of a generic falling object with certain resistance and bounciness qualities. We implemented a simple spring-dumper system to control the speed and dynamics of that playback back to the common frame.

ShoogleIt.com Shoogle Builder - Browser Application For Editing Shoogle Videos

A flash based web browser application called ShoogleIt Builder for creating and hosting interactive videos was created by Stefano Padilla as described by Padilla and Chantler (2011). Shoogle videos created with this tool were hosted on the shoogleit.com website as seen in Figure 30, which provided a free portfolio platform for artists and e-commerce to showcase their work with interactive videos. Content created with this tool could be embedded onto other websites and enabled interaction by horizontal or vertical dragging.

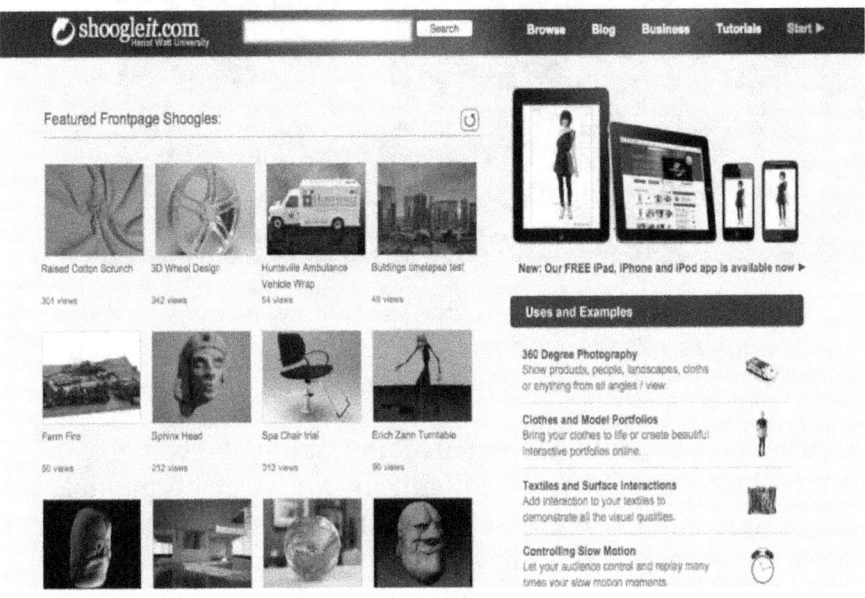

Figure 30 – ShoogleIt.com website and examples of usage of shoogle videos with either horizontal or vertical drag interaction.

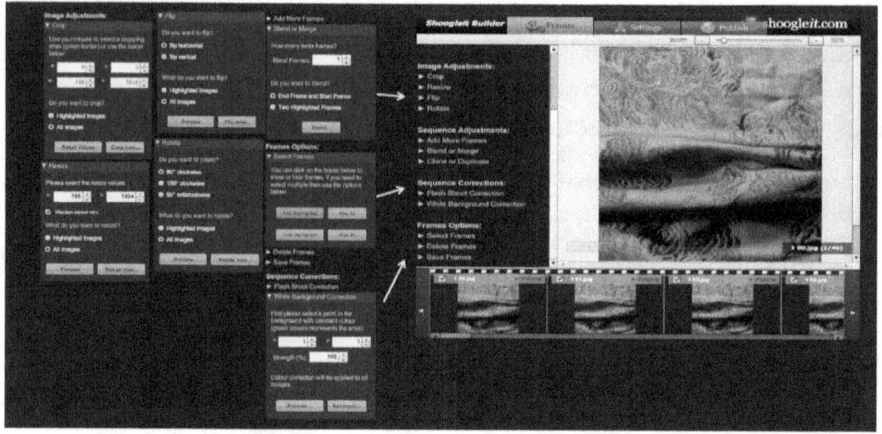

Figure 31 – ShoogleIt Builder. Frame editing screen. Here users could add, remove and reorder frames as well as crop and edit them to achieve seamless playback of shoogle videos.

Our iShoogle fabric simulator required the ability to combine a number of videos and interact with them with use of multiple gestures. Unfortunately using shoogleit.com it was only possible to interact with one movie at a time with use of one gesture (only horizontal or vertical drag were available, the mouse equivalent of touchscreen Stroke). We used a number of simple methods to adjust the ShoogleIt Builder for our needs without modifying the actual website. We created our multi-gesture iShoogles by editing each of the one-gesture movies separately and then using the movie names to indicate which ones belonged to the same multi-gesture iShoogle. For example when we created a multi-gesture shoogle for fabric RedBuckram, we would call respective videos RedBuckram_HPINCH, RedBuckram_VPINCH, RedBuckram_CRUNCH, etc. where the word appended at the end of each movie described which gesture should trigger that particular video within a multi-gesture iShoogle. In the above example, our iShoogle Player iPad app would identify and download all the

199

shoogle videos starting with RedBuckram and then combine and display them as a single iShoogle interactive fabric. Within each video we used the ShoogleIt Builder's setting for the starting frame (the frame that should be displayed on the screen before user started interacting with the shoogle video) to indicate which frame within each video depicts the fabric laying flat. Editing and publishing settings of ShoogleIt Builder can be seen on Figure 31 and Figure 32.

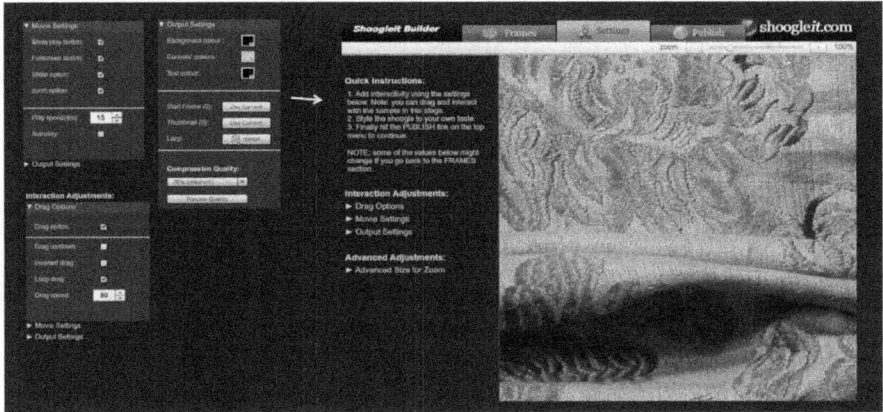

Figure 32 – ShoogleIt Builder. Output settings screen. Here users could select direction of drag, playback and loop modes and initial video frame.

We used shoogleit.com's infrastructure as an editing tool for fabric videos, as a cloud storage solution and as an API to power our iPad iShoogle player application. The ShoogleIt Builder was build using Adobe Flash platform which was not compatible with mobile devices, which meant that it was impossible to create and play ShoogleIt videos on smartphone's and tablet's web browsers. In the later, HTML5 based version of shoogleit.com, basic playback features were available on some mobile devices.

Introduction To Recording Physical Fabrics

As well as building a touchscreen interface, we also aimed to create a system in which a researcher or a manufacturer could record a fabric and share it with a user or a customer instantly, repeatedly and over large distances. This was why we imposed a series of constraints on the recording technique used to capture fabric videos for iShoogle. We aimed to create a solution feasible for the real world fabric sharing scenario, hence we needed to:

- Use off-the-shelf and inexpensive equipment for recording and editing videos;
- Require only a small amount of time and training to operate the setup;

The iShoogle was designed from the ground-up for cheap creation and consumption. We focused on inexpensive camera and stop-motion animations approach, rather than industrial fabric measurement, 3D scanning or force feedback equipment as attempted by Takahashi et al. (2009).

Below we also outline the system we devised to record and distribute the digitized fabrics over the Internet and play them back on iPad devices.

4.4.5 Creating Content

Setup For Recording Physical Fabrics

The deformation video recordings of each fabric had to be made in consistent conditions and the common frame had to look as similar as possible on each movie. We tested two recording setups, a high fidelity dark room setup and a low fidelity home recording setup described in Figure 33 and Table 11.

The high fidelity setup consisted of a basement room with no windows, a ceiling mounted camera tripod, a Canon 5D high-end digital LCR camera, professional lighting setup, with a MacBook Pro acting as a preview of the image from the camera lens. To achieve consistency of the common frame between all the movies, we drew guidelines on a semi-transparent foil covering the laptop screen, and made sure that each movie started or finished with fabric fitting into those guidelines exactly. Once the movies were recorded, they were separated into frames with the open source image manipulation library ffmpeg (www.ffmpeg.org), batch edited with XNView (www.xnview.com) software and the smooth playback of movies was achieved by removing some of the frames by hand.

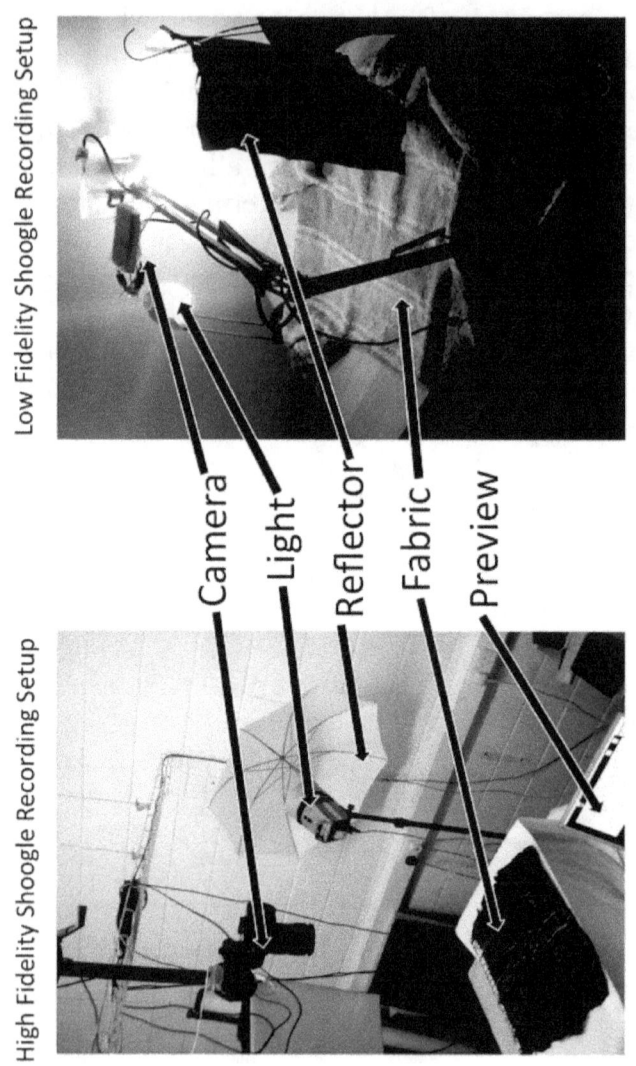

Figure 33 – High Fidelity and Low Fidelity camera recording setup.

The low fidelity setup consisted of a room with the window blinds closed, an IKEA desk lamp repurposed as a simple camera stand, a Sony Xperia Mini android phone or iPod touch as a recording device, two desk lamps as sources of light and a tinfoil sheet as a light reflector. The smartphone screen was used as the preview of recordings. All the postproduction (separating into frames, batch editing, removing frames to achieve smooth playback) was performed with the use of shoogleit.com browser application on an Internet connected laptop. To achieve a consistency of the common frames between all the movies, we recorded all the deformations with slightly larger margins, and then used Pan and Crop tools within shoogleit.com builder.

Element	High Fidelity Setup	Low Fidelity Setup
Room	Light isolated photography room	Any room, with a mix of natural and artificial light
Camera stand	Ceiling-mounted camera stand, with built in cables. Cables were used to provide live preview of camera frame on a laptop positioned below.	Simple IKEA night lamp with 3 degrees of freedom and stripped of electric components. Camera/phone holder was fitted in a place of light bulb fixture
Fabric stand	Square table with adjustable height positioned below the ceiling mounted camera stand	Any flat surface allowing sufficient access. We used a simple desk.
Camera	Professional LCR Canon	Sony Ericsson Xperia

		5D camera with the ability to preview via connected computer screen	Mini mobile phone with 5Mpx camera connected to a laptop, without ability to preview on an external device.
Light		2 sets of professional grade lights with dissolving filters positioned at the top and left of the frame and a small halogen light positioned underneath the fabric (to highlight transparency of some materials)	Two halogen lights positioned at the top and the left of the frame and a reflective sheet of tinfoil bouncing some light back into the frame.
Consistency of common frame (image of a fabric laying flat that had to be present in all of the movies)		Since we could see the preview of camera recordings on the laptop screen, we covered the screen in transparent foil and annotated some features of the fabric on the foil (patterns, buttons, etc.), this allowed for precise positioning of the common frame in all of the movies	Because of the inability to preview the frame accurately during the shooting, we recorded videos with large margins and used post-production cropping to achieve the same positioning of the common frame
Separating movie into		Because of the high resolution and their size,	Movies were uploaded to shoogleit.com and

frames	movies were not uploaded to shoogleit.com but separated with ffmpeg command line tool	separated into frames with its built-in tool, seen on Figure 31.
Batch editing frames	Frames were batch edited (cropped and resized) with open source batch editing software XNView	Frames were cropped and resized with built in functions of shoogleit.com
Removing frames to improve flow	Some frames were removed manually using Picasa as a tool for quick preview of large number of images in quick succession	With the built-in preview as movie tool of shoogleit.com, some frames were removed with built-in delete function
Processing hardware	A powerful laptop capable of multitasking	Any computer with a modern Internet browser and Flash Player to access shoogleit.com
Internet connection	No internet connection was required for processing	Internet connection was crucial for processing with shoogleit.com
Time taken	20h for a shoogle consisting of 5 movies	1.5 h for a shoogle consisting of 5 movies
Control	High control over every aspect of the process	Only as much control as shoogleit.com software provides

Learning curve	Complex software installation and dependency stack required specialist knowledge	After a 5 minute tutorial user should be ready to use the recording setup, shoogleit.com and all of its features
Mobility	Not possible to move the recording and editing setup	Very mobile recording and editing setup

Table 11 – Elements of High Fidelity and Low Fidelity recording setups.

ShoogleIt Builder and shoogleit.com (described above in section 4.4.4) were used in both setups to create and edit shoogle videos (in low fidelity setup) and to host the final shoogle videos (in both setups).

4.4.6 Proposed Mobile iShoogle Maker App

Both of the recording setups we described above have created comparable results, with the high fidelity setup giving a lot of power to the editor, but at a high price, demands of space and very time-consuming postproduction. At the same time, the low fidelity set up provided less control over the results and required a separate laptop constantly connected to high-speed Internet to access shoogleit.com.

A superior solution would be an iPad application that would enable the user to record, edit and publish movies from one device without the need for constant Internet connection. Videos could be recorded, edited and combined together on the same device that would be later used for interacting with them. Such a tool would make creation of iShoogle videos easier, faster and more accessible. The ultimate goal would be to make archiving a textile swatch so effortless that it would not take longer than simply recording a video of a fabric. While creating such a tool was not possible within the budget and time constraints of our research, we estimated that it would be possible to create it within a year long project.

4.4.7 Combining Gesture Recogniser And Visual Stimuli Into A Textile Simulator

iShoogle Interface And ShoogleIt Player App

The algorithm that recognised gestures and the method for controlling multiple movies from one interface element were combined into a textile simulator interface called iShoogle. At standby, the iPad tablet iShoogle displayed the common frame of all textile deformation movies for one fabric. Once it recognised a gesture input as detailed in Figure 28, the iShoogle triggered playback of a movie corresponding to the recognised gesture. The speed and direction recognised by the gesture recogniser were then interpreted by software and translated into the speed and direction of the visual presentation. Our interface also included the physics simulation which controlled the 'gravity' which made all movies return to the flat frame when the user was not touching the screen.

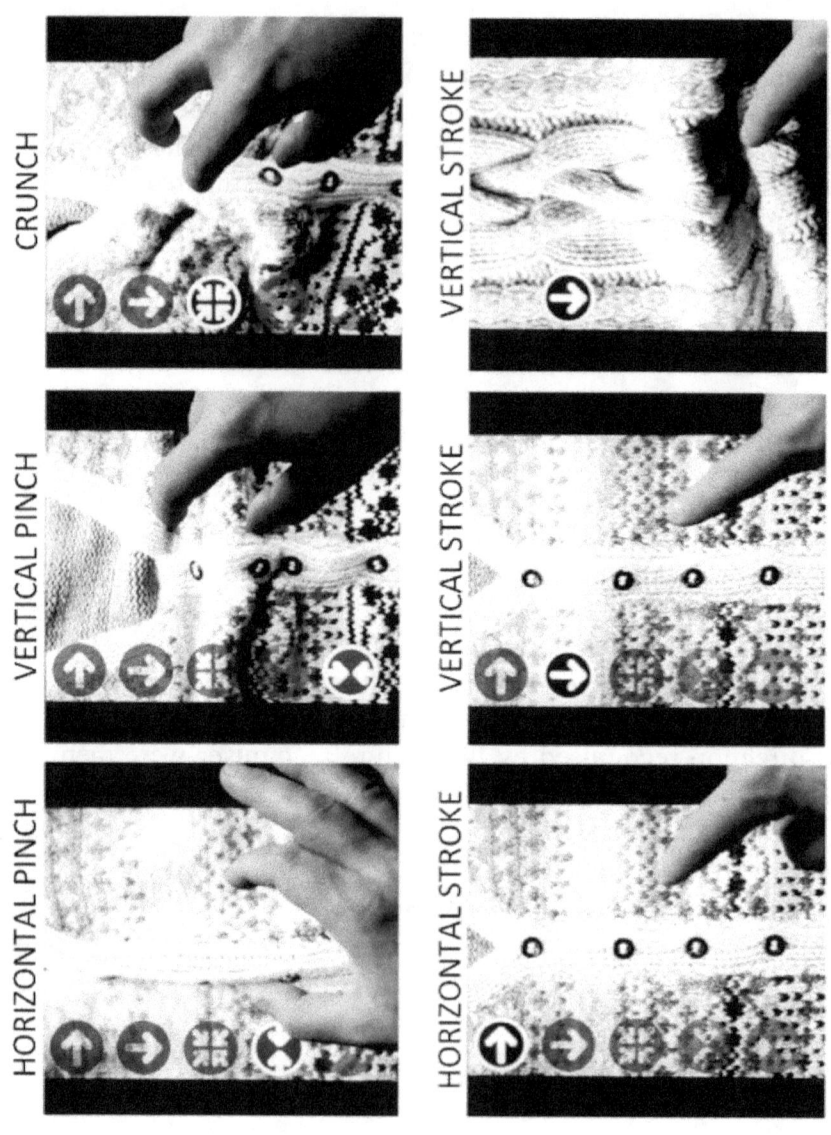

Figure 34 – Gestures in iShoogle interface.

The iShoogle interface was used as a part of the ShoogleIt Player app, which we released for free on the Apple App Store. With this app it was possible to browse previously recorded fabrics, download them onto the iPad device and interact with them with the use of our multi-gesture iShoogle simulator.

On Screen Elements And Interface Discovery

The iShoogle interface did not require any additional visual interface elements (apart from the video of the fabric itself) for controlling the playback of the movies. Throughout the prototyping process, we realized that it was necessary to hint at possible interactions to simplify the interface discovery. Icons on the side of the screen were used to hint at all the possible gestures. While it was possible to create a textile simulation of a fabric by recording only some of the enabled gestures, only the icons for enabled gestures were displayed as in Figure 34. These icons were not clickable, but they lit up when a given gesture was performed. During testing of the interface we noticed that users were intrigued with the icons, and would attempt to perform all the gestures mimicking movements represented by the icons.

4.5 Extending iShoogle With Sound Stimuli

4.5.1 Introduction To Sound Stimuli

Introduction To Sound Stimuli

Sound was the next modality we considered for further expansion of the iShoogle fabric simulator. The purpose of adding sound feedback would be to better communicate qualities of simulated fabrics in the least obtrusive way. This could be achieved without adding any visual clues, but rather complementing the visual feedback with audio feedback. Such feedback had to mimic not only the behaviour of physical fabric in terms of how it sounds, but also had to provide the level of interactivity present in all other aspects of our fabric simulator. If implemented in an unobtrusive way, such sound feedback might be relevant to non-expert users who, despite the lack of expert training in handling and evaluating fabrics, would have experience of the sounds that fabrics make when handled.

Therefore, the challenge in terms of interface design and HCI was to create an impression that sound generated by the fabric in a textile simulator was similar to the sound generated by the original fabric being deformed. For that purpose, a software solution was built to work with the textile simulator interface, which manipulated pre-recorded sound samples in response to user actions. We also described the sound recording techniques that we used.

4.5.2 Recording Sound Stimuli

Sound Recording Setup

We needed sound recordings that we could use in our prototypes of sound enabled iShoogle. We used four fabrics to record sound samples: Ripstop, Latex, (Raised) Cotton and Buckram as seen on Figure 35. We selected those fabrics because they represented a range of visual and sound behaviours and qualities. With a wide variety of used samples we aimed to be able to answer our research questions and generalise our results onto fabrics in general.

Fabrics samples used in the studies

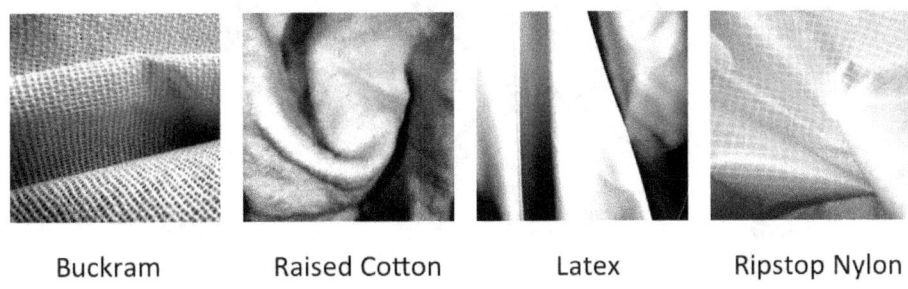

Buckram   Raised Cotton   Latex   Ripstop Nylon

Figure 35 – Fabric samples used to record videos and sound samples for our studies. See Appendix III for larger photos of these fabrics.

Mp3 audio files of the physical fabrics Buckram, raised Cotton, Latex and Ripstop were recorded. Three samples were recorded for each fabric by moving the physical fabrics in front of a microphone (without contact with the microphone). Three types of sounds were recorded for each fabric:

- **Scratching**: fabric was scratched with a fingernail, while the microphone was attached to the finger. This provided a constant distance of the microphone from a source of sound and removed the Doppler effect.
- **Crunching**: fabric was crunched and straightened in front of a microphone
- **Rustling**: fabric was rotated in a crank-like movement in front of a microphone

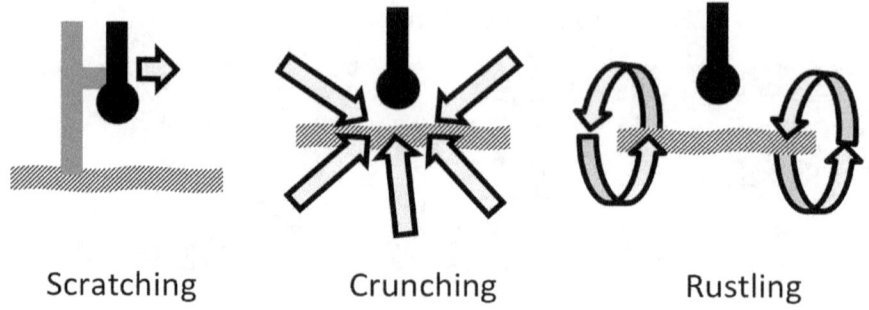

Scratching Crunching Rustling

Figure 36 – Microphone setup and movements used in recording three sounds of fabric sound stimuli: Scratching, Crunching and Rustling.

Audacity (www.audacityteam.org) sound editing software was used for recording and editing sounds, and the samples were amplified with the default increase volume filter. Recordings were taken in a sound isolated room with a stage-quality microphone and external microphone amplifier.

Each sample was trimmed down to 5 seconds in a way that provided the most seamless playback. Once samples were edited, the beginning and end of each sample were merged, creating a loop with no obvious beginning or end, which could be played back on a loop for an extended period of time without jumping and crackling effects. Once this process was finished, samples were again amplified to the audacity's optimum volume level, so that there would be no visible changes in volume during the sound playback for different trials of the experiment.

4.5.3 Sound Interactivity

Sound Interactivity: Algorithm translating User's Actions into Sound Playback

For the consistency of the iShoogle textile simulator, we considered that the sound playback should change in response to user's actions in a similar fashion to the visual feedback. We explored and prototyped a number of sound interactivity algorithms that translated user's actions into sound feedback.

We experimented with changing the following characteristics of the sound in response to user's movement speed and direction:

- Volume (faster movement causing higher sound volume). This produced a realistic and simple to implement algorithm which varied the volume depending on the current movement speed of the virtual touch points. Because we used the speed of the simulated virtual touch points, we benefited from the same spring-dumper speed simulation as the visual content. Thanks to that mechanism the changes in playback volume were smooth and sounded natural.
- Pitch (faster movement causing higher pitch). This produced the effect of a rubbery material and seemed unrealistic for natural fabrics (i.e. cotton),
- Speed of playback with correction for pitch (faster movement causing faster playback). This seemed very unrealistic and was difficult to implement,
- Dynamics of the sound frequencies (the speed of movement changed Hi-Low balance). The effects were not satisfying, as there was no resemblance to real changes in sound during fabric handling.
- Effects (such as echo or muffled sound indicating direction of movement). This algorithm would have to be custom

designed for each gesture separately and was hence not selected,
- Directionality of right-left stereo channels (direction of movement changed the balance between channels). This algorithm worked well only for horizontal Stroke gesture where the volume split between channels was from 30% left channel, 70% right channel during stroking right, and the opposite during stroking left),

After prototyping all of the above algorithms we decided to use a simple translation of the movement speed to the sound volume to achieve sound interactivity. The speed of movement (calculated as a percent of the highest ever recorded speed) was directly changing the playback volume (as a percent of max available volume) in real time.

4.5.4 Sound Interactivity Conclusion

Above we described the way the iShoogle interface could be expanded with sound stimuli. The audio recording setup and procedure for recording a variety of sounds for each fabric were also described and tested. We also described our investigation of playback and interactivity methods that could be combined with fabric sound recordings to create the same level of simulated interactivity as with the visual aspect of iShoogle.

Recordings and interface described above were later used for the studies Study 8 and Study 9.

4.6 Chapter Conclusions

Recording, Presentation and Interactivity Of Visual And Audio elements of iShoogle

The iShoogle textile simulator interface described above combined our knowledge of gestures acquired from previous chapters with lessons from direct manipulation of video literature. We described in detail two recording setups to create video materials for shoogle interactive videos: a high fidelity complex expensive recording setup and a low fidelity simple and cheap setup. Further we described how a number of videos sourced from the same fabric sample can be combined into one iShoogle interface and how software will decide which video to play based on user's actions. Furthermore we described how the interactivity itself will be simulated in response to the dynamics of user's interaction and how we corrected for possible lag caused by hardware limitations. We also recommended other possible gestures and ways to record the visuals that would accompany them. Finally, we described recording and playback techniques for audio feedback displayed in iShoogle alongside visuals of deformed fabrics.

Later in this thesis, based on the contributions of this chapter, we compared our natural gesture interface with its alternatives.

Strengths: Narrow Scope Enables Specialisation

The iShoogle Interface has been designed and built with the sole purpose of providing the experience of interacting with fabrics on a touchscreen. One of the key strengths of the iShoogle was that it aimed to fulfil a very specific need, hence we did not need to compromise by making it universal and feature rich. Since we aimed to enable people to perceive only fabrics (rather than also metals, concrete, paper, etc.), there was no need to compromise in terms of the gestures we enabled or the vocabulary of the qualities of which perceptions we evaluated during the studies.

Strengths: Use Of State Of The Art Consumer-Available Hardware

We decided to use the most advanced hardware that was available off-the-shelf to the general public. Other solutions in this area of research have often used very specialised, expensive and delicate hardware, which meant that the prototypes could not be scaled or used outside of the laboratory environment. The other extreme would be to create a solution that would work on every piece of hardware (even such as mouse and keyboard computer), but would limit the possibilities of multimodal and free interaction. We chose the iPad devices because at the time of the first prototypes they were vastly superior in terms of sensors (tracking 11 independent touch points/fingers), screen size and processing power.

Strengths: Economically Viable Recording And Creation

We strived to provide an accessible way to create iShoogle content. Another strength of our solution was that it provides a simple, cheap and scalable recording mechanism. The low fidelity recording setup described in this chapter would be suitable for small research teams and artists, while the high fidelity recording setup would be able to meet the needs of more demanding users who need higher quality recordings. It was also possible to upgrade the simpler setup to meet user's needs, matching the budget and effort that they were willing to invest.

Strengths: Proof Of Concept Easily Expandable With More Gestures And Modalities

iShoogle was a proof of concept and a platform that would enable years of research and innovation. The flexibility and the ease of expansion was the leading concept not only in the playback and recording setup - the iShoogle interface itself was designed to be expandable. While the interface served its purpose with as few as two gestures, it could be expanded to 5 gestures (as in the studies described in this chapter) or even more than 9 gestures (in one of the prototypes, abandoned due to time constraints). While we demonstrated a simple sound-augmentation of iShoogle, it was possible to expand it with other forms of sound or even different modalities available in the hardware that was becoming available (sound-based vibration, gyroscope point-of-view changes, front-facing-camera reaction to the light conditions.

An example of a gyroscope gesture would be rocking the iPad held in both hands that would trigger an animation of a falling fabric as if it were pulled down by gravity. An example of using light conditions to change a gesture would be turning the iPad laying flat on a table around the middle of its screen, so that the source of light (i.e. the sun or other light perceived by the front facing camera) would change its position in relation to the displayed fabric. The visual effect of such gesture would be displaying a video of fabric being illuminated from respectable position or angle. This gesture would potentially provide rich information about irregularly patterned textiles, such as corduroy. Additionally, given the data from new senses providing information about pressure of individual fingers it could be possible to further describe gestures closer to the original on-fabric gesture set (such as Scratch and Pull).

Limitations: Hardware

Interacting with fabrics remotely required a creative approach to using existing hardware devices and the hardware limitations shaped this research and the final version of iShoogle. While at the time of writing there was no existing hardware solution for emulating the behaviour of fabrics (resistance, feedback, vibration, fine texture, etc.), we investigated solutions providing these sources of feedback separately. We found those either too fragile or limiting as well as unsuitable for a wider audience.

We decided to imitate the aforementioned stimuli using a touchscreen, specifically an iPad2 device because of its superiority in terms of sensitivity, processing speed, number of touch-points and correct size. The limitations of using a touchscreen were: a lack of point-exact and built in vibration hardware; no force feedback or resistance/roughness control. We investigated whether the lack of vibration could be aided with attaching a device to the iPad which translates its sound output into vibrations. Unfortunately, we did not encounter a dependable device of such kind and found that building it from the scratch with an Arduino microchip proved to be complicated and the results were bulky and unreliable.

Limitations: Technical And Programming Expertise

Some hardware limitations could be overcome with expertise in electronics or advanced programming. Unfortunately in the beginning of the development, that expertise was not available, hence some solutions that appeared viable were not implemented: external hardware was not used to translate sound to vibrations; the front-facing camera was not used to identify the direction and strength of the ambient light; the gyroscope was not used for rocking gestures; we did not interpret multiple fingers on screen as applying more pressure. In fact, the number of gestures was reduced from seven to five to achieve more stable software in the face of limited development time, skills and resources.

4.6.1 Future Directions

Future Directions: Interface Development

Further steps in the development of the iShoogle Interface would involve expanding the currently existing interface and adding different modalities. A number of gestures that were drafted within this thesis could have been implemented given more development time and technical know-how. They would only involve expanding on the currently existing module of software gesture recognisers.

The second major interface development area could be adding new modalities, using both the built in hardware within the iPad device (gyroscope, light sensor/camera, microphone, speakers) as well as custom-made external devices producing vibrations or force feedback. Progressing with this angle of interface development would require substantial amounts of time, training and budget for equipment.

Future Directions: Recording Setup

The setup and interface for recording and editing iShoogle videos could also be an interesting research and development avenue. It presented a range of separate challenges which were beyond the scope of this thesis. A mobile, cheap and universal recording setup would need to be designed and built (lights, background, camera stand).

Optimally, a mobile phone video editing app could also be created that would record and edit single gesture videos, as well as aid in stitching multiple movies into one iShoogle interactive video. Software could also upload the finished product to the ShoogleIt.com server, where other users could download and interact with the recorded materials.

This project would require substantial amounts of time and development; however, it could make the iShoogle interface available to the general public, justifying more research in this area.

Future Directions: Sound Recordings Suitable For Gestures

Sound recording techniques could be further developed to create sounds that would be most suitable for each particular gesture. For example, the sound Crunching may be suitable to accompany the gesture of Crunch, while the sound of Scratch may be suitable for Stroke gestures. Additional research and prototyping would be required to discover the best mappings between gestures (and visual deformations caused by them) and the sound samples that could be played along side them in a sound enabled iShoogle simulator.

Future Directions: Design Space Trade-offs

Other areas of the same design space could be considered and alternative solutions to iShoogle could be created. There is a need for a thorough analysis of the current research into haptic feedback devices and 3D simulation of fabrics. Possibly prototypes of alternatives to iShoogle that use these technologies could be created and used to attempt communication of fabric qualities.

Additionally most trade-offs that shaped the design of iShoogle were driven by the state of the art hardware in 2009, which was when this research was started. In recent years new devices, including VR helmets, became available to general public and it is possible that some of our design space analysis should now be updated.

4.7 Chapter Contributions

> CONTRIBUTION 4.1 – iShoogle Interface – Multi-Gesture Touch-Screen Interactive Fabric Simulator

In this chapter we described the design of our interactive touch-screen fabric simulator iShoogle. iShoogle combines gesture recognition with stop-motion animation to provide a visual experience of interacting with a swatch of digitised fabric. From the analysis of on-fabric gestures used by non-experts to evaluate fabrics (Chapter 3), we devised a set of corresponding on-screen gestures. Those gestures were used in the iShoogle interface to deform fabrics on screen. The type, direction and speed of the gestures were translated into the movement of an on-screen fabric, to mimic responses of a real fabric.

Videos of the iShoogle interface are available at the author's website http://www.macs.hw.ac.uk/texturelab/people/pawel-michal-orzechowski/

The iShoogle interface created by the author of this thesis was not only used for research in this thesis, but also in other published research such as work described by Atkinson et al. (2013).

The proof of concept of iShoogle app for iPad devices was released it to the public using Apple App Store, enabling general public to download and interact with fabric samples.

CONTRIBUTION 4.2 – High Fidelity and Low Fidelity Recording Setup For Video Recording Fabric Deformation Videos

To record the video content that could be used within iShoogle interface we devised two recording and processing setups. The high fidelity setup required expensive and complicated equipment, room setup, and lights. Using it required training and expertise and was time consuming, however it provided complete control over the final effect. The video recordings it created were of higher quality and gave the video creator more freedom and control. The low fidelity setup used cheap, off-the-shelf components and was small and easy to transport. It used shoogleit.com website for all of it's processing and a mobile phone for video recording. The low fidelity setup produced videos of lower quality and took away a lot of freedom from the creator, however it introduced the benefit of being easy and cheap to use.

CONTRIBUTION 4.3 – Extending iShoogle Interface With Sound: Interface Interactivity And Sound Recording Setup

We extended the iShoogle interface by adding sound feedback to fabric deformation videos. Sound samples describing currently performed gesture were played in response to user's movements. The playback qualities (volume, pitch etc.) were modified in response to the speed and direction of user's movement. To acquire the sound samples we created a sound recording setup and devised three ways to record sounds (Crunching, Scratching and Rustling) that could be used as a sound feedback for different gestures.

Chapter 6 – iShoogle's Ability To Accurately Communicate Fabric Qualities

Goal:
Identify the visual and sound elements of iShoogle that close the perceptual gap between textile qualities perceived when interacting with a digital fabric and those perceived when interacting with a physical fabric

Literature:
Cross-modal interfaces help users reduce uncertainties about the qualities of objects. Modalities of vision, sound and responsiveness can provide information that was incomplete in other modalities

Study 8:
Sound-enabled iShoogle is used to rate fabric qualities. Ratings made using iShoogle with sound and without sound are compared with fabric quality ratings from Study 5

Study 7:
A simplified one-gesture iShoogle is compared with an image, a slideshow and a movie of the same fabric. The accuracy of ratings is measured for these four interfaces

Study 9:
Fabric quality ratings made using iShoogle with sound and without sound are compared with ratings of physical fabrics

Contribution:
The type of interface used to present fabric digitally influences the accuracy of textile quality ratings. The accuracy increased or decreased depending on the rated textile quality. The simplified one-gesture iShoogle (used in this study) is not better than other interfaces

Contribution:
Depending on the fabric (and possibly sound recording and production), adding sound to iShoogle has the capacity to increase or decrease the accuracy of textile quality ratings

5. Evaluation Of iShoogle Interface In Terms Of Gesture Performance And Sound Interactivity

5.1 Introduction

5.1.1 Context

Context Within The Thesis

In this thesis we reported on our investigation of interfaces that digitally communicated the qualities of fabrics. Such interfaces should enable non-experts to evaluate textile qualities described in Chapter 2. We identified gestures investigated in Chapter 3 as a promising foundation of a digital interface to interact with fabrics on the screen. In Chapter 4 we designed and implemented an iShoogle interface which interpreted user's on-screen gestures and displayed visual and sound feedback similar to fabric behaviour.

In this chapter we investigated the performance of our multi-gesture fabric simulator interface iShoogle. The study described below compares iShoogle with an alternative interface and evaluates its performance, accuracy and whether it caused excessive cognitive load. In another study, we investigated perceived usefulness and interactivity of the sound feedback. In all of the studies we use the iShoogle interface, often simplified so that it would respond only to one gestures or with removed sound feedback.

5.1.2 Chapter Goals And Motivation For Goals

> GOAL 5.1 – Examine The Performance Of The Digital Fabric Simulator In Fabric Handling Tasks And The Cognitive Load It Induced

An interface was considered superior to its counterparts if the advantages it offered outweighed its disadvantages and cost. The gesture based iShoogle simulator had to be compared to its alternatives in terms of performance (speed, accuracy) and effort it required (cognitive load it induced and its change over time). Given no decrease in performance when compared to its counterparts, iShoogle would be considered superior given the unique advantages it offers. To investigate if a gesture-based interface indeed performed no worse than alternative designs, we performed a study comparing a gesture-based interface with a GUI based on-screen sliders interface in terms of performance, learning and cognitive load. During our investigations we considered the intricacies of learning the new interface (such as length and type of instructional materials) and the impact of the practice effect on cognitive load.

> GOAL 5.2 – Examine How Augmenting A Digital Presentation Of Fabrics With Interactive Sound Changes The Perceived Usefulness Of The Interface

We identified sound feedback as a next achievable step in improving the interactive fabric-handling interface. Later in this thesis we investigated whether providing an interactive audio feedback made the interface more suitable for communicating fabric qualities and whether sound-enabled interface made the simulated fabric appear more realistic. In response to user's actions, the sound of the simulated fabric could be played with varied playback attributes (e.g. pitch, speed and volume) to imitate changes in the sounds of a physical swatch. In Study 6, participants decided which of the interfaces was more realistic and suitable for communicating fabric qualities: the one with non-interactive sound (sound not adjusting to user's actions) or the one with interactive sound (sound adjusting to user's actions).

5.1.3 Goals We Did Not Pursue

Due to time limitations we did not investigate the following promising avenues of research:

- What would be the impact of the simulated physics on the perceived realness of the digitally presented fabric? Would the optimal simulated physics differ depending on the fabric and, if so, how could it be measured?
- Would the perceived value and usefulness of the interface improve if we added more gestures and interactions? What would be the minimum number of gestures and which of them are perceived as the most useful?
- What would be the most beneficial way to teach users how to use gesture-based textile interfaces and what visual clues would make this process most effective?
- In what conditions was the Germane Cognitive Load induced by using gesture-based fabric interfaces the smallest?

Some of these queries were partially explored during our research; however, they are considered to be beyond the scope of this thesis.

5.1.4 Contributions And Acknowledgements

Unless otherwise specified, all the intellectual input into this thesis comes from the author. The sound interactivity study was run in collaboration with Nadia Berthouze from UCL in connection with the Digital Sensoria project, published by Atkinson et al. (2013). The Cognitive Load work was run in collaboration with Nadine Marcus from UNSW, Sydney.

5.2 Literature Review

Why This Chapter Shares Literature Review With Chapter 4

In this chapter we evaluate the design of iShoogle interface that we described in Chapter 4. Because both design and evaluation of iShoogle interface draw inspiration and methodology from the same literature, there is no dedicated literature review in this chapter. Instead we used and referenced papers that we describe in excessive literature review of Chapter 4.

5.3 Study 5 – Gesture Performance, Learning Curve And Cognitive Load

5.3.1 Introduction

Enabling Complex Interactions Without Adding Interface Complexity

Direct manipulation of objects on a touchscreen is a radically new way to communicate real world artefacts, and as such it comes with the price of being unknown to untrained users. A trade-off of the ability to perform completely new interactions is usually a need to learn them. When an interface is not familiar, it requires a substantial amount of concentration and often causes higher mental load and a steeper learning curve. Blackler, Popovic, and Mahar (2002), Mohs et al. (2006) and Israel et al. (2009) describe research investigating connections between intuitiveness, familiarity and successful usage of an interface. There seems to be a consensus that learning of interfaces happens on a multitude of levels of familiarity from natural familiarity (innate and sensory) to cultural familiarity (cultural and expertise based). The more natural types of familiarity (inspiring intuitiveness) are available to even the untrained users, hence making it accessible to a greater amount of people, not only those from a specific cultural circle or with expert skills. In this section we compared the iShoogle multi-gesture interface with an alternative solution created from popular GUI elements.

The main challenge with displaying multiple movies within one interface was to provide a means for the user to select a movie to play and to control its playback at the same time. Traditionally, movie playback would be controlled with a GUI slider (used for example in YouTube or QuickTime player): an axis represents the timeline and a draggable marker represents the current position on that timeline. In the following study we compared mental effort and efficiency in using gesture-controlled fabrics with the mental effort and efficiency when using a separate slider for each fabric deformation.

In our touchscreen gesture interface, the type of performed gesture indicated which movie should be played, while the speed and direction of that gesture controlled the movie's speed and position. In a slider interface we devised for controlling multiple movies, users interacted with a set of sliders, each controlling the playback of another movie.

The most important differences between the two tested interfaces were the consistency of interaction with the visual feedback it caused in gesture interface and lack of that consistency in the slider interface. Gestures were designed to give the impression of direct manipulation when on-screen fabric deforms in a way similar to how a physical artefact would. For example in the gesture interface, vertically pinching the screen would trigger and control a movie of the fabric being vertically pinched. In the slider interface the same vertical Pinch deformation would be controlled by horizontally moving the 'Pinch' slider.

Using Affordance To Minimise Germane Cognitive Load

Cognitive Load refers to the mental resources of a person used to perform a given task. Available working memory capacity and a person's attention are both limited resources. As described by Cierniak et al. (2009) the Cognitive Load Theory (CLT) separates the mental load into three types of load: Intrinsic (active; used to understand and absorb the material), Extraneous (invested; used to interact with the interface and absorb the presented information) and Germane (wasted; spent on using inappropriate and confusing interface elements).

Cierniak et al. (2009) explained how appropriately designed interfaces could minimise Germane (wasted) cognitive load and give opportunities for increasing Extraneous (invested) cognitive load. Intrinsic (active) cognitive load is specific to the difficulty of the problem at hand and can not be changed by interface design. Since a person's cognitive capacity is limited, any mental resources used up on interpreting a bad interface can not be simultaneously used for absorbing information, hence a bad interface will impede the perception and absorption of that information.

In the interface design scenario, minimising the Germane cognitive load could be achieved by creating an interface that is simple to use, learn and understand. While it is speculative and should be researched independently, we believe that gesture based interfaces have the advantage of the user not needing to engage with visual GUI elements. Additionally it is not important to touch any particular part of the screen during the interaction. Both paying attention to the visual elements and to the area of the screen could be a source of Germane cognitive load.

In the fabric handling scenario, the ability to perform familiar gestures anywhere on the screen could give the user more spare mental resources to invest into perceiving and analysing fabric qualities.

5.3.2 Study Design

Introduction

We hypothesized that a novel gesture-based interface could be learnt quickly and used efficiently if gestures correspond to actions visible on the screen, acting as a simulation (a digital representation of a real object). We created an iPad interface, iShoogle, which displayed movies of fabric being deformed (pinched, hugged, crunched, turned and stroked) when a user performed corresponding gestures (Pinch, Hug, Crunch, Turn, Stroke). Those gestures were spatial, not symbolic, and were used to smoothly control the state of application rather than invoke commands. We simplified and changed the names of some gestures from the previous chapter for the purposes of this study into Hug (once Horizontal Pinch), Pinch (once Vertical Pinch), Turn (once Horizontal Stroke), Stroke (once Vertical Stroke) and Crunch (once Crunch).

We decided to investigate whether iShoogle offered an improvement in terms of accuracy, interface performance and speed as well as whether that improvement came at a price of a more difficult and longer learning period. In this context by accuracy we meant how well participants can use the interface for the task at hand (whether they completed the task successfully), by interface performance we meant how quickly and accurately users can trigger the desired behaviour of the interface (e.g. how long it takes to start controlling deformation they wanted to trigger) and by speed we meant time to successfully complete a task with that interface. To achieve our goal, we compared iShoogle gestures with on-screen sliders in a simple task of spotting fabric imperfections. Below we describe the task in detail and describe possible alternatives and our rationale for selecting it. We also aimed to investigate the change in performance over time, to examine whether accuracy and speed improved with practice in the same way for both interfaces.

Tested Interfaces: Gestures Vs. Sliders

During the experiment, participants interacted with a set of movies depicting one fabric being deformed. All movies started with the same frame and the interface allowed users to select which of the movies would be played.

In the iShoogle interface there were no visible components (i.e. buttons, sliders) to control the movie playback, but instead performing gestures on the screen would control which movie is played and its playback. Each of the fabric deformation movies was assigned to its own gesture. Performing that gesture activated its respective movie and controlled the playback of the movie frames. The direction, type and speed of gestures corresponded to the type of deformation that was shown on the movie. For example, the horizontal pinching of the screen triggered and controlled a movie of the fabric being horizontally pinched.

This interface gave the illusion that the user was actually deforming the fabric, because the deformation and speed of playback was controlled by the user's actions. Each animation started with the same image of a flat fabric, so that switching between animations was unnoticeable. After the user stopped performing a gesture, the movie played back to the initial first frame of fabric being flat, giving the impression of fabric falling back onto a table.

In the slider interface, each of the movies was assigned one slider that controlled its playback. When the user started to move any of the siders, the movie assigned to that slider was played (i.e. Crunch slider would control the playback of movie of a fabric being crunched). Unlike in the iShoogle, there was no physics simulation in this interface – moving the slider had an immediate and linear effect on the playback of the movie, and the position of the slider exactly corresponded to the playback timeline of the movie.

The slider interface was very similar to the multi-gesture iShoogle interface described previously, with the difference that it used more familiar GUI elements. Along the left edge of the screen five icons of gestures were displayed: Crunch, Hug (Horizontal Pinch), Pinch (Vertical Pinch), Turn (Horizontal Stroke) and Stroke (Vertical Stroke). User operated sliders with one finger touching the touchscreen as in Figure 40. User would put their finger on one of the icons and slide the finger right and left as if they were using a slider to trigger any of the five animations. Icon did not move to follow user's finger, not to obscure the fabric on the screen. Just as in the iShoogle, when user stopped performing an action, the animation played back to the initial flat fabric state.

Familiarity Vs. Efficiency Trade-Off

Since slider interfaces were familiar to all the users, we expected the slider interface to be faster and easier to use with very little amount of training. On the other hand, the gesture interface could appear to be difficult in the beginning, but once participants were familiar with gesture interfaces they would become faster and more accurate in using it. The iShoogle interface had a unique set of advantages: it did not obscure content with visible GUI elements; it was not constrained to any one part of the screen (gestures could be performed anywhere); it was easily expandable to many more gestures than the five that were enabled at the point of the study without decrease in clarity.

Those unique advantages could justify the initial effort of learning a new interface only if there was no decrease in accuracy and speed of the task performance. In other words, the new interface should be adopted if it was better or the same in terms of performance, and introduced additional features.

In this study, we had to take into consideration what amount of training was required for gesture interfaces to give comparable results to the sliders interface and how the performance was affected by interruptions or changes in difficulty.

Experimental Task – Recognizing A Hidden Stain

To evaluate the usefulness of textile simulators in a realistic scenario, we designed a task that emulated looking for imperfections in a garment. Often while shopping, consumers would evaluate seams, buttons and quality of textiles by inspecting them closely, either in certain light, position, angle or stretchiness level.

We needed an experimental task which would evaluate how well participants can operate a fabric simulator interface, how quickly and accurately it allowed them to perform the fabric deformations that they intended to perform and how intuitive such interface was.

In this study it was of no interest to us how the fabric itself is perceived, but rather how well participants could use a fabric simulator as an interface between them and the digital fabric.

We envisaged a task during which participants needed to correctly identify a particular detail of a digitised fabric in front of them. An example of such fabric detail to identify could be its colour, pattern, weave technique, imperfections or structural elements such as buttons, seams or edges. One of the possible ways to achieve this goal would be to record a large number of shoogle videos of feature rich fabrics (i.e. Christmas jumpers, beaded sweaters) and ask participants to identify details of these garments on the screen. However we were concerned with a number of problems with such task (scalability, preparation, cultural relevance) as we attempted to create a task in which:

- all detail recognition episodes would have similar difficulty and would not require cultural or textile knowledge to identify,
- the task difficulty would not be inherent to the fabric recordings and could be changed if our experimental design required it,
- we could prepare a large number of tasks and digitised content in a reasonably short amount of time, preferably reusing the same shoogle videos in different experimental tasks,
- the nature of the task would be analogous to searching for details or imperfections in a physical fabric, even if it could not be a perfect representation of such task.

To achieve the above qualities of an experimental task we decided to superimpose the images of imperfections onto already recorded shoogle videos. This allowed us to have complete control over the position, size, complexity and animation dynamics of the superimposed imperfections, which made it possible to implement a more complex study design. We could also control at which point in the shoogle video (at which point of the fabric deformation) the stain would appear.

Another alternative for testing the iShoogle interface's performance would be to not display fabric videos at all (i.e. they would see white screen with a black line moving across it in response to their gestures or slider movement) and we would only test participant's ability to perform actions accurately and quickly. An example of task in this scenario would be to find a moment of the video where the black moving line is at certain position, i.e. static line in the middle of the screen. A study using videos of animated lines instead of shoogle videos of deformed fabrics would have a clear and easy to justify design. Participants would use gestures and sliders to find a particular frame on a movie, and we would measure the speed and accuracy of their actions. However we argued that such design would test performance of individual gestures and sliders, rather than the performance of the iShoogle interface itself. In our opinion using such simplified videos would remove iShoogle's core feature of the visual feedback mimicking behaviour of a physical object. Because of that we believe that above design would evaluate person's performance in using multi-touch gestures (which is not within a scope of this thesis), rather than evaluating person's performance while using iShoogle.

In our study we digitally added an image of a grey stain (in real time, rather than in pre-processing of video) hidden in one of the frames of the fabric deformation movie. This stain was designed to symbolise a fabric imperfection that the consumer might be searching for in the shopping process. In each task we always displayed one stain (from 6 different stain types) and it was the participant's task to identify which stain was present in the fabric video that they interacted with. This task could be considered somewhat artificial, because the behaviour of a stain on a wrinkled fabric would be more dynamic (e.g. the stain would wrinkle with the fabric). Nevertheless we believe that our stain finding task offered the best balance between being quantifiable and easy to modify (i.e. to increase difficulty, change position and type of stain) and between representing the simplified process of searching for fabric imperfections while deforming a fabric in a shopping scenario.

Process

Participants were told to interact with the movie and find the stain hidden somewhere within the footage of deformed fabric. We programmed the stains to appear in a random position on the screen (excluding a 20% margin on all sides) and on a random frame of the movie (excluding the first 20% of frames). There were six different stain images (see Figure 37 and Figure 38), and the challenge given to the participants was to recognise which of the six stains was hidden in this particular movie. When a participant identified the correct stain, they had to press a button at the top of the screen with the image of that stain. A row of software buttons representing all the possible stain types can be seen on Figure 39. Clicking on a stain button would finish a trial and move the participant onto the next trial. Stains were designed in a way that the grey area they occupied on the screen was exactly the same for each of them (i.e. equivalent to a grey circle with radius 1 unit, would be a square with a side 1.77 unit, both occupying 3.14 square units of the screen).

We expected that participants would experience the practice effect throughout the study and become better at the experimental task. To counterbalance that effect and keep the participants challenged, motivated and performing as well as they could, we steadily increased the number of stain shapes that participants had to recognise. Initially participants had to distinguish between 2 stains (Easy difficulty), then 4 stains (Medium Difficulty) and finally 6 stains (Hard difficulty). The analysis of Self-Reported Cognitive Load and task performance (both below) showed that this increase in objective difficulty succeeded in generating a constant subjective difficulty of the task and succeeded in motivating participants to perform well. As participants became better at using the interfaces in the stain recognition task, we made the task more complex, so that the perceived difficulty remained constant.

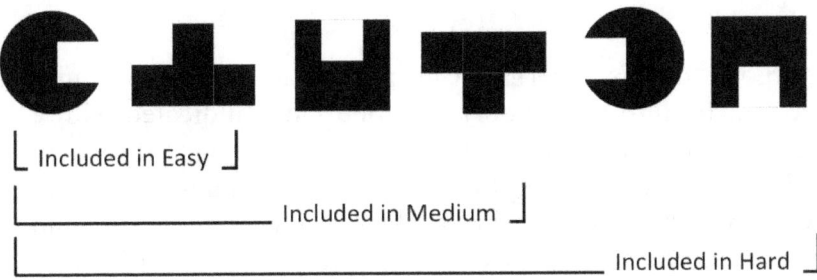

Figure 37 – Stain designs and their presence on different task complexity levels.

Each movie contained only one stain in only one frame of the movie, but on four neighbouring frames there were smaller versions of the same stain: next and previous frames had the same stain in 66% of the original size; one after next and one before previous frames had the same stain in 33% of the original size. This way during the playback, the stains seamed to appear, grow, and disappear from the screen smoothly over the period of five movie frames as explained in Figure 38.

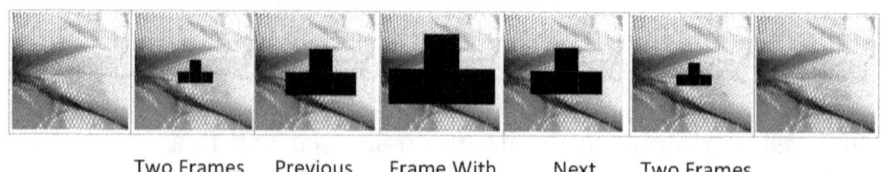

| Two Frames Previous | Previous Frame | Frame With The Stain | Next Frame | Two Frames Next |

Figure 38 – Stains were present in full size on one frame only, but were also displayed on four neighbouring frames in smaller sizes.

Measurements: Accuracy, Time-to-Start, Efficiency, Self-Reported Cognitive Load

For the purposes of this experiment we asked participants to trigger (with a correct gesture or a slider) only one video indicated with a prompt at the top of the screen. Apart from the requested gesture/slider, all the other gestures/sliders were enabled as well, and it was possible to perform a different gesture/slider than prompted for. We considered such failures to perform a task to be an important part of the learning of the interface.

We measured how many milliseconds after the prompt participants took to start performing a fabric deformation, which could be considered an indication of how well they knew the interface. Participants were told to find the stain as quickly as possible, so that they would be motivated to start using the gesture/slider quickly.

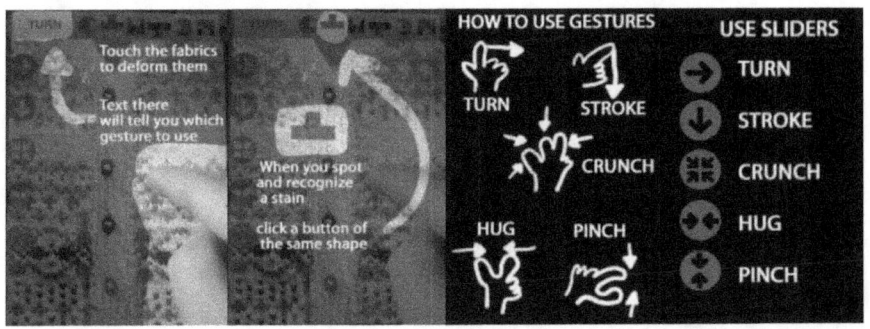

Figure 39 – Stain study: tutorials and an image of interface in use.

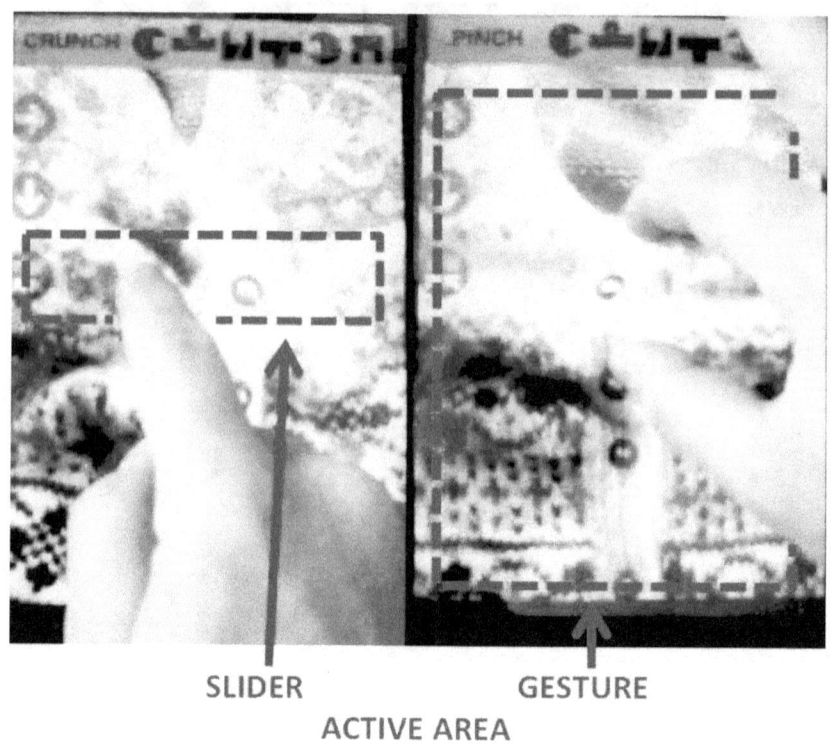

Figure 40 – Stain study, example of a Slider interface performing Crunch deformation (left) and a gesture interface performing Pinch deformation (right).

Once a participant started interacting with the fabric deformation movie, their task was to find a stain hidden in one of the frames and to click a button corresponding to the stain they just saw as quickly as possible. We measured how long it took them to perform the stain-finding task, which was the time between starting the playback of the correct movie (with gesture/slider interface) and tapping the correct stain button. This measured time indicated how efficient each participant was in using a given interface for performing this particular task, hence indicating how useful the interface itself was.

We also measured whether the recognition of stains was accurate, i.e. whether the stain selected by the participant was the same as the stain they have seen on the movie. At any point in the study there were a number of different stains that participants had to choose between. To keep a consistent level of difficulty throughout the experiment, participants started with only two stains being shown in the beginning, and then that number increased up to four and six during the study. All the participants experienced the increase in the difficulty at the same two points in the study as seen in Table 12.

Additionally, every 40 trials participants were asked about their Mental Effort with a 7 point scale displayed on the screen.

We measured task Accuracy (correctness of stain recognition), Time-to-Start (time taken to start a task with each interface), Efficiency (time taken to performing the task) and the Self-Reported Cognitive Load. The logging mechanism in the experimental app submitted all the results to our results database.

Experiment Flow

Both tested interfaces were presented interchangeably during the study with a random interface presented first. In total participants performed 280 trials, 140 in each of two interfaces (20 training tasks, then 3 x block of 40 tasks). Within each block of 40 tasks, the data from the first 10 were discarded, because we expected the participants to need a few trials to get into the flow of efficiently completing the tasks. Video podcasts explaining how to use the interfaces were presented before each block of 40 trials. A reminder screen explaining how to use the interface was presented in the middle of each block, after the first 20 trials.

Instruction video podcasts were prepared to explain to the participants how to use both interfaces. They were played in the beginning before each training session.

Interface	Action	Trials	Difficulty
A	Movie podcast explaining Interface A		
A	Practice session	20 trials	2 different stains
A	Task session	20 trials + 20 trials	2 different stains
A	CL Questionnaire		
B	Movie podcast explaining Interface B		
B	Practice session	20 trials	2 different stains
B	Task session	20 trials + 20 trials	2 different stains
B	CL Questionnaire		
A	Task session	20 trials + 20 trials	4 different stains
A	CL Questionnaire		
B	Task session	20 trials + 20 trials	4 different stains
B	CL Questionnaire		

A	Task session	20 trials + 20 trials	6 different stains
A	CL Questionnaire		
B	Task session	20 trials + 20 trials	6 different stains
B	CL Questionnaire		

Table 12 – Design of the stain finding study: practice, tasks and CL questionnaire.

Gesture Prompt

In each trial the participant was prompted to trigger and control only one fabric deformation video. We wanted the prompt to communicate a need for action that the participant would interpret and act on (as it would be the case in a fabric evaluation scenario where a need for stretching fabric causes stretching action). We considered a number of prompt techniques using video, text, icon and sound stimuli. In terms of the mental process, we wanted the participant to understand the deformation they were asked to trigger ('I am supposed to Crunch the fabric now') and then use the interface to achieve that goal.

This was the reason why we decided against the use of the same gesture icons to prompt the task as we used on the slider interface, since there was a danger that participant would simply recognise the prompt icon on one of the sliders, and use that slider. This would turn using the slider interface into a pattern recognition task, which was not what we intended to test.

We also decided against audio prompts, because we anticipated difficulty in creating a set of prompts that would take the same time to absorb (both in terms of them being of the same length and requiring the same time to distinguish between them). We appreciated that the sound prompts could be more appropriate and less distracting than visual prompts, since the participants could focus their visual attention entirely on the iShoogle, without glancing at the prompt bar at the top of the screen. However, since we planned to crowdsource the data for this study by releasing it on Apple App Store, we anticipated that using sound in this study would introduce sources of noise connected with us having no full control over the environment (external noise, speaker's volume or using different types of earphones). Because of these reasons we decided against sound prompts and opted for only using visual prompts in this study.

5.3.3 Stain Study Results

Data Analysis

This study was intended as a preliminary pilot study that would highlight improvements needed to design and perform a larger app based study. Our initial intention was to release that second version of the study as a game on the Apple App Store, but because of time constraints it was not possible. Below we present the findings from our pilot study and a series of improvements that we believe would be necessary to expand this study. We believe that thanks to our initial findings we could develop and run a more focused and simplified version of this study that would provide further answers to our research questions.

We ran this experiment with six participants (four male). One (male) participant was discarded because of a corrupted data file. Each participant completed 240 non-training trials. Three participants started with the gesture interface and two started with the slider interface. As described in the study design, the first 10 trials in each 40 trial block were discarded. This was the case because it took a number of trials after the interruption or training to get back to the efficient flow of completing the experimental task.

Data indicated that removing the first 10 trials of each block was justified. Inspection of the means revealed a practice effect, such that first 10 trials of each block after training or instructions had a much longer time to start a task, and so we deleted these trials from the dataset (regardless of the interface). Within each block the remaining 30 trials consisted of 6 trials for each of the 5 fabric deformations. These interface-deformation combinations were averaged for the analysis.

Time To Start The Task – Gestures Faster, But Only Marginally Significant Trend For Turn

In order to examine the effect of the interface type, deformation type and difficulty level on time to start the task, we conducted a within-subject analysis of variance. We found a non-significant trend where it took participants marginally longer to start the task when they were using the sliders rather than gestures ($F(1,4)=5.27$, $p=.083$). This finding is consistent with our expectation that gestures would be not slower than sliders.

Deformation type showed a significant effect on the time it took to start the task ($F(4,16)=2.98$, $p=.05$). The difficulty level had no effect ($F(2,8)=1.26$, $p=0.34$).

We then conducted a separate analysis for each Deformation type, in order to explore the effect of Interface type for each Deformation as seen in Table 13.

Deformation	Mean Slider	SE Slider	Mean Gesture	SE Gesture	p value	Mean Difference
Turn	1589.90	257.02	1099.53	106.10	.04*	490.37
Stroke	1863.03	390.26	1049.90	102.06	.10	813.13
Crunch	1376.82	269.93	1275.79	123.98	.56	101.03
Hug	1626.72	255.54	1483.51	164.44	.59	143.21
Pinch	2276.08	542.80	1591.48	186.07	.15	684.60

Table 13 – Time to start the task in the stain finding study.

For Turn there was a significant effect of the interface type on the time to start the task: when participants were using the slider, it took them significantly longer to start the task. There was no such effect for Stroke, Crunch, Hug and Pinch.

Time To Complete The Task – No Significant Effect

In order to look at the effects of Interface Type and Deformation Type on time to complete the task (time between starting a deformation and choosing a correct stain button), we conducted a within-subjects analysis of variance. We found no significant effect of Interface type ($F(1,4)=0.91$, $p=.39$), deformation type ($F(4,16)=0.25$, $p=.91$), or difficulty ($F(2,8)=0.05$, $p=.95$). We still decided to conduct a separate analysis for each deformation type presented in Table 14 in order to mirror the analysis of time to start the task (detailed above).

Deformation	Mean Slider	SE Slider	Mean Gesture	SE Gesture	p value	Mean Difference
Turn	1914.18	486.81	1872.58	224.43	.91	41.60
Stroke	1836.06	404.93	2091.43	449.59	.15	-255.37
Crunch	1740.23	251.07	2109.46	398.18	.10	-369.23
Hug	1879.48	271.88	1908.94	404.76	.94	-29.46
Pinch	1808.30	313.27	1927.30	405.94	.46	-119.00

Table 14 – Time to perform the task in the stain finding study.

As expected, there was no significant effect of interface type on the time it took to complete the task for none of the five deformation types.

Self-Reported Cognitive Load – No Significant Effect

In order to look at the effects of Interface Type and Difficulty Level on Self-Reported Cognitive Load, we conducted a within-subjects analysis of variance. We found no significant effect of either variable on the Self-Reported Cognitive Load (interface $F(1,4)=0.286$, $p=.62$; difficulty $F(2,8)=0$, $p=1$). Even though objectively the task was getting more complex, the participants were getting more practiced and did not perceive the increasing task difficulty in either the slider or in the gesture condition.

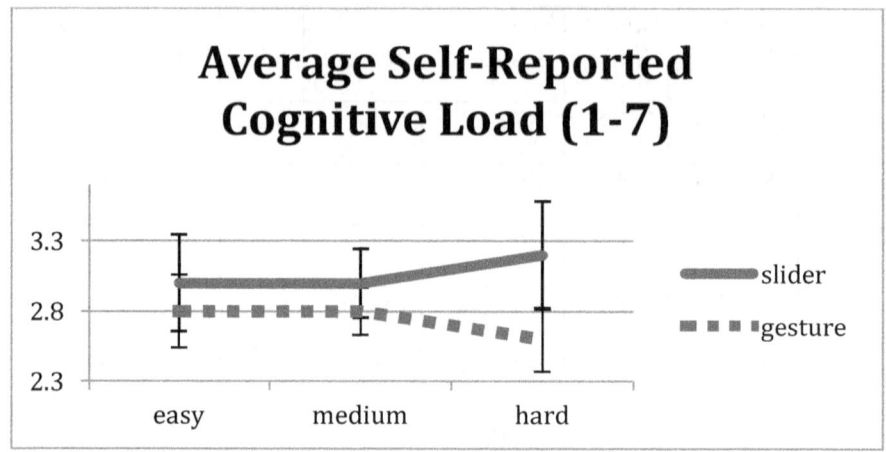

Figure 41 – Average self-reported cognitive load on a 1-7 scale. Data for three task complexity levels for two interfaces. Error bars depict standard error.

Discussion Of Stain Study

We expected to see that gestures would not be any worse than sliders, as far as the time to start the task and the time to complete the task were considered. Statistical analysis failed to show statistically significant differences between the two compared interfaces on the two time measures. Since we found no evidence that the Sliders interface is better, and the Gestures interface has some qualitative advantages, we believe that there is support for the use of a Gestures-like interface for this problem.

Starting the task required an understanding of the command presented on the screen, to identify the way to perform that task on a given interface and to touch the touchscreen in an appropriate way. Over time and practice, participants became faster and more efficient for both interfaces. We observed that effect in our study: the training trials were slower than the rest of the study, which would indicate that participants learned to use the interfaces efficiently over the course of the study.

No statistically significant differences were found in the time taken to complete the task (between starting a deformation and successfully completing the trial, i.e. identifying the stain). The task described by this measurement was a recognition task, and its performance was dependant on efficiency in using the interface, difficulty of the task and the confidence the participants had in the interface. Gestures were no slower than sliders, which again was a substantial achievement given the novel nature of the iShoogle.

Compared with traditional interfaces, the gesture based interface for handling fabrics presented unique advantages: savings in terms of screen estate (no need to display additional artefacts on the screen); required less distraction and thus possibly less Germane Cognitive Load (no need to pay attention to the interface elements); enabled ease of expansion (no real maximum limit on the number of possible gestures).

The results of this study did not show a statistical decrease in performance for iShoogle. This would mean that iShoogle's advantages did not come with a decrease in performance, hence making the iShoogle interface superior to a traditional slider-based interface. This was the case for the tasks that we were using in our studies and assuming that the advantages iShoogle introduced were relevant. In the study, performance of the gesture interface was not worse than the GUI interface in a task designed to imitate an online shopping scenario. Tasks within the study that we considered relevant to a shopping scenario were: evaluating the fabric in the way that the user intends to (triggering a particular deformation) and spotting a detail of the fabric or garment that was important to the user (recognizing the stain).

5.4 Study 6 – Evaluation Of Interactive Sound Extension Of iShoogle

5.4.1 Introduction To iShoogle Sound Stimuli

Introduction

In the previous chapter we described how sound interactivity was added to the iShoogle interface. In this chapter we describe a study investigating user's acceptance of interactive sound accompanying iShoogle. We realised that adding sound to a fabric simulator has the potential to improve or impair the experience of using that interface. To test user's reactions to sound interactivity we designed a simple pairwise comparison study in which participants had to perform a large number of comparisons between interactive and non-interactive versions of sound stimuli in iShoogle, and decide which of them is more "Realistic/Suitable" for representing fabrics on screen. Below we describe the design and outcome of this study.

Research Question

We conducted the study described below to answer the following research questions:

- Was the difference between interactive movement-driven sound playback and non-interactive (movement independent) sound playback noticeable to non-experts in terms of the suitability for representing fabrics on the screen,
- Which version of the sound extension in iShoogle interface was considered more realistic and suitable for communicating fabric qualities by non-experts: interactive or non-interactive sound?

5.4.2 Study Design – Does Movement-Driven Sound Feedback Appear More Realistic Than Simple Sound Playback?

Task

To test which way of presenting sound in the iShoogle interface appears more realistic, we decided to run a pairwise comparison study. During each trial, two competing interfaces (differing only by sound interactivity) were presented side by side as in Figure 42. In each trial the participant's task was to choose which of the two compared interface appeared to be more realistic and suitable for representing fabrics. Both compared interfaces were identical in terms of behaviour (both used only Horizontal Pinch gesture) and visuals (both depicted the same fabric) displayed on the screen, but differed in terms of the way sound was presented. The sound was always interactive or non-interactive.

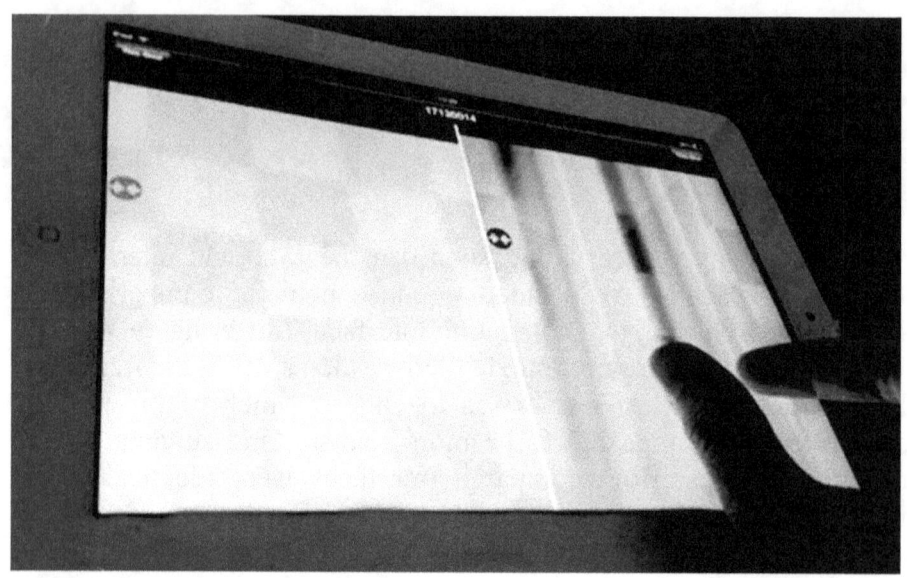

Figure 42 – Example of side-by-side shoogle interfaces. During each trial participant decided which sound was more realistic after horizontally pinching both interfaces.

The study used four different fabrics seen in Figure 35, each with three different sound samples recorded while fabric was Scratched, Rubbed and Crunched with different sound recording techniques described in Figure 36. Within each pair of interfaces both were identical in terms of visuals and behaviour, but differed in terms of sound. There were 6 possible options for the sound stimuli, since we used every possible combination of three sound recording techniques (Scratch, Rub, Crunch) and two different playback techniques (Interactive, Non-Interactive). Each fabric had three sound samples, each played with one of the two playback techniques, giving a total of six different sound stimuli to be presented per fabric.

Variables

In this experiment we sought to establish which sound addition to the iShoogle interface was perceived as more realistic and suitable for presentation of textiles: the interactive sound or a non-interactive sound. The variable we evaluated was Sound Interactivity and the two evaluated conditions were: Interactive Sound (attributes of playback depended on the user's movements) and Non-Interactive Sound (only the presence of sound depended on user's movements, while playback attributes, such as volume, pitch and speed, were constant).

We decided to vary fabrics and sound stimuli (as described above) rather than to use the same fabric and sound every time and only vary the interactivity. We did this to provide more general results that would apply to a range of fabrics and their sounds. We were also concerned with the participants realizing the purpose of the study if there was not enough variability in the tasks. Finally, if the study were to be too repetitive, the participants would get bored and fatigued, making less careful choices and in effect decreasing the quality of data that we gathered.

We believed that providing such variety of stimuli would improve the quality of gathered data, and the noise that it could introduce would be counterbalanced by the benefits.

Fabric Samples

We used all the possible combinations of 6 sound stimuli options (each fabric had 3 sound recordings x 2 interfaces). There were 15 possible combinations of pairs without repetition of 6 sound stimuli (5 + 4 + 3 + 2 + 1 = 15). Each pair was presented side by side on a horizontally oriented iPad, one on the right side of the screen, one on the left side of the screen as in Figure 42. During each trial the right-left position of interfaces was randomised, to remove possible preference to choose right or left option. Possible sources of bias could be choosing the dominant hand side more, or choosing the interface that was used first (usually interfaces were used in the direction that the English language is read – from left to right). Since we used 4 fabrics in this study, each of them was presented in 15 sound stimuli combinations, giving a total of 60 possible pairs to compare.

Each participant was presented with those 60 choices and in each instance was asked to perform the horizontal Pinch gesture more than once on both interfaces, while listening to the sound stimuli and decide which interface was more "Realistic/Suitable".

Sound And Visual Stimuli

The four fabrics that we used in this study were: Ripstop, Latex, (Raised) Cotton and Buckram as seen in Figure 35. Mp3 audio files of the physical fabrics in three recording setups for each fabric: Scratching, Crunching and Rustling, described in more detail in 4.5.2. Each sample was trimmed down to 5 seconds and looped seamlessly. Once this process was finished, samples were again amplified to Audacity's optimum volume level (see Section 4.5.2), so that there would be no audible changes in volume during the sound playback for different trials of the experiment.

Each visual stimuli used in the iShoogle interface was created from a video of a fabric being pinched horizontally. 40 frames were extracted from each video in a native iPad 2 resolution (1024x768 pixels) and transformed into a shoogle stop motion animation. Shoogle videos were loaded into the iPad iShoogle app modified for the purposes of this a study.

As in previous studies, fabrics were recorded on a transparent table with a built in backlight and a checkerboard pattern. Thanks to this process, the transparency of fabrics was clearly visible. Two more lights pointing from the top and left of the view point were used with white paper diffusers. This setup simulated a natural fabric handling lighting and viewing conditions as explained in Figure 33.

Procedure

Individual participants were sat at a table in a library or a computer lab and were provided with an iPad tablet and noise cancelling earphones as seen in Figure 46. Once participants were briefed, they were instructed to tap a 'start study' button on an interface, at which point the first trial started. During each trial, the participants were asked to interact (by horizontally pinching the interface) with both versions of iShoogle interface and to chose the one that they considered to be more 'Realistic/Suitable'. The words 'Which One was More Realistic/Suitable' (always both of the words) were written on the cover of the agreement form in front of them. During the introduction we explained to participants that we meant whether the interface was 'Realistic' as a digital representation of a physical fabric and 'Suitable' to represent a physical fabric digitally. The choices were made by pressing one of two software buttons saying 'THIS ONE' in the corner of the screen, one next to each of the interfaces. The participants interacted with 60 pairs of interfaces and made a choice for each pair. In each pair they were comparing the types of sound stimuli, since the visual stimuli was identical. After completing the study participants were paid and debriefed and their data was automatically submitted to a secure server. The room and equipment setup was identical as in Study 9.

5.4.3 Interactive Sound Study Results

Measurements

Fifty undergraduate students from Heriot-Watt University participated in the study and 48 participants (31 male) completed the study successfully (two sets of data were lost due to a software failure). We recruited such a large number of participants to achieve meaningful results, despite possible sources of noise in the study. Each of the participants made 60 choices, hence we gathered 2880 data points in total. The experiment took on average under 6 minutes (around 6 seconds per trial), plus time for introduction and debriefing.

Since we evaluated every possible combination of sound interfaces, some of the data points were comparisons between two interactive or two non-interactive interfaces. These data points were discarded, as we were only interested in the Interactive vs. Non-Interactive Choices, i.e. choices where a participant was choosing between two levels of our experimental variable (participants compared an interactive sound with a non-interactive sound). Because 9 out of each 15 pairs were such Interactive vs. Non-Interactive Choices, we gathered 1728 data points where participants were comparing an interactive and non-interactive interface. These were the data points on which we tested our hypothesis.

Statistical Analysis: Binominal Test

The data was analysed using a binominal test in SPSS with the null hypothesis of equal probability of participants' choosing sound interactive and sound non-interactive interface (50% and 50%) as the more realistic one. Altogether there were 1728 trials where participants were choosing between the two different interfaces, and in 1176 (67%) of them participants indicated that the sound interactive interface was more realistic than the sound non-interactive interface. The binominal test indicated that this proportion was significantly different from 50% (p < .01).

Discussion Of Findings - Interfaces With Interactive Sound Were Considered More Realistic/Suitable

The data gathered in this experiment support the hypothesis that participants preferred interactive sound rather than non-interactive sound to accompany the iShoogle interface. This finding was meaningful, because even though the algorithm used to add interactivity to sound was very simple, it already improved the 'Realistic/Suitable' perception of this interface, according to the data.

Using the speed of movement to modify volume of playback (i.e. Interactive sound) was perceived as more Realistic and Suitable than a solution with constant volume (i.e. Non-interactive sound), as a sound component of iShoogle interface for interacting with digital fabrics.

5.5 Chapter Conclusion

Chapter Context

In this chapter we focused on evaluating a usable textile simulator interface. We investigated the capabilities of direct manipulation interfaces and examined which of them could be applied to the iShoogle interface. We also investigated the acceptability and perceived realism of different ways to enrich iShoogle with sound feedback. An attempt was made to understand the challenges around learning of the new interface and the Cognitive Load necessary to use it.

Highlights: Study Data And Findings

During the stain finding Study 5, participants explored the simulated fabrics on a tablet in search of a detail hidden within the video. The study compared the iShoogle Interface with a GUI slider interface in terms of Time it takes to start performing an action, time it takes to complete an action, and the cognitive load introduced during the process. According to the study findings, gestures were as fast as sliders in both starting the gestures (recollection task) and finding the hidden stain (recognition task). This means that iShoogle did not cause a decrease in performance while it introduced unique advantages (no screen space used, natural gestures, direct manipulation). This could be interpreted as iShoogle interface being superior to its alternative.

The interactive sound Study 6 evaluated the impact of sound interactivity on the perception of the interface itself. The results of the binomial test showed that there were significant differences in perception of two sound interfaces (interactive and non-interactive) with the interactive sound interface rated as more realistic and suitable.

Limitations: Access To Fabrics And Expert Manufacturer's Knowledge

To investigate a full range of sensations and qualities experienced while touching fabrics, we needed to use a wide variety of fabrics for our research. Thanks to the collaborators from various design and textile departments, we obtained a wide range of fabrics. However due to time and organisational constraints, we never reached the full potential of these cooperations. For example, we tried to use fabrics that differed in stretchiness or roughness, but were identical in every other aspect. The potential for testing the interface with such closely matched fabrics was not achieved due to time constraints and difficulty in sourcing such fabrics.

Limitations: Access To Users And No Remote Studies

Once the iShoogle interface reached a stage in which it could be tested, we needed access to participants to perform our studies. We believe that the research could be stronger if for certain studies we released a free app to the Apple App Store and allowed people from around the world to use iShoogle in return for us gathering their usage data. Unfortunately, copyright constraints, organisational disagreements and some technical difficulties made that impossible.

The need to have participants on site with our own iPad devices with pre-loaded iShoogle app made it possible for us to recruit in total only around 200 participants for all the studies, rather than estimated tens of thousands, if we were using the App Store as a distribution channel. We were aware that running studies on unknown hardware and in unknown conditions would introduce new and unexpected unknown variables. These sources of noise might, or might not be counterbalanced by larger number of participants.

Future Directions: Research

Future research could include: the acceptability and discoverability of gestures in iShoogle; interface design and hinting on gestures that users had not discovered yet; ways to increase perceived usefulness of iShoogle, lowering the technology's adoption threshold.

iShoogle was successfully released on the Apple App Store, becoming available to every iPhone and iPad user in the world. We released iShoogle to the general public primarily as a demo and a companion to shoogleit.com, however it could be also released in a modified form as a globally accessible study. Henze et al. (2011) described successful attempt to add game mechanics to a research project, to gain an unprecedented amount of participants and data, with a cost of losing some of the control over the participant's setting.

Designing a study to be distributed as a game or fabrics catalogue (with all the ethical disclaimers and information that usually accompany studies) could be a source of invaluable insight into the usage of iShoogle. Such studies, because of their scale, would enable insight and results unavailable otherwise.

5.6 Chapter Contributions

> CONTRIBUTION 5.1 – When Comparing iShoogle Gesture Interface With A Slider-based Alternative, iShoogle Was Not Slower Than Sliders In Terms Of Time To Start And To Complete The Interaction.

Sliders, despite of being a priori more familiar to users, were not significantly faster than gestures in terms of time it took to start the task and in terms of time it took to complete the task. This confirmed our hypothesis that the gesture interface would not be significantly slower than the slider interface. In fact, there was a trend suggesting that participants took less time to initiate interaction in the gesture interface and the type of deformation had marginally significant effect. However, these results were not conclusive. Only for one of the deformations was the gesture interface significantly faster than sliders interface.

It is possible that if we were to increase or simply vary the number of different gestures in future versions of iShoogle that this might change. Whilst we see an advantage for at least one deformation being represented in a gesture based interface, we cannot rule out the possibility that there might be more deformations better interacted with via gesture, or indeed, some deformations that are easier to interact with via sliders.

CONTRIBUTION 5.2 – In Sound-Enabled iShoogle, Users Notice The Difference Between Interactive And Non-Interactive Sound: Participants Consistently Chose Interactive Sound As More Realistic/Suitable.

Participants testing sound-enabled iShoogle found varying sound volume (interactive) to be more realistic/suitable than constant sound volume (non-interactive). The sound interactivity was achieved with an algorithm that translated user's real-time actions into the volume of sound playback.

Chapter 6 – iShoogle's Ability To Accurately Communicate Fabric Qualities

Goal:
Identify the visual and sound elements of iShoogle that close the perceptual gap between textile qualities perceived when interacting with a digital fabric and those perceived when interacting with a physical fabric

Literature:
Cross-modal interfaces help users reduce uncertainties about the qualities of objects. Modalities of vision, sound and responsiveness can provide information that was incomplete in other modalities

Study 8:
Sound-enabled iShoogle is used to rate fabric qualities. Ratings made using iShoogle with sound and without sound are compared with fabric quality ratings from Study 5

Study 7:
A simplified one-gesture iShoogle is compared with an image, a slideshow and a movie of the same fabric. The accuracy of ratings is measured for these four interfaces

Study 9:
Fabric quality ratings made using iShoogle with sound and without sound are compared with ratings of physical fabrics

Contribution:
Depending on the fabric (and possibly sound recording and production), adding sound to iShoogle has the capacity to increase or decrease the accuracy of textile quality ratings

Contribution:
The type of interface used to present fabric digitally influences the accuracy of textile quality ratings. The accuracy increased or decreased depending on the rated textile quality. The simplified one-gesture iShoogle (used in this study) is not better than other interfaces

6. Impact Of iShoogle's Visual And Sound Elements On Accurate Perception Of Fabric Qualities

6.1 Introduction

6.1.1 Context

The goal of this thesis was to understand how non-experts could perceive fabrics via digital interfaces and to create and evaluate an interface that could communicate the qualities of fabrics accurately. In this final chapter we combined the outcomes of all previous chapters to achieve that goal. We investigated what textile qualities can be perceived (Chapter 2) when interacting with fabrics using gestures (Chapter 3) incorporated into a touch and sound interface (Chapter 4 and 5). The ultimate goal of this investigation was to provide a feasible way of communicating fabric qualities via digital means.

In three described studies we investigated the impact of varying the visual interface in Study 7 and the presence of a sound interface on perceived fabric qualities in Study 8 and Study 9.

6.1.2 Chapter Goals And Motivation For Goals

> GOAL 6.1 – Establish Which Visual Interface Of A Fabric Simulator Results In The Most Accurate Perception Of Fabric Qualities.

In this chapter we compared the interfaces currently used for communicating fabric qualities with the iShoogle interface developed and evaluated in previous chapters. In Study 7 we compared four visual methods of displaying fabrics and evaluated which of them communicates fabric qualities most accurately. The optimal accuracy would occur when the perceptual gap is the smallest, i.e. the qualities users perceived when touching the on-screen fabrics differ the least from the qualities they perceived when touching the physical swatch .

We tested the accuracy of the interface (lack of perceptual gap) by asking participants to rate a fabric on textile qualities scales (Soft, Rough, etc.) in both a digital and physical condition. Study 7 described in this chapter has been published as a joint paper by P. M. Orzechowski et al. (2011) and is further described there.

GOAL 6.2 - Examine If The Sound Interface For A Fabric Simulator Provides A More Accurate Perception Of Fabric Qualities.

In this chapter we also evaluated whether sound could further enhance iShoogle's ability to communicate fabric qualities. We investigated whether the interactive sound (described in detail in Chapter 4) increased the accuracy of communication of textile qualities for a range of fabrics.

Similar to the investigation of the impact of visual presentation on the perceptual gap, we conducted a study which compared the perception of fabric qualities in sound and no-sound conditions with the rating of real fabrics. Study 7 in this chapter was a collaboration with Martonjak further described by Martonjak (2011) and the Study 8 was a collaboration with Nadia Berthouze (paper in review).

6.1.3 Contributions And Acknowledgements

Unless otherwise specified, the entire intellectual input into this thesis comes from the author. The visual interface study was a collaboration described by P. M. Orzechowski et al. (2011), sound studies were collaborations with Martonjak (2011) and Nadia Berthouze. Most of those collaborations were a part of Digital Sensoria project, as detailed by Atkinson et al. (2013).

6.2 Literature Review

6.2.1 Literature Review Introduction

We identified a number of relevant papers in the area of online commerce that investigated the opportunities created by using interactive digital presentation tools. In particular, we identified studies and findings that were related to shopping for textiles and interacting with them.

The literature search highlighted that online retail needed a tool that would enable shoppers to make good informed decisions while purchasing textiles. 'See-touch-handle' factor was being frequently highlighted as important in the evaluation process; however, it was understood to be non-existent in an online shopping environment. Some researchers attempted to achieve better textile representation by adding more modalities to their interfaces. Expanding the visual presentation of products by adding sound and other interaction types increased shopping enjoyment, trust towards the retailer and confidence in purchase decisions.

We also mentioned studies that investigated using sound to expand the possibilities of digital presentation tools to communicate object qualities.

Literature Review Criteria

We reviewed recent research concerned with using interactive simulations of fabrics to communicate fabric qualities. We specifically looked for literature which:

- described the challenges of shopping for clothes online, especially in the context of using the interface to create a better shopping experience.
- described the impact of touch and tactile interaction on enjoyment and decision making in an online shopping context.
- Investigated using sound to communicate qualities of objects

6.2.2 Consumer Need For Tactile Input: An Internet Retailing Challenge

When consumers purchase goods on the Internet, they cannot touch the products before ordering them. Citrin, Stem, Spangenberg, and Clark (2003) described a survey of 272 respondents which investigated how likely they would be to use tactile input while purchasing products over the Internet. The analysis investigated what role in the decision-making process the tactile feedback took, and also whether it had an impact on the actual purchase of a product.

The findings indicated that consumers who took the tactile qualities under consideration in their decision-making were more likely to purchase products online. Findings also suggested that women put more weight than men on tactile investigation of a potential purchase. In the absence of tools for communicating tactile qualities online, there is a population of potential online shoppers who are not making online purchases of garments, because they cannot evaluate fabric qualities without physically holding the garment. Citrin et al. (2003) believe that enabling consumers to investigate online purchases using tactile input would expand the population of online shoppers by including consumers for whom tactile evaluation is important. They also discuss strategic implications of their findings for online retailers.

6.2.3 The Affective Experience Of Handling Digital Fabrics: Tactile And Visual Cross-Modal Effects

Wu et al. (2011) investigated the emotions associated with touching and manipulating fabrics during purchasing textiles in the real world. They aimed to recreate the same affective states during online shopping with use of interactive fabric animations. These animations attempted to bring digital shopping experience closer to reality. Wu et al. (2011) investigated the impact on pleasure and engagement of the order in which digital and physical fabrics were presented to the participants. The study found that handling the physical fabric first increased the enjoyment of handling the digital animation afterwards, but handling the digital animation first did not influence the later experience of handling the physical swatch (which was used in our digital-first accuracy measurement method). Gender and body awareness seemed to be moderators.

6.2.4 Product Category Dependent Consumer Preferences For Online And Off-Line Shopping Features And Their Influence On Multi-Channel Retail Alliances

Levin et al. (2003) investigated which aspects of the purchasing process were important for which types of goods. They looked especially at the comparison of online and offline shopping experience, because both of those platforms provided different advantages and disadvantages relating to scale, physicality and price. The presented analysis of strengths and opportunities of textile shopping online was relevant to this thesis. Levin et al. (2003) also reported on the high importance of touching and inspecting textile products prior to the purchase, while at the same time considering touch an exclusively offline evaluation method. Their paper highlighted the need for providing touch evaluation in the online environment, but did not suggest any solutions to this problem.

6.2.5 Capturing Product Experiences: A Split-Modality Approach

Schifferstein and Cleiren (2005) compared the role of four modalities (vision, sound, smell and touch) in interacting with products and perceiving their qualities. In the study, participants were exposed to products using only one modality at a time and were asked to describe those products. Those unconstrained language descriptions of products were then analysed in terms of: words used to describe the experience on mono-modal interaction with the object; correct identification of what type of object they were interacting with; and memories and associations triggered by the experience. The touch and vision modalities appeared to enable participants to create the most detailed descriptions. The touch and vision modalities also triggered the most memories and enabled greater product recognition. Participants who interacted with objects via vision alone took much less time to investigate products than those who used touch.

Findings described by Schifferstein and Cleiren (2005) suggested that while vision is a convenient and dominant way to communicate products, the touch modality might wield a promise as well. It was of relevance for this thesis, since combining two main modalities in a seamless fashion might improve the shopping experience.

6.2.6 Affective And Cognitive Online Shopping Experience: Effects Of Image Interactivity Technology And Experimenting With Appearance

Lee, Kim, and Fiore (2010) analysed the impact of Image Interactivity Technology on the perceived risks of online shopping. The findings suggested that improving the visual presentation of products increases enjoyment of the shopping experience. Improving visual presentation of products also seemed to increase the perceived trust in the online retailer (associated with the likelihood that the product will match the description and will not have to be returned). Perceived risk also influenced the relation to the online retailer, which meant that using better product presentation technology could be used as a brand strengthening exercise. Lee et al. (2010) demonstrated that the interfaces preferred by the study participants were often those described as innovative yet playful.

6.2.7 It Just Feels Good: Customers' Affective Response To Touch And Its Influence On Persuasion

Peck and Wiggins (2006) investigated the role of touch in purchase decision-making (evaluating quality and value), especially in scenarios where there was not enough information about the product. The study found that people motivated to touch products (those who considered touch to be fun and interesting) did report an affective and persuasive impact of touching the product. Participants who valued touch liked the products more and were more likely to buy them after touching them. These effects were particularly visible when the touch feedback was positive or neutral, i.e. touch was not unpleasant.

6.2.8 Consumer Decision Making In Online Shopping Environments: The Effects Of Interactive Decision Aids

Häubl and Trifts (2000) performed a large study where participants had to choose from a large number of products in a realistic simulated online shop. This study concentrated on two stages of decision-making: the initial screening to narrow down the choices to a smaller shortlist and the detailed examination of the shortlisted items to make the final decision. Participants used digital decision aiding tools of varying sophistication levels, designed to help participants narrow down the choice and make the final decision. The more sophisticated tools were found to create smaller lists of shortlisted products, and the choices made with their help were later considered to be better choices by the participants themselves. Häubl and Trifts (2000) concluded that developing better decision-making and product comparison tools for online shopping could increase the quality of choices and could possibly make the online shopping experience faster and less frustrating. The authors also described the possibilities and potential increase in revenue (more sales, fewer returns) that can be brought by improvements in the digital decision making tools.

6.2.9 When Sound Affects Vision: Effects Of Auditory Grouping On Visual Motion Perception

Watanabe and Shimojo (2001) designed a set of studies that presented identical visual stimuli with varying sound, and evaluated how sound changed the perceived qualities of visual objects. In one study, two visual dots travelled on a colliding course on the screen and the exact timing of the sound sample (just before, or just after the collision) determined whether the participants thought that the dots bounced off each other or passed through each other.

This paper presented, on a very low level, the principle that sound could be used to solve perceptual ambiguities. Participants used acoustic information to decide on physical qualities and behaviour of the visual stimuli and interpreted visual content as a different behaviour just because of the type and timing of the sound. This principle could possibly be applied to perceived qualities of fabrics.

We tested this principle in Study 8, Study 9 and also Study 6, designed to influence the way people perceive the qualities and interpret behaviour of fabric by changing the sound it emits.

6.2.10 Crossmodal Correspondences: A Tutorial Review

Spence (2011) reviewed crossmodal correspondences where acoustic and visual input were connected in unexpected ways. A number of described patterns were relevant to this thesis. When sound was considered to not be connected to the visual stimuli (non congruent), it had less influence on participants' perception of the stimuli. Applied to our research, whenever the sounds used in textile simulators would be not suitable, or not created with care, they could have a negative or no effect on the accuracy of ratings.

Spence (2011) identified three main benefits of crossmodal presentation: Structural (coming from the objects themselves), Statistical (coming from the past experience of objects) and Semantic (based on the understanding of the objects). This indicated that positive effects of crossmodal perception could be acquired through repeated experience of objects (Structural and Statistical), rather than only through formal education (Semantic). In the context of fabrics, this means that even untrained, non-expert fabric handlers would have a mental model of a connection between fabric visuals and fabric sounds.

6.2.11 Sound Enhances Visual Perception: Cross - Modal Effects Of Auditory Organization On Vision

Vroomen and Gelder (2000) investigated the impact of simple sound tones in a variety of visual contrast detection tasks. The speed and accuracy of participant's responses were evaluated. Visual tasks were accompanied either by sounds or by silence. The results indicated that the presence of sound feedback improved the speed with which participants performed rating tasks. However, accuracy improved only when the sounds were meaningful (e.g. pitch height corresponded to brightness) and participants were aware of the connection between sound tone and the visuals on the screen.

Findings described by Vroomen and Gelder (2000) were relevant for this thesis, as they indicate that enhancing a visual presentation of objects with sound stimuli can aid perception of presented objects. For the sound stimuli to aid perception of visual qualities, the presented sound stimuli (e.g. fabric sounds) need to correspond to the presented acoustic stimuli (fabric video).

6.2.12 Literature Review Summary

The main lessons learned from the literature review, were:

- People consider tactile feeling of the garments while buying them, even when they had to derive fabric's tactile qualities from photographs and descriptions as detailed by Citrin et al. (2003),
- Interacting with fabrics digitally is influenced by previous experiences of physical interaction with similar fabrics, but not the opposite as described by Wu et al. (2011),
- Whilst making purchase decisions online for various types of products, shoppers missed the ability to evaluate tactile qualities for textile products as investigated by Levin et al. (2003),
- While vision was the primary way to experience objects online, combining it with other modalities (vision, sound, smell and touch) could enrich the experience as in the work described by Schifferstein and Cleiren (2005),

- More advanced interaction interfaces used during online shopping increased shoppers' trust in their purchasing decisions as reported by Lee et al. (2010),
- Touch was used to evaluate quality and value of products in conditions where not enough information was available through other means as observed by Peck and Wiggins (2006),
- Better digital tools for decision making and product comparison could help shoppers to increase confidence in their decisions and decrease frustration as detailed by Häubl and Trifts (2000),
- When evaluating objects, sound stimuli was used to fill the missing qualities of objects and could change perceived qualities of objects as detailed by Watanabe and Shimojo (2001),
- The benefits of crossmodal interaction can be structural (coming from the interaction with objects) and statistical (coming from the past experience of objects) rather than only semantic (acquired via formal education) as investigated by Spence (2011),
- Auditory feedback improved perception of visual objects only when auditory feedback was relevant and participants understood the connection between visuals and sounds as in work described by Vroomen and Gelder (2000).

6.3 Organisation Of This Chapter

We conducted three studies to investigate the impact of visual and sound enhancements of our digital textile simulator iShoogle, on its ability to communicate textile properties. While we were not interested in purely emulating a shopping scenario, we anticipated that our findings would be readily expandable and applicable to online shopping interfaces research.

In order to investigate the impact of the visual element of an interactive fabric interface on perception of textile qualities, a Study 7 was performed, comparing four different fabric simulation interfaces. We focused on the differences in perception of fabric qualities between different interfaces, to understand what the impact is of the fidelity (number of frames), interactivity or the ease of use.

In order to investigate the impact of sound (its type and interactivity) on the perceived qualities of the simulated textile, studies Study 8 and Study 9 were performed in collaboration with UCL researchers. The main contributors and the work they have done were listed in the descriptions of studies. The first study was concerned with the difference in perception of textiles when they were presented with their own sounds, as compared to when they were presented with the sound of another fabric. The second study investigated how the presence and absence of a correct sound changed the perceived qualities of fabrics, especially when they were compared with qualities perceived during the interaction with real physical swatches.

6.4 Study 7 – Impact Of Presentation And Interaction On Perceived Fabric Qualities

6.4.1 Introduction

Acknowledgements

This study was co-designed and run together with Douglas Atkinson and acknowledgements are made wherever his work is cited. The results of this study were published in a P. M. Orzechowski et al. (2011). Study design and running the study were shared effort of Douglas Atkinson and Pawel Orzechowski, while Software used was fully developed by Pawel Orzechowski. The write up and analysis were a cooperation between the authors of the aforementioned paper.

Introduction

We aimed to create technology that could communicate textile qualities better than technologies used currently in online retail. Despite the advancement in features and availability of mobile devices, the best way to present textiles to a consumer was still a photo or in certain instances a video. Both of these technologies had their own advantages and disadvantages connected with the amount of visual detail and interaction that they provide. Häubl and Trifts (2000) and Levin et al. (2003) suggested that consumers missed the Textile Hand qualities and that they had fears of the textile qualities being badly represented on the photos and movies.

The next successful generation of interfaces to interact with textiles had to communicate textile qualities more accurately (more similarity with the actual textile qualities of the communicated fabric). We decided to compare whether our iShoogle interface, described and evaluated in previous chapters, could communicate textile qualities better than image and video interfaces.

6.4.2 Evaluating Fabric With Visual Interfaces

Study Design

In this Study 7 we compared four digital interfaces for presenting fabrics digitally, to determine which of them produces a more realistic presentation of fabrics. Participants interacted with fabrics using: an Image, a Slideshow, a Movie and an iShoogle as described in Table 15. The differences between these interfaces are described below in terms of visuals, interaction and simulated physics. We considered each of the next interfaces as an improvement over the previous one: Slideshow provided more visual content than Image; Video provided continuity and movement information to the visual content; iShoogle provided interactivity and control as well as responsiveness to familiar gestures to Video. We hoped to identify to what degree it was one of those cumulatively improving steps that enabled more accurate communication of fabrics.

We considered an interface to be realistic when it enabled perception of the same levels of qualities (Rough, Soft, etc.) as qualities perceived when handling a physical sample of fabric. When participants described a digitally presented fabric as similar to the original physical sample, it meant that the digital presentation communicated true qualities of that fabric and hence was realistic.

We used the eight quality rating scales created in Chapter 2 to evaluate fabric qualities. Participants rated fabrics along the dimensions of Hard, Furry, Rough, Textured, Crisp, Flexible, Soft, Smooth (Figure 17). Participants used two iPad devices side by side, one to interact with the interfaces and one to rate fabric qualities. Participants rated the fabric qualities on a digital form with sliders (Figure 43) displayed on an second iPad device (not the one they used for interacting with the interfaces). Sliders had no visual clues about the middle or particular number of steps and were set to register position on the slider between 1 and 100. We used a photo of the checkerboard pattern that we recorded the fabrics on as a background for the sliders screen. This way the participants had a better opportunity to judge the transparency of fabrics.

Each fabric was evaluated twice by the same participant, first in digital form and then as a physical swatch (to provide a control for that fabric). To avoid experience and learning, we did not ask participants to interact with the same fabric four times (once using each interface). Instead, we used a different fabric for each interface. Participants interacted with a different fabric for each interface and we used the same four fabrics as in other studies as seen in Figure 35. All four digital rating sessions happened first, followed by all four physical rating sessions, because we wanted participants to estimate fabric qualities (guess how a fabric would look from interacting with it digitally), rather than simply recall them (remember how fabric felt during interactions with the physical swatch). Additionally findings described by Wu et al. (2011) suggested that interacting with an object physically first did have potential to change participants' reaction to the digital equivalent later, but seeing the digital version first (like in our studies) did not have impact on participants' reaction. Interface-Fabric pairs were randomized and so was the order of interfaces. Order of presented interfaces and fabric-interface pairings were balanced with use of latin squares.

Once participants evaluated each fabric digitally and physically on the eight quality rating scales, we compared the ratings on each scale for the ratings of digital and physical interaction. We refer to the difference between physical and the digital ratings of that fabric as the Accuracy of those ratings. In this study we aimed to look for patterns in the average accuracy of each interface, to identify which interface produces most accurate ratings and is therefore the most realistic.

	Image	Slideshow	Movie	iShoogle
Visuals	A single frame from a movie of the fabric being deformed was	Like the image condition, but at any given point a random frame	A movie of the fabric being deformed played on the screen.	A movie of the fabric being deformed controlled with a

	displayed on the screen	from the fabric deformation movie is on the screen (out of a set of 10 frames)		pinching gesture of the iShoogle interface
Interaction	No user interaction	User taps an on-screen button to move to the next frame of the slideshow	User taps an on-screen button to play the movie again.	Direction and speed of the movie is controlled by the user's gesture
Simulated physics	No physics	No physics	No physics. All movie frames played in identical time intervals. Constant playback speed.	Simple spring-damper system described in Section 4.4.4, acting as an in-between factor between user and the movie.

Table 15 – Comparison of four visual fabric presentation methods.

6.4.3 Evaluating Fabric With Visual Interfaces – Results

Results And Analysis

A total of 21 participants (15 male) between 19 and 31 years old from Heriot-Watt University took part in the study, each rating four fabrics twice and completing the study. Each fabric rating consisted of 8 values (one for each quality rating scale) producing a total of 1344 data points. The data was analysed using repeated-measures Analysis of Variance ANOVA. We used the interface (image, slideshow, movie, iShoogle) as the within-subjects factor and analysed the scores on each scale separately. This analysis was also published by P. M. Orzechowski et al. (2011).

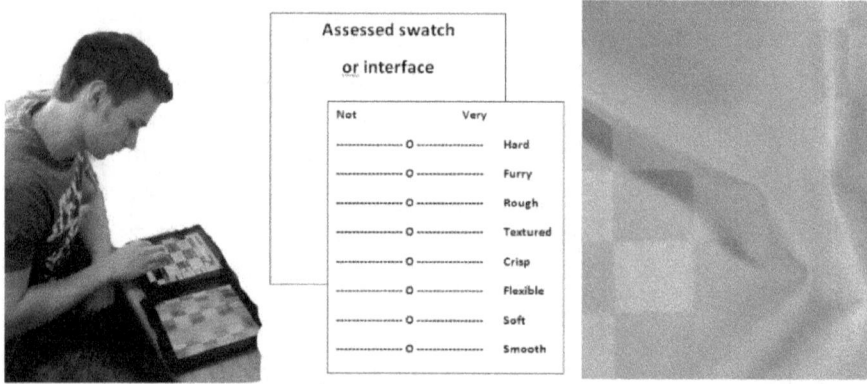

Figure 43 – Images used by P. M. Orzechowski et al. (2011) from left to right: Participant using interface on one iPad and rating fabrics on the other iPad; diagram of our two iPad setup and rating sliders; example of what Latex looked like when displayed on the screen.

Means and standard deviations of fabric quality ratings showed large differences between rating accuracy between interface types, but also the errors associated with the means were large. Interestingly for most dimensions (as seen on Figure 44) the difference in ratings was smallest for the Movie interface. This could be caused by the fact that Movie combined the benefits of both groups of interfaces: the simplicity of interaction (Image and Slideshow) and the rich communication of how fabric behaves while moving (iShoogle).

iShoogle was not the most accurate interface in communicating fabric qualities, however the iShoogle version used in this study was not the final version of iShoogle described in this thesis. It is worth mentioning that this was chronologically the first study that used iShoogle and so the interface was still in development and also it only used one gesture to interact with digitised fabrics (horizontal Pinch). Because of these two constraints (software in development and one gesture) the iShoogle interface described in this study did not present the full set of benefits that its final version did, while introducing new challenges (need for learning and obscuring some of the screen with the hand that performs a gesture).

Our study was exploratory in nature and we did not find the desired results, however the data analysis suggested some interesting research avenues, which could be followed up on.

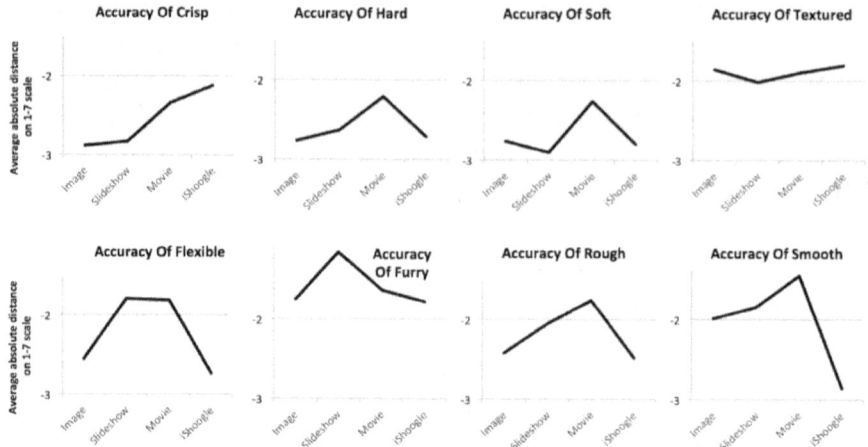

Figure 44 – Rating Accuracy (the difference between fabric quality ratings of a swatch and digital version of the same fabric) across the 4 interfaces. For scale, accuracy is presented as average absolute distance of physical and digital ratings as if they were presented on 1-7 scale.

Results suggest that interface type influenced rating accuracy (the difference between digital and physical ratings) but not for all textile qualities. The positive or negative impact of interface type on quality ratings could be explained by how each quality is evaluated when touching a physical fabric.

The effect of interface type on accuracy of Crisp ratings showed a trend with F(3,60)=2.32, p=.084 and a planned contrast analysis showing a linear effect F(1,20)=6.41, p=.020. One of the promising trends in data was iShoogle's positive impact on accuracy of Crisp ratings. The Crisp quality describes the behaviour of fabric during movement, rather than when it is stationary. Also Crisp could be considered a quality that was best evaluated by repetitive small movements. This could explain why the rating accuracy of Crisp benefited from the more visual and animated interfaces (Movie and iShoogle). The iShoogle interface was designed to communicate textile qualities with movement of the fabric, which could help to interpret this trend.

A planned contrast analysis of scales Rough and Smooth showed a quadratic effect of medium $F(1,20)=9.08$, $p=.007$ and $F(1,20)=4.19$, $p=.054$ respectively. The results of within-subject ANOVA for those scales were $F(3,60)=1.47$, $p=.23$ and $F(3,60)=1.95$, $p=.13$ respectively. An interesting trend is iShoogle's negative impact on accuracy of tactile qualities evaluated with fingertips – Rough and Smooth. This trend could be explained by the fact that the smooth glass surface of the iPad tablet might have created an impression that the fabric did in fact feel like smooth glass surface. This would decrease the perceived Rough and increase the perceived Smooth qualities of the digitally presented fabric. This could be caused by the fingertip sensations not only missing from the iShoogle interface, but indeed being replaced by the inconsistent sensation of touching a hard, cold surface of the glass screen, hence confusing user's perception of digitised fabric.

Conclusions

Since the results of this study did not achieve statistical significance, the interpretation of this study is highly speculative. The most important lesson learned was that potentially not all textile qualities could benefit from iShoogle interface. In follow-up studies, we expected that:

- the Accuracy for different fabric qualities can vary within the same interface. For example, the iShoogle interface could be very accurate in communicating Crisp, but misleading in terms of Smooth ratings,

- adjusting the interface settings can cause changes to fabric quality rankings. Some participants commented on the speed of fabric animations (when fabric returned to the central frame) and that it influenced the qualities they perceived, especially the Flexible quality.

Future Work

Future work should focus on improving the limitations of the study and following up on the study findings. We recruited relatively few participants for quite a complex study design, hence creating small effects and an underpowered study. To address the sources of noise in gathered data we would: simplify our study design with a smaller amount of interfaces and improve the iShoogle interface to use multiple gestures and hence to make use of its full potential. Additionally we might require participants to rate fabric qualities twice or for them to have an opportunity to improve their initial ratings during a second handling episode, which could produce more consistent ratings. Additionally rating scales rather than being represented by one word, could use an icon or a small word cloud to promote common and consistent understanding of fabric qualities.

While the results did not reach statistical significance and the above analysis is highly speculative, future work could still follow up on the trends suggesting that iShoogle could have either a positive or negative impact on the rating qualities when compared with other interfaces. We decided that in further studies, analysis should always be performed separately for each of the fabric qualities. We believed that it was likely that different mechanisms influence ratings of different fabric qualities.

6.5 Study 8 – The Impact Of Sound On Perceived Qualities Of Fabrics

6.5.1 Introduction

Background

We considered the modality of sound to be a promising addition to the pre-existing interactive and visual modalities of the iShoogle interface. In the following part of this thesis we describe the investigation of how the Accuracy of fabric quality ratings changes when sound modality is added to the iShoogle interface. Two studies were performed in collaboration with UCL researchers, in order to investigate the impact of sound (its type and interactivity) on perceived qualities of the simulated textiles. The main contributors and the work they have done are listed in the descriptions of studies.

6.5.2 Presence And Correctness Of Sound Compared With Physical Swatch Ratings

Introduction And Collaboration

In the next two studies, we used a sound-enabled version of the iShoogle textile simulator. We presented participants with visual stimuli of four fabrics, enriched with the sound recordings of those fabrics. In the first study, run by and co-designed with Martonjak and further described by Martonjak (2011), we compared quality ratings between three conditions: fabrics paired with their own sound recordings; fabrics paired with a sound recording of another fabric; and fabric paired with no sound recording (silence). In the second study, run by the author of this thesis and co-designed with

Nadia Berthouze, we repeated that procedure, but we expanded it by the rating of physical fabrics as well as digital ones. We asked participants to rate real physical swatches of the textiles after they interacted with the same fabrics in the simulator. The aim of this study was to identify conditions in which adding a sound recording playback to iShoogle increases the Accuracy of fabric quality ratings.

6.5.3 Correct Sound Study – The Exploratory Study – Collaboration With Liina Martonjak

Acknowledgements

This study was co-designed and run together with Liina Martonjak and acknowledgements were made wherever her work is cited. Study design and running the study were shared effort of Liina Martonjak and Pawel Orzechowski, while Software used in the study was fully developed by Pawel Orzechowski.

Sound Samples

As in Study 7, the stimulus set consisted of four visually similar fabrics that differed in terms of the sound they made and their tactile qualities. We selected bright cream-colored samples of Buckram, (raised) Cotton, Latex (rubber) and Ripstop (nylon) (see Figure 35). Samples were digitized in the lighting conditions and resolution described in Chapter 4 into shoogle movies of 40 frames each. The sounds of crunched fabrics were recorded following the guidelines described in (Section 5.4.2) with a stage-quality microphone and an amplifier in a soundproof room. The audio recordings were edited in Audacity software, in order to achieve seamless loops and consistent volume of the sound.

Experiment Design

In this study, participants were interacting with digitized fabrics via a sound-enabled iShoogle interface. We were interested in the impact of the sound on perceived qualities of the fabric. We tested three different iShoogle versions which varied by the sound feedback, but were otherwise identical. The three sound conditions were:

- fabric with no sound feedback (silence),
- fabric with correct sound feedback (sound originated from the same physical swatch as the visuals on the screen),
- fabric with incorrect sound feedback (sound originated from substantially different physical swatch than the visuals on the screen).

Participants interacted with digitised fabrics via a modified iShoogle interface version which always used one of the three above sound conditions. Participants' task was to describe the fabric qualities that they perceived during interaction with each digitised fabric sample. For each digitized sample, we asked the participant to rate the presented fabric on our eight 7-point textile quality rating scales (Crisp, Hard, Soft, Textured, Flexible, Furry, Rough, Smooth). These were the rating scales that we created previously in section 2.8 and used in previous studies.

Over the whole experiment each participant was asked to rate 40 digitized fabric samples. Each digital fabric sample consisted of visual and sound stimuli coming from the same or different fabric. We used four fabrics as sources of visual and sound stimuli (Buckram, Latex, Raised Cotton and Ripstop as seen in Figure 35) as in our other studies. Each of four visual stimuli (fabric movies) was accompanied by one of five different sound options: silence; its own sound; sound of the remaining three fabrics. We aimed to present participants with all the possible combinations of visual and sound stimuli. Since each of 4 visual fabric recordings was presented with 5 sound options, participants rated 20 different versions of digitised fabric. During the study each possible combination of stimuli was presented twice, thus participants interacted with the total of 40 trials, rating each on the textile quality scales. In order to avoid learning effects, the trials were randomised.

Data Analysis

Nineteen students (8 male) age 19-31 took part in the study recruited at UCL, London. For this analysis we only used ratings recorded in silence and correct sound setup (visual and audio stimuli originated from the same fabric) and we did not use ratings for conditions where fabrics were presented with incorrect sounds. For clarity we modified a table created by Martonjak (2011) (p. 58) into the Table 16. On it, p values of Wilcoxon's Matched-Paired Signed-Ranks test results showed a p value for the significance in ratings' difference between silence and sound conditions for different fabric types. The colours describe whether sound provided more realistic (green) or less realistic (orange) ratings of the fabric. We compared the ratings of digitised fabrics with the ratings of their physical originals, but because participants did not rate physical fabrics as a part of this study, we used physical fabric ratings from Study 7, which used a similar design and the same fabric swatches.

	Buckram	Latex	Raised Cotton	Ripstop
Crisp	.029* ↑	.030* ↓	.179	.002** ↑
Hard	.006** ↑	.001** ↓	.577	.049* ↑
Soft	.033* ↑	.001** ↓	.714	.025* ↑
Textured	.273	.813	.431	.926
Flexible	.061	.021* ↓	.275	.035* ↑
Furry	.546	.042* ↑	.021* ↓	.026* ↑
Rough	.427	.083	.251	.001** ↑
Smooth	.803	.041* ↓	.616	.047* ↑

Table 16 – Addition of sound can improve or undermine communication of fabric qualities.

In Table 16 colours signify if sound provided more realistic (green) or less realistic (orange) ratings of the fabric. This graph is a modified version of the graph from Liina Martonjak's thesis and includes only comparison of ratings for the correct sound and silence conditions. Incorrect sound data were excluded. In this table * represents p<0.05 and ** represents p<0.01.

Results

Table 16 indicates that the addition of sound, in the way we implemented it, can improve the identification of some types of fabric's qualities, and hinder others. Buckram and Ripstop seem to be more accurately described when accompanied by matching audio. However, for most qualities, Latex accuracy actually decreases, while Cotton is not significantly affected either way.

This was primarily an exploratory study, conducted to investigate whether there is scope for further research into the effects of adding sound to the iShoogle interface. These results highlight that the possible variables that changed perceived qualities of fabrics when the sound is added were: the type of fabric recorded; the quality being described; and sound recording/post-production method. In post-study interviews participants suggested that amplifying all sounds to the same level is misleading, since different fabrics produce different sound volumes in real life. For example, amplifying the sound of the soft and quiet Raised Cotton to the same level as the sound of the squeaky and loud Latex, makes the Raised Cotton sound unrealistically loud. We performed this study in hope of finding patterns that could guide future work and during the data analysis we identified a number of potential patterns described above.

Discussion

The impact of the presence of sound on perceived qualities was the strongest for the two fabric with the most distinguishable sounds: Ripstop (sound often increased Accuracy) and Latex (sound often decreased Accuracy). Ripstop is a gently ribbed, synthetic fabric used to produce umbrellas, tents and waterproof jackets. Ripstop emits a very crisp and sharp sound, which could be used to identify Ripstop's qualities. Latex, on the other hand, is used for the production of rubber gloves and balloons, and emits a sharp, squeaking, unpleasant sound, which may have been disorienting to participants. Additionally, these differences in accuracy of the ratings may have been caused by Ripstop being more common in everyday life. Interestingly, the effect of adding sound on the ratings of Buckram (which is a grooved fabric, hard and difficult to bend) was noticeable only in some qualities. There was no effect of adding sound on the accuracy of ratings of Raised Cotton, which is soft and fluffy, and hence produces almost no sound. As raised cotton sounds were amplified to an unnaturally loud volume, the sound appeared to not be associated with the visual stimuli and it may have been disregarded when participants evaluated fabrics. This idea is supported by the work of Spence (2011), who concluded that irrelevant sounds had no impact on perception. Textured was the quality whose ratings were the least affected by adding sound, possibly because it represented a large set of words on the initial grouping, thus giving a large scope for misunderstanding of the term.

6.5.4 Study 9 - Correct Sound Study And Real Fabric Comparison – Collaboration With Nadia Berthouze

Acknowledgements

This study was co-designed and run together with Nadia Berthouze and acknowledgements are made wherever her work is cited. At the time of writing this thesis this study is being written up and for publication in TOCHI Journal. The study design, Software development and running the study were done by Pawel Orzechowski with advice and supervision of Nadia Berthouze and Mike Chantler. Analysis and write up for the journal version were a collaborative effort between Nadia Berthouze and Pawel Orzechowski.

Connection With The Previous Study

In the previous Study 8 we investigated the difference in the ratings of perceived qualities when participants interacted with a sound enabled iShoogle interface in different sound conditions. Study 8 was an early exploratory study, additionally investigating other aspects of iShoogle and sound, such as the impact of audio samples of incorrect fabrics on perceived fabric qualities, the emotional reaction of users to sound enabled iShoogle, and the intention to purchase goods. Most of that data was gathered with a combination of questionnaires and interview questions conducted with participants before and after the experiment. The analysis of these elements of Study 8 is not within the scope of our thesis, however it was described in Liina Martonjak's thesis and published by Martonjak (2011) with their own work.

Study 9 described in this section follows from the initial findings of Study 8 and treats it as a pilot. We decided to remove everything apart from comparison of presence and absence of sound in iShoogle interface. We narrowed down our focus to only presenting iShoogle interfaces with their sound or without any sound with hope of discovering in what conditions and for what textiles sound has ability to improve the communication of textile qualities.

Research Question

The goal of this study was to investigate how adding sound to the iShoogle fabric simulator may affect perceived textile qualities of fabrics. Specifically the research question that we wanted to ask was: can adding sound to the iShoogle interface improve its ability to communicate textile qualities accurately, and would such a benefit vary between fabrics and between textile qualities that were being evaluated? We were especially interested in the comparison of the perceived fabric qualities when touching a physical swatch, a silent digital simulator, and a sound enabled digital simulator. If enabling sound in a textile simulator increased the Accuracy of ratings (brought the perceived qualities closer to the ratings of a physical swatch), it would indicate that the sound made the simulated fabric appear more realistic and life-like. In this study we investigated what types of fabrics and textile qualities would benefit from adding the sound to the digital textile simulator.

Study Design

As in the previous study, the experiment was conducted on iPad 2 devices and used a sound-enabled iShoogle interface. We simplified the iShoogle iPad interface, so that it only enabled participants to control interactive movies of pinched fabrics with a two-finger Pinch gesture. The speed and direction of the Pinch gesture controlled the movie playback and sound volume. This was designed to imitate an interaction with a real fabric swatch. Once participants interacted with each fabric, they were asked to fill a short paper questionnaire. When done, participants would turn the questionnaire to the next page and press the 'next' button on the iPad with the study software as seen in Figure 45. Pressing that button opened the next simulated fabric. To avoid annotation problems, each fabric had a randomly generated unique ID code, which was displayed at the top of the iPad interface and printed above each questionnaire.

The study was run in an open plan computer lab using iPad 2 devices and UrbanEars noise cancelling earphones as seen on Figure 46.

At the end of the study participants interacted with four real physical swatches of the same four fabrics that they had seen previously with the iShoogle interface. No software was necessary during the interaction with real physical swatches.

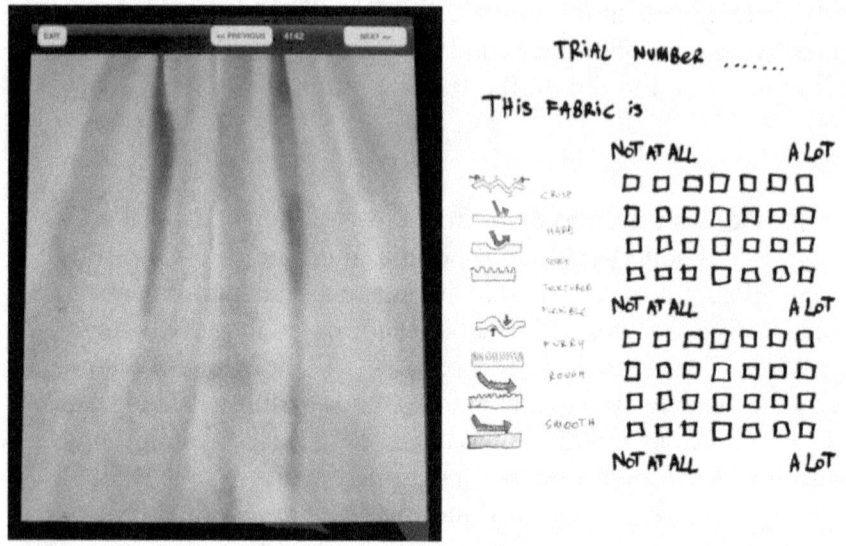

Figure 45 – Study 9. Software and the questionnaire.

Measures

While interacting with each digital or physical fabric, participants filled out a paper questionnaire about the perceived qualities of each swatch. Each questionnaire consisted of 8 scales for describing fabric qualities seen on Figure 17 and participants indicated their rating by making a mark on each scale's axis. Each participant used an A6 notebook, which included the 20 paper questionnaires (each on a separate A6 page), a consent form and debriefing information, all bound together.

Participants were instructed to estimate the properties of textiles as they interacted with the digital or physical swatches. Each of the eight rating scales was described with the word and an icon as seen on Figure 17. We used seven-point Likert scales anchored with words 'not at all' and 'a lot' for Crisp, Hard, Soft, Textured, Flexible, Furry, Rough, and Smooth.

Participants were instructed to press the 'next' button on the iPad interface when they turned the page of the questionnaire booklet. Participants were instructed not to look at the previous pages that they had already filled in, so that they could not compare their current ratings with their previous ratings. Figure 45 (right) depicts what the form looked like and Figure 46 (right) shows a participant filling the form. The unique ID codes of each fabric and sound combination were displayed at the top of an iPad interface and participants were asked to write them down at the top of the paper questionnaire. This procedure made it easier to avoid transcription mistakes or participant errors.

After a short introduction each participant was asked whether they understood the eight fabric qualities, or whether they needed further explanation. No one requested any help in understanding the eight textile qualities that they were asked to evaluate.

Participants were instructed to take as much time as they needed to interact with the digital fabrics and fill out the questionnaire. Participants took on average 30 seconds to complete one trial of interacting with a fabric and rating it on each of eight scales, on average completing the study within 15 minutes.

Procedure

The four digitized fabrics from the stimulus set were presented to participants in a randomized order, one after another, as described above. All fabrics were presented either silent or with sound. After that, fabrics were shown again, but in the opposite sound/silence condition (if the first four were silent, then the next four were with sound, and vice versa). Throughout the study, the complete set of 4 fabrics was shown 4 times, interchangeably with sound and silence. Within each set of fabrics, the order was randomized. A random sound/silent condition was presented first.

The software was designed to shown 16 digital fabric samples in groups of four. Each group consisted of all four fabrics in a randomized order (Buckram, Latex, Cotton, Ripstop depicted on Figure 35), and all fabrics in a group were either silent or voice enabled. Silent and sound enabled groups were presented interchangeably, with half the participants starting with sound and half with silence. For example, if a participant was in a 'silent first' group, they interacted with four silent fabrics, and then four sound enabled ones, then four silent ones and finally with four sound enabled ones.

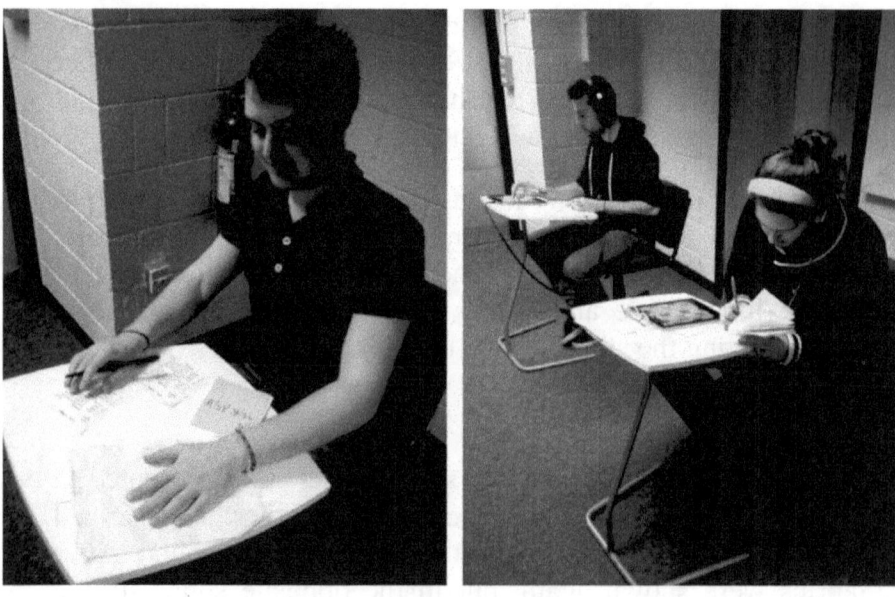

Figure 46 – Study 9. Handling the swatch and experimental setup.

After 16 trials grouped that way, a final batch of four physical fabrics was presented to the participant. These were not presented on an iPad, but they were physical textile samples placed in front of the participant on the table. In each trial, the task given to participants was to rate each of the digitized or physical fabrics on eight scales representing their perceived textile qualities.

6.5.5 Data Analysis

Gathered Data

Twenty participants (13 male) were recruited from Heriot-Watt University in Edinburgh. We only recruited native English speakers, because the rating scales we used were described with English words, which needed to be immediately familiar to the participants. All participants received two large chocolate bars for participating in the experiment.

Each of the 20 participants completed 20 trials, creating altogether 400 completed questionnaires, each with ratings on 8 scales, resulting in 3200 (20x20x8) data points to analyse. Since participants evaluated each fabric twice for sound and twice for silence, we used averages of the two ratings in each sound/silence condition. We treated the ratings of each physical swatch as a baseline rating for that fabric, because handling fabric in one's hands could be considered the most true and realistic way to perceive its qualities.

We were interested to see if introducing sound to the digital interface changed the perceived qualities, moving them further from the baseline ratings (decreasing the Accuracy, making the interface less realistic) or closer to the baseline ratings (increasing the Accuracy, making the interface more realistic). During the analysis, we compared each fabric-quality combination for silence and sound with values for the same fabric-quality combination for physical swatch.

Statistical Analysis

As indicated by our exploratory study described in Section 6.5.3, a Wilcoxon signed-rank test confirmed once again that adding sound to digital presentation of textiles significantly changed the perceived qualities of some fabrics for some qualities – results of the test are shown in Table 17. Some fabrics and qualities appear to be more often significant than others (see discussion below). The analysis of the data and interpretation of the results is outlined below.

Does the presence of sound have impact on perceived qualities and moves them closer (up) or further (down) from the physical swatch rating				
	Buckram	Latex	Raised Cotton	Ripstop
Crisp	(Z=-2.854) ** ↑	(Z=-2.907) ** ↓	(Z=-2.304) * ↓	(Z=-3.234) ** ↑
Hard	(Z=-2.710) ** ↑	(Z=-1.858)	(Z=-.994)	(Z=-2.031) ** ↑
Soft	(Z=-2.301) * ↑	(Z=-1.842)	(Z=-1.369)	(Z=-.837)
Textured	(Z=-.769)	(Z=-.312)	(Z=-.556)	(Z=-.290)
Flexible	(Z=-3.189) ** ↑	(Z=-.463)	(Z=-1.486)	(Z=-1.263)
Furry	(Z=-2.080) * ↑	(Z=-.794)	(Z=-.371)	(Z=-.632)
Rough	(Z=-.995)	(Z=-2.344) * ↓	(Z=-2.897) ** ↓	(Z=-.361)
Smooth	(Z=-.058)	(Z=-2.158) * ↓	(Z=-1.433)	(Z=-.889)

Table 17 – Presence of sound moves perceived qualities closer or further from the real rating.

In Table 17 colours signify if sound provided more realistic (green) or less realistic (orange) ratings of the fabric. In this table * represents p<0.05 and ** represents p<0.01.

Discussion

The ratings of Buckram appeared to be influenced by the sound for most qualities, especially those evaluated by moving the fabric (Crisp, Hard, Soft, Flexible, Furry). This influence was always positive - ratings made in sound-enabled condition were closer to the real ratings than ratings made without sound. A similar effect was visible for Ripstop, but only for Crisp and Hard qualities. A possible explanation of these findings is that both Buckram and Ripstop produce a distinguishable sound when deformed. Possibly for those fabrics the sound aids correct evaluation of deformation-connected qualities (Crisp, Hard, Flexible), but the sound impedes correct evaluation for touch-evaluated qualities (Smooth, Rough).

An opposite effect was observed when introducing sound for fabrics that do not produce distinguishable sounds or that produce sounds that participants may not find familiar (uncommon squeaking sound of Latex and over amplified sound of Cotton). For these fabrics, adding the sound confused participants and decreased Accuracy, making the ratings with sound further from reality than perception with no sound. For example, the Accuracy of ratings for Latex and Raised Cotton was decreased for Rough (and also for Smooth for Latex). Since those two fabrics produce more sound when stroked and rubbed, it could explain why it was the Smooth and Rough qualities that were most influenced by the sound.

Across the qualities, the ratings of Crisp seemed to always significantly change when sound was added. This could be because that particular quality can be connected with noise that the fabric makes.

The ratings for the silent interface, sound-enabled interface and real swatches are presented for each fabric separately in the Figure 47. If the rating made with the sound-enabled interface was closer to the real rating than rating made with the silent interface, it was interpreted as improving the ratings (degree of significance is depicted with asterisk). The size and top-bottom order of markers was chosen to make them more distinguishable wherever they are overlaying.

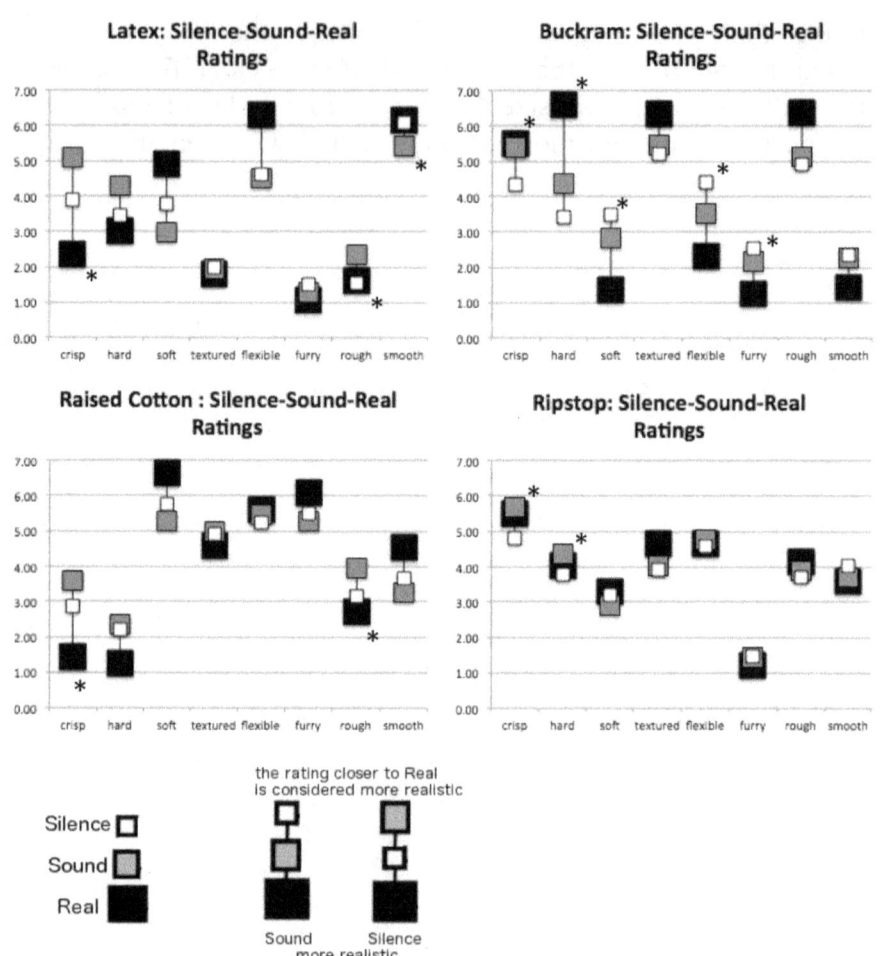

Figure 47 – Did sound improve or undermine the communication of fabric qualities? Asterisks indicate statistical significance.

6.6 Chapter Conclusion

Chapter Context

In this chapter we investigated the impact of visuals and sound in the iShoogle digital textile simulator on Accuracy of perceived fabric qualities. We described three collaborative studies that investigated the changes of rating Accuracy depending on iShoogle's visual Study 7 and sound Study 8, Study 9 attributes.

Highlights: Literature Review

The reviewed literature suggested that visual and interactive digital presentation of fabrics could have an impact on the perceived qualities of presented fabrics. There was also evidence that combining modalities, and especially adding sound to visual presentations, can have an impact on perceived qualities.

According to the work by Citrin et al. (2003), in an online shopping scenario, the ability to evaluate textile qualities prior to the purchase would make people more likely to purchase products. Wu et al. (2011) and Peck and Wiggins (2006) stated further that emotional response to garments can be influenced by interactive digital presentations of textiles. Further, Schifferstein and Cleiren (2005), Häubl and Trifts (2000) and Lee et al. (2010) investigated how combining modalities and providing interactive presentations of textiles delivered with digital means could improve their perception and self-perceived satisfaction of shopping decisions. Watanabe and Shimojo (2001), Vroomen and Gelder (2000) and a review described by Spence (2011) described how adding sound to visual presentations can change and enhance the perceived qualities of objects on the screen.

Highlights: Study Data And Findings

Study 7 highlighted that the accuracy of fabric quality ratings depended on the digital interface used to present the fabrics. There were no significant results to indicate that iShoogle was overall either better or worse than other interfaces. The results for Crisp (higher accuracy) and Soft (lower accuracy) indicate that digital simulators might be more accurate with movement-based qualities and less accurate with friction-based qualities.

In Study 8 we investigated the difference in perceived fabric qualities between using interactive sound versus silence within the iShoogle interface. There was a statistically significant difference in the accuracy of silent vs. sound ratings. For some fabrics (Buckram, Ripstop), adding sound improved the rating accuracy of some qualities, while for other fabrics (Latex) the accuracy decreased for some qualities. One possible reason for no significant results for Cotton was that the fabric sound was too amplified (too loud), because we used an automatic amplification feature of the Audacity software which over-amplified only the most quiet fabric sound (Cotton). This mistakes was not avoided because even though the interactive sound algorithm was piloted, the final audio mixes of fabric sounds were never piloted or tested prior to the study.

The analysis of the final Study 9 indicated similar findings: the accuracy of some ratings for Buckram and Ripstop ratings improved with sound, while accuracy decreased for some Latex and Cotton ratings. Additionally, some qualities (Crisp, Hard, Soft, Furry) were more influenced by the presence of sound than others.

Possible Improvements And Future Directions

The best way to further develop the research presented in this chapter would be to replicate the above studies with a more varied set of fabrics. Some of the results seemed to be caused by participants being unfamiliar with the presented fabrics (especially Latex) and their sounds. Improving the sound editing method and piloting the sounds prior to the experiments could remove another source of noise. For example, sounds of the fabrics should have been recorded in a number of conditions, with different microphone recording setups and postproduction methods, as described in Figure 36. All of these recording versions could then have been evaluated during a pilot study to find the most suitable samples for each fabric.

Further research could be conducted in the following areas: using different sounds to illustrate different fabric deformations; evaluating fabric qualities with the use of sound-only interfaces and how that impacts ratings accuracy; evaluating a sound-enabled iShoogle simulator in a realistic textile shopping setting. It would be also interesting to ask participants about their trust in the quality ratings, since Lee et al. (2010) implied that digital tools improve people's trust in their own decisions.

Another way to approach the presented research questions in follow up studies would be to find a set of promising qualities (e.g. Crisp, Hard, Soft, Flexible, Rough) and evaluate them across a large number of fabrics (around 10-20 different fabrics grouped in the fabric families of natural, artificial, industrial and novelty). The choice of fabrics and qualities should be guided by previous findings and aim to create useful guidelines for research and industry application of sound enabled textile simulators.

6.7 Chapter Contributions

In this Chapter we investigated the impact of visuals and sound on the accuracy of perceived qualities of simulated fabrics. During three studies we evaluated whether the type of visual stimuli (image, slideshow, movie, iShoogle) and a type of sound stimuli changed the perceived qualities of fabrics and brought them closer to the actual qualities of these fabrics. The goal of our investigation was to decide which interface conditions made the appreciation of the fabric qualities more realistic (i.e. brought the on-screen quality ratings closer to the ratings of physical fabric).

> CONTRIBUTION 6.1 – There Was A Trend For Some Textile Qualities Of Video Increasing The Accuracy Of Fabric Qualities' Perception When Compared With Image And Slideshow. Results Were Inconclusive For iShoogle, Since For Some Qualities iShoogle Introduced Improvement To The Accuracy Of Quality Ratings While For Others It Decreased That Accuracy.

In Study 7 we compared perceived qualities of fabrics when the fabrics were interacted with via a number of digital interfaces. We exposed participants to a Movie recording of a moving fabric, a Slideshow of frames from that movie and a single Image from that movie. The fourth condition was an interactive iShoogle interface using the same video footage as the other three interfaces. Participants rated fabric qualities most accurately in the movie condition, i.e. movie-based ratings of fabric qualities were most similar to their swatch-based ratings, however results were inconclusive and analysis was highly speculative.

We found some trends in the data where the iShoogle interface improved or decreased the accuracy of quality ratings, depending on the quality we looked at. The possible reasons were: the imperfections in the iShoogle's early prototype we used; lack of cognitive resources, since a large extraneous cognitive load was caused by the novelty of the iShoogle interface; screen visibility, since sometimes considerably large parts of the visual stimuli were obscured by the hand performing the on-screen gestures.

CONTRIBUTION 6.2 - A Sound Has Varying Impact On The Ratings Of Fabric Qualities Depending On A Type Of Fabric And The Rated Quality.

There were significant differences in perceived qualities of fabrics depending on whether the sound was present or not, improving the accuracy of the interface for some fabrics, but not for others. The hypothesis that would need to be tested further was that the sound of familiar, noisy fabrics was more consistently enhancing perception of qualities because the sounds were recognised and trigger memories of everyday experiences of handling these fabrics.

However for fabrics that were familiar, but produce quiet sounds in everyday life (e.g. Cotton), there was no impact of sound on quality perception. Possibly, an unfamiliar sound stimuli was disregarded and judgments were purely based on the visual stimuli. Additionally, the sounds of fabrics that were not encountered on everyday basis occasionally confused people, causing some textile qualities ratings to be less accurate than in the silence condition. Sound of unfamiliar objects seemed to distract the participants' intuitive, visual-only judgment, hence producing less accurate quality ratings. Both familiarity and natural noisiness theories would need to be further researched.

7. Thesis Discussion and Conclusion

7.1 Synopsis And Discussion

7.1.1 The Reason For This Thesis

The Process Of Creating And Evaluating The iShoogle Fabric Simulator

Over the course of this research we designed and evaluated a number of prototypes on the iShoogle interface that used a Direct Manipulation principle (where on-screen finger movements are directly translated into simulated movements of the object) to provide a realistic presentation of fabrics digitally. With iShoogle, fabric movements on the screen could communicate fabric qualities without the need to touch the physical fabric. We wanted for our simulator to communicate fabric qualities as accurately (Realistically) as touching the physical fabric. Throughout the thesis we tested and enhanced iShoogle's ability to communicate qualities with natural gesture control, realistic bouncing physics simulation and audio feedback.

Within this thesis we described the process of evaluating and improving a digital fabric simulator that could communicate fabric qualities accurately.

7.1.2 Tool For Evaluating How Realistic An Interface Is: Textile Quality Rating Scales (Chapter 2)

Why We Needed Words Describing Fabrics For Evaluating Interfaces

One of the core concepts in our research was the Realistic communication of fabric qualities, i.e. whether the textile qualities perceived when interacting with a digitised fabric via iShoogle were similar to the textile qualities perceived when interacting with a physical swatch of that same fabric.

Following the method used by Dillon et al. (2001) we asked participants to rate fabric qualities on Likert scales and examined the difference between the ratings of digitized and physical fabrics to estimate how Realistic the given interface was. In Chapter 2 we identified terms to use as anchors on the Likert scales in our questionnaire in a two stage process: firstly identifying expert words that are known and used by non-experts, and secondly adding non-expert words that were frequently used in unconstrained speech. After we removed words inappropriate for describing fabric qualities (i.e. words describing emotions, temporary states, comparisons or which were ambiguous), we ran a word sorting study on the remaining set of 78 words. The final fabric qualities rating questionnaire consisted of 8 Likert scales, each labelled with one term (chosen to represent a group of fabric descriptive terms) from the following set: Crisp, Hard, Soft, Textured, Flexible, Furry, Rough and Smooth as seen on Figure 17.

Participants used these 8 rating scales in all the fabric evaluation studies in this thesis, primarily by rating each fabric in its digitised and physical form. Intraclass Correlation Coefficient analysis indicated that participants used our questionnaire consistently or reproducibly for quantitative measurements of fabric qualities.

7.1.3 The Language Of On-Fabric Gestures That Could Be Translated Onto On-Screen Gestures (Chapter 3)

An Annotation Scheme For On-Fabric Gestures: Why We Needed It And How We Created It

To guide the design of touchscreen fabric simulator we needed an understanding of how people evaluate fabric qualities with touch. We observed that during the evaluation of fabrics, non-experts touched fabrics and performed a variety of gestures to evaluate fabric qualities (e.g. Stroke to evaluate Roughness, or Stretch to evaluate Stretchiness).

We created our own on-fabric gesture annotation scheme based on the literature and used it to identify the most common gestures used by our participants in a fabric handling study. We used the types of gestures (e.g. Tap, Crunch, Stroke) and their qualities (e.g. Speed, Area) to create guidelines for on-screen gestures that were designed further along this thesis. Our final gesture dictionary consisted of 7 gestures with modifiers see Figure *21*.

We did not observe the co-occurrence of gestures and textile descriptive words (e.g. people performing the Stroke gesture, as they described the fabric as Rough). Although we did make preliminary observations showing some types of fabrics affording certain gestures more (i.e. Soft fabrics were Crunched more often than Hard fabrics).

7.1.4 Textile Simulator Interface iShoogle (Chapter 4)

How On-Fabric Gestures Were Translated Into On-Screen Gestures In The iShoogle Interface

The key concept behind the iShoogle fabric simulator was the principle of Direct Manipulation described by Dragicevic et al. (2008) in which user's actions are mapped as directly as possible into the movements of the on-screen object. Touchscreen software recognised on-screen gestures (inspired by real life on-fabric gestures) and translated them into the movements of the on-screen fabric. The visual, sound and reaction feedback aimed to imitate how a physical swatch would behave when touched by the user. Our goal was to mimic and recreate digitally the exact response that physical fabric would exhibit – e.g. for the Pinch on-screen gesture to produce visual and sound feedback as an on-fabric Pinch gesture would.

Our visual stimuli consisted of stop-motion animations of a number of fabric-deformation videos, all of which shared a common frame of the fabric laying flat. A simple physics simulation (spring-dumper system) controlled the fabric's responsiveness and its ability to fall back to the common frame, from which other gestures could be triggered.

Audio feedback additionally translated user's actions (gesture and speed) into the playback qualities of fabric noises (type, pitch, volume, speed were evaluated). We developed and evaluated a number of techniques to add sound interactivity to iShoogle and found a simple algorithm for translating user's movements into sound volume. We also devised an appropriate recording rig for visual and auditory feedback.

7.1.5 Evaluating iShoogle's Acceptability And Performance (Chapter 5)

Acceptability And Performance Of The iShoogle Interface

An interface can only be considered successful when the benefits of using it outweighs the required effort to use it and time investment required to learn it (like in Advantage/Disadvantage breakdowns described by Sutcliffe (2013)). In Study 5 we compared performance and effort of iShoogle and an alternative interface. Data highlighted a possible trend that participants took a shorter time to start the task with iShoogle rather than with sliders, however there was no significant difference in time to perform the task, task accuracy or perceived effort. With no decrease in performance we considered iShoogle to be superior to its alternatives, given the unique advantages that it offered (natural gestures, multiple movies, full user control, fabric sounds).

Following the findings of Watanabe and Shimojo (2001) that sound has the potential to adjust perception of visual objects, we investigated user's perceived appropriateness of sound interfaces. In our further research we continued to use the interactive sound interface that was found to be superior in Study 6.

7.1.6 Using iShoogle To Communicate Fabric Qualities (Chapter 6)

Impact Of Presentation And Interaction On Perceived Fabric Qualities

The goal of this research was to create and evaluate a digital fabric simulator that would be capable of communicating fabric qualities.

At this point in the research process we had created an iShoogle textile simulator based on the natural on-fabric gestures (Chapter 3), we knew it could be successfully used to interact with digitised fabrics (Chapter 5). We also evaluated what fabric qualities could be communicated with such a digital fabric simulator (Chapter 2) and we devised a method of testing whether an interface can communicate fabric qualities correctly by comparing textile quality ratings of digital and physical fabrics.

When we compared iShoogle without sound with other visual interfaces for communicating fabrics (Image, Slideshow and Movie) during Study 7, we found that the communication accuracy of the iShoogle interface differs between fabric qualities (the qualities perceived via iShoogle were more accurate for Crisp, and less accurate for Soft when compared with ratings of alternative interfaces). Results were inconclusive. A possible explanation of these differences was an additional Germane mental effort as suggested by Cierniak et al. (2009) would be involved in learning a new interface such as iShoogle. Additionally, the early iShoogle prototype that this study utilised, used only one gesture (horizontal Pinch) during which the user obscured a substantial part of the screen, which could have led to less accurate ratings when compared with the video playback (where the whole screen was visible at all times).

Impact Of Sound On Perceived Fabric Qualities

In Study 8 we evaluated the differences in fabric qualities perception when fabrics were presented with and without sound. Results suggested that the presence of accompanying sound could improve the accuracy of perception of fabric qualities for everyday fabrics (Ripstop) but decrease accuracy for unusual fabrics (Latex).

In Study 9 participants evaluated the same digitised fabrics twice using iShoogle, with and without sound, and then evaluated the original fabric swatches. As before, fabrics with familiar and distinguishable sound (Buckram, Ripstop) improved the accuracy of some qualities' perception, while fabrics with unusual sound (Latex, over amplified Cotton) decreased the rating accuracy of some fabric qualities. Sound improved ratings for qualities evaluated by deformation (Crisp, Hard, Flexible) while it decreased the accuracy of ratings for qualities evaluated with finger-tips (Smooth, Rough).

The overall outcome of the above studies was that it is possible to communicate fabric qualities with iShoogle and that sound can further enhance that communication when used appropriately. The positive and negative effects on ratings accuracy differed between fabrics and communicated qualities.

7.2 Strengths And Limitations

7.2.1 Strengths

Full Journey In Research Design And Test-First Development

One of the unique qualities of this thesis was that in it we reported on a complete journey of research, design and development that lead to solving a real world problem. To create a new fabric simulator interface we had to define the research tools, design space and run studies that tested a series of more advanced prototypes.

We were inspired by the test-driven development described by Janzen and Saiedian (2005) when we decided to create our criteria for evaluating success at the beginning of the research process. Once we had a set of well-defined goals and an evaluation strategy we applied our success criteria at different stages towards improving the iShoogle simulator interface. The success criteria measured how realistic the presentation of fabric qualities was. Our evaluation strategy was to compare the users' ratings of perceived qualities of the same fabric when touched with the iShoogle simulator and when touched as a physical swatch. The smaller the difference between simulator based and swatch based ratings, the better we considered the interface to be. Additionally we had to identify what qualities of fabric we should ask our participants to evaluate. The initial part of our research was concerned with identifying these qualities (and in effect our interface fitness test) by combining literature and our own studies focused on fabric qualities.

We believe that a thorough description of this process, especially the lessons we learned through our successes and failures while exploring a novel field, contributes to the pool of knowledge of HCI research.

Holistic Approach To The Fabric Handling Experience (Gestures, Qualities, Touch, Sound)

We identified a problem of a lack of digital means to communicate fabric's touch and feel qualities. However instead of arbitrarily starting to develop a software solution to the problem, we decided to step back and consider the whole complex reality of interacting with fabrics. We believed that if we only had understanding of some aspects of a problem, then our solution would only address the parts of the problem that we understood. Following Kouprie and Visser (2009) we decided that stepping back was necessary, and we clearly defined the scope of our research.

When we defined what fabric qualities were of interest to us we decided to initially investigate every aspect of fabric that an untrained person perceived: touch-handle, movement dynamics, responsiveness, sound, emotional and preference responses.

During the evaluation of gestures we did not limit our investigation just to movements possible on a touchscreen, even though it was likely that the final interface would use touchscreen technology. We set off to observe every possible interaction that non-experts perform to evaluate fabric qualities, and even though some of them could not be translated into touch screen gestures, we believed that they could still give us a better understanding of what constitutes the experience of fabric evaluation.

The fabric qualities we considered were not only limited to the qualities that could be objectively measured or qualities that describe a subset of tactile qualities. Just as with the gestures, we gathered all the possible words that people used to describe fabrics and only then limited the word set to those that were suitable for our purposes.

We also aimed to create the most wholesome cross-modal experience of interacting with fabrics with our iShoogle interface that was possible: using gestures that are known from interacting with physical fabrics, adding realistic sound feedback, taking care to create video recordings that reflect real life fabric interactions.

User Centred (Perception, CLT, Understanding Non-Trained Participants Rather Than Training Them)

We aimed to create a textile simulator that was built for the needs of its target demographic (non-experts) and user-centred. We recruited non-experts for all of our studies, and extracted knowledge about how they interact with fabrics using gestures and words they used to describe those fabrics. We tested how the perception of fabric qualities of non-experts changes for different digital fabric presentation methods. Finally we evaluated non-experts' acceptability, mental effort and perceived usefulness of iShoogle and sound stimuli.

There could be advantages to not using non-experts and instead to focus on expert words, gestures and evaluation strategies. This would require less exploration, provide less uncertainty and most likely give us better data from experiments. However we decided against focusing on expert fabric evaluation primarily because the findings would most likely not be relevant to non-experts handling fabrics.

Additionally, we decided against taking a middle route of educating non-experts in evaluating expert fabric qualities. Expert agreed fabric qualities have advantage of being objective and hence easier to evaluate for correctness, as they could be compared to established machine measurements used as industry standards of Roughness, Stretchiness etc. We decided against teaching non-experts the expert fabric evaluation convention, because it would have potential to bias participants' opinions (by training them incorrectly in using the evaluation scales). This solution could also omit some fabric qualities that are important to non-experts (e.g. because we had no access to the equipment to objectively evaluate these qualities).

From the beginning of our research we focused on the demographic (fabric non-experts) that our research outcomes would be relevant to and aimed at investigating textile simulators for that demographic.

Blueprint For Research In A Novel Area

At the beginning of the investigation described in this thesis, there was little published research on the subject of touchscreen fabric simulators. In our research we identified the inventive step required to enable touchscreen fabric simulation (combining natural gestures, stop motion animation and our filming rig) and we used the tools and methodology from HCI-related areas to evaluate and improve the fabric simulator interface.

All of the research presented in this thesis was not only replicable, but could also be used as a blueprint for similarly in-depth and complete investigation of a different HCI area. Throughout this thesis we described not only details of our method, annotation and recording techniques and analysis, but also how we arrived at those, through literature searching and experimentation.

Publically Available iShoogle App

We released a customer-ready publically available iShoogle fabric browsing app for iPad and iPhone. This outcome of our investigation was unintended, but nevertheless important strength of our work. Our app's primary value was the fact that it served as a proof of concept, demonstrating that interacting with fabrics on consumer-available devices was possible.

Taking an experimental design and releasing it to the general public required work that would otherwise not be necessary for laboratory-only interface. We had to make the iShoogle work on various models of hardware and OS; we tested and optimised download times and file seizes; a user experience was designed around browsing and interacting with fabrics; finally the iShoogle app had to respond gracefully to device and environment events such as receiving a call, empty battery or low storage.

We created and evaluated the iShoogle app so that it could be readily applied in online commerce and communication of textiles for other purposes (e.g. archiving, education). Turning the iShoogle into a usable, market-ready product was outside of the scope of this thesis. However, it happened nevertheless, and could be further improved.

7.2.2 Limitations

Scope Was Too Wide And There Were Too Many Avenues To Provide Any Definite Results About Many Of Them

Because of the holistic approach that we took, there were too many avenues of research to provide definitive and insightful research into many of them. The research described in this thesis touched upon many questions that were left unanswered and issues that could be turned into a full thesis in their own right.

Given the time scale of this thesis we have we were not able to do any more research, or report on any more aspects of touchscreen fabric simulators; however, we believe it could be an avenue worth pursuing given more time and resources.

Underpowered Studies And The Participant Demographic

Power calculations were not performed. It is likely that our studies were underpowered and even though we used within-subjects design to maximise power, it is still likely that we were not able to detect differences even when they existed.

Our participants were mainly students in their 20s and the data we gathered might have been different if we recruited amongst people from other age groups and other backgrounds.

Using Subjective Fabric Quality Ratings Or Real Fabrics As A Baseline (Rather Than Objective Mechanical Rating Methods)

To evaluate interfaces' accuracy of fabric presentation, we needed baseline ratings of all fabric qualities that we could compare with ratings acquired while using tested interfaces. For these baseline ratings of fabric qualities we used ratings from participants handling the original physical swatches of digitised fabrics.

A baseline value for each quality-fabric combination (i.e. baseline of Crisp for Ripstop) was the average of individual ratings of all participants that rated this quality for that fabric. Ratings were averaged because they differed between participants. There were multiple reasons for differences in participants' ratings: participants' background, subtle differences in understanding of the rating scales, or even a tendency to answer Likert scales in a particular manner as indicated by Garland (1991).

An alternative solution would be to take objective baseline measures with specialist equipment used in the textile industry to evaluate different types of roughness, stretchiness and other qualities. Unfortunately it would be challenging to identify which of the non-expert rating scales should be compared with which objective expert quality.

Alternatively, we could train participants in using expert rating scales identical to those used for objective machine-measured ratings. Unfortunately we believe that this approach could create the danger of evaluating expert-only qualities that non-experts do not pay attention to, and hence creating and evaluating an interface that would be usable only by experts.

Since the purpose of this thesis was to develop a textile simulator usable by non-experts, we believe that this limitation could not have been avoided, or indeed was desired.

7.3 Future Directions

7.3.1 Research Avenues That Could Be Explored Further

Connection Between Fabric Qualities And Gestures Used To Explore Them

In Section 3.5.6 we briefly explored the co-occurrence of gestures and fabric qualities. Unfortunately the study during which we gathered data to run that analysis was not designed for the purpose of researching co-occurrence of words and gestures. The data from this study did not answer the fundamental questions that would help us explain co-occurrence or causality between gestures, fabric qualities and fabric types.

For example any time a gesture (e.g. Crunch) and a fabric quality (e.g. Soft) appeared frequently together it was unclear if any of the following interpretations of this co-occurrence could be true:

- A given fabrics inspired/afforded certain gestures (i.e. a Soft fabric inspired Crunch gestures),
- A given gesture enables evaluating certain fabric qualities (i.e. whenever users Crunched a fabric, they commented on its Soft quality),
- A given quality is evaluated with a certain gesture (i.e. when users aimed to evaluate Soft quality they frequently used Crunch gesture)

Given the available data, it was unclear whether any of the above statements were true. In section 3.5.6 we drafted a design of a study to investigate this which is described alongside of our initial analysis of one instance of co-occurrence from our available data.

Additional Gestures And Ways To Present Them On Off-The-Shelf Devices

A number of gestures were not implemented in iShoogle due to time constraints and lack of technical skills. Gestures that required analysis of small scale movements and repetitive patterns (Tap) as well as those that had potential to conflict with existing gesture recognisers (Rotate interfered with Pinch). Also gestures that used sensors other than the touchscreen (gyroscope, proximity sensor, front facing camera) were not implemented. Further research could evaluate the acceptance and performance of these gestures once they had been implemented.

Additionally it would be an interesting avenue of further research to run another observational study aiming at identifying a larger dictionary of possible touch screen gestures that are inspired by on-fabric movements, or were indeed identified in our gesture annotation study in Chapter 3.

Performance And Algorithm Of Fabric Simulation In Response To Gestures

A simple spring-damper system controlled the responsiveness of gestures (how virtual touch-points moved in response to physical touch points), and the movement dynamic of animation playback when the user stopped performing a gesture and fabric fell back to its initial state. All of the spring-damper attributes in our studies were identical, which means that light and heavy fabrics would fall back with the same speed to their initial state of laying flat on the table. The movement dynamics of that falling movement could have had an impact on the perceived qualities of the fabric as a result.

The final version of iShoogle was capable of simulating different settings of spring-damper system, however settings were never set to non-defaults to avoid additional variables in the studies. It would be an interesting avenue of further research to investigate textile qualities perceived in response to a varying simulated physics of fabric. Additionally we could explore methods to record stretchiness and return-rate of fabrics and to use these settings in the iShoogle interface. Preferably these fabric quality measurement methods would be simple, cheap and available rather than expensive and complex as the method described by Kawabata and Niwa (1991).

Sound Performance And Different Sounds For Each Gesture

We created a number of sound types (differing by recording setup) that could correspond to gestures. Unfortunately we only used these sound stimuli in studies where participants performed only one gesture, a horizontal Pinch. Types of played sound were not dependant on the performed gesture. In the studies described in Chapter 6 we observed that adding the sound of fabrics to iShoogle had changed the perception of these fabrics. In these studies, participants only used one gesture to interact with iShoogle, but it could be a very promising avenue of research to enable different sounds for different gestures. We believe that varying sound stimuli so that they would be suitable for the visual stimuli could further improve the capacity of iShoogle to communicate accurate fabric qualities.

E-Commerce, Impact Of Digital Presentation On Trust And Purchasing Decisions

It would be very interesting to apply the findings of our research to empower online retail with novel digital presentation tools. An effective communication of the touch and feel qualities of fabrics with digital means would be highly beneficial to e-commerce. That is why a more accurate way to communicate products to consumers would be especially needed in online shopping for garments. Possibly utilising the iShoogle textile simulator and our evaluation methods described in this thesis would be of interest to e-commerce researchers and could result in fruitful collaborations and research.

7.4 Conclusions

7.4.1 Contributions Of This Thesis

7.4.2 Did We Achieve The Goals Of This Thesis

Enabling Interaction With Textiles Via Digital Interface And Closing The Gap Between Fabric Qualities Perceived During On-Screen And On-Fabric Interaction

The goal of this thesis was to investigate the possibilities of textile simulator interfaces that could enable the communication of textile qualities via digital means. A textile simulator that could communicate textile qualities as accurately as handling original textiles in one's hands could have the potential to revolutionise e-commerce, education and archiving of fabrics. If textile simulators were as realistic as physical fabrics, it would no longer be necessary for the customer to visit the location of where the fabric is stored, or for the supplier to send swatches of fabric to the customer

Individual Goals And Contributions

Our goal in Chapter 2 was to identify textile quality dimensions on which non-experts could describe fabrics in our further studies. This goal had to be achieved in order to compare different interfaces' abilities to communicate textile qualities accurately. The primary contribution of Chapter 2 was a set of 8 terms describing textile quality dimensions: Crisp, Hard, Soft, Textured, Flexible, Furry, Rough and Smooth as seen on Figure 17. These terms were used throughout this thesis for evaluating textile qualities of fabrics when using digital interfaces and when handling physical swatches.

Our goal in Chapter 3 was to catalogue and understand on-fabric gestures that non-experts use to evaluate textile qualities. This goal had to be achieved in order to design on-screen interactions for iShoogle interface described in later chapters. The primary contribution of Chapter 3 was a dictionary of on-fabric gestures that consisted of 7 gestures with modifiers as seen on Figure *21*.

Our goal in Chapter 4 was to design and implement the iShoogle digital touch-screen multi-gesture fabric simulator. Once this goal was achieved we were able to investigate whether the new interface was accepted and successfully used by non-experts. In further work we also investigated whether iShoogle enabled participants to perceive textile qualities accurately. The primary contribution of Chapter 4 was the iShoogle interface combining stop motion animations of fabric deformations with gesture recognisers for on-screen equivalents of on-fabric gestures. iShoogle also included interactive sound where type and playback qualities of audio were controlled by user's gestures. Additionally a recording and production rig was designed for video and sound content for iShoogle simulator.

Our goal in Chapter 5 was to evaluate the acceptability, performance and speed of iShoogle. iShoogle had to be not worse in terms of performance in order to be considered an improvement to alternative ways of communicating textiles digitally. The results from Study 5 suggest that iShoogle might be comparable in time performance to an alternative slider interface. Additionally in Chapter 5 we had the goal of evaluating whether interactive sound was more acceptable to participants than non-interactive sound. Findings of Study 6 confirmed that participants considered interactive sound more realistic and suitable for representing fabrics than non-interactive sound.

Our goal in Chapter 6 was to evaluate whether iShoogle could be used to accurately communicate textile qualities and what visual and sound variables have impact on the rating accuracy. This goal had to be achieved in order to improve iShoogle and to establish what fabrics and qualities was iShoogle most suitable for communicating. The primary contributions of Chapter 6 were the results of our studies evaluating the impact on rating accuracy of visual elements (Study 7) and sound elements (Study 8, Study 9) of iShoogle. We found that the type of visual and sound feedback could change perceived accuracy of textile qualities by making it consistently more or less accurate depending on the particular fabric and quality described. Results were inconclusive, however they pointed towards trends in terms of some fabrics and qualities that were more likely to react in positive or negative way to changes in visual and sound features of iShoogle.

iShoogle Digital Textile Simulator That Enables Perceiving Fabric Qualities On A Touchscreen

As an outcome of this thesis, we created and evaluated the iShoogle interface – a touchscreen textile simulator which uses natural fabric-handling gestures to control interactive movies of deformed fabrics accompanied by fabric sounds. We evaluated the iShoogle in terms of how realistically it presents fabrics (how similar peoples' ratings of on-screen and physical fabrics are). We also evaluated the mental effort that is required to learn and use iShoogle, as well as user's accuracy, ease of control and performance.

We believe that at the time of writing of this thesis, the iShoogle interface is the state of art method to communicate textiles on publicly available touchscreen devices and that it is capable of communicating textile qualities digitally.

8. Appendices

Appendix I. Private communications with Douglas Atkinson – Literature Review Of Words That Fabric Experts User

Chart With Expert Words Analysis

TERM	SUGGESTED OPPOSING TERMS (ANTONYMS)	FREQUENCY AND RELEVENCE			REFERS TO:		ARE EVALUATORS:				IS TERMINOLOGY CHOSEN BY:			BLIND TET Y/N?		FABRIC TYPE(S) EVALUATED	SORTING METHOD:				APPEARS IN TEXT(S):	ORIGINAL LANGUAGE OF TEXT/TERM(S):
		Incidences Of Term	Related HESC Term	Is Term Hedonic? (Y/N)	Surface	Handle	Trained	Un-trained	Both	Given Training for Heightened	"Expert"	Untrained Evaluators	Both	Y	N		Bipolar Scale	Unipolar Scale	Grouping (inc. Difference /Triads)	Other		
Cold/Cool	Warm	8	Shari	N		X		5	2	1	3	4	1	4	4	Various x 4, Shirting, Bag Fabrics, Car Seat	3	4	4	1	1,2,3,6,7,11,12,13	French x 3, Korean and English (US), Taiwanese, French and Portuguese, English (US) x 2
Warm/Hot	Cold	7	Fukurami	N		X		4	2	1	2	3	1	4	3	Various x 4, Bag Fabrics, Car Seat	3	3	4	1	1,3,6,7,11,12,13	French x 3, Taiwanese, French and Portuguese, English (US) x 2
Thick	Thin	8	Fukurami	N		X	2	4	2	1	4 (1x?)	2 (1x?)	1	4, 1 x ?	3, 1 x ?	Various x 5, Shirting, Bag Fabrics, Men's Suiting, Car Seat	5	4	3	1	1,2,3,5,6,7,10,11	French x 3, Korean and English (US), Taiwanese, Turkish, French and Portuguese, English (US)
Thin	Thick	7	Fukurami	N		X	2	3	2	1	3 (1x?)	2 (1x?)	1	4, 1 x ?	2, 1 x ?	Various x 4, Bag Fabrics, Men's Suiting, Car Seat	5	3	3	1	1,3,5,6,7,10,11	French x 3, Taiwanese, Turkish, French and Portuguese, English (US)
Light	Heavy	5		N		X	1	2	2	1	1 (1x?)	2 (1x?)	1	4	1	Various x 4, Car Seat	3	3	3	1	1,6,7,10,11	French x 3, French and Portuguese, English (US)
Heavy	Light	7		N		X	1	4	2	1	2 (1x?)	3 (1x?)	1	5	3	Various x 5, Shirting, Car Seat	3	4	4	1	1,2,6,7,10,11,12	French x 3, Korean and English (US), French and Portuguese, English (US) x 2
Supple	Rigid	4	Hari	N		X		2	2	1	1	2	1	3	1	Various x 3, Car Seat	2	3	3	1	1,6,7,11	French x 3, French and Portuguese
Rigid	Supple, Drapable	4	Hari	N		X		2	2	1	1	2	1	3	1	Various x 3, Car Seat	2	3	4	1	1,6,7,11	French x 3, French and Portuguese
Hairy		1		N	X				1	1	1			X		Various,	X	X	X		1	French
Soft	Tough, Stiff, Hard, Harsh	9	Fukurami	N	X		2	4	2	1	5 (1x?)	1 (1x?)	1	4, 1 x ?	3, 1 x ?	Various x4, Shirting, Bag Fabrics, Men's Suiting, Car Seat	5	4	3	1	1,2,3,5,6,7,10,11,13	Korean and English (US), Taiwanese, Turkish, French x 2, French and Portuguese, English (US) x 2
Granulous		2	Numeri	N	X			1	1	1	1	1		2		Various x 2	1	2	1	1	1,7	French, French and Portuguese
Sticky	Slippery	2		N	X			1	1	1	1	1		2		Various x 2	1	2	1	1	1,7	French, French and Portuguese
Raised		1	Numeri	N	X				1	1	1			X		Various,	X	X	X		1	French
Greasy		2		N	X			1	1	1	1		1	1	1	Various x 2	2	1	2		1,11	French x 2
Slippery	Obstructed, Sticky, Harsh	6	Hari	N	X		1	2	2	1	3	1	1	2, 1 x ?	2, 1 x ?	Various x 3, Bag Fabrics, Men's Suiting	4	2	2	1	1,3,5,7,11,13	French x 2, Taiwanese, Turkish, French and Portuguese, English (US)
Falling		2	Hari	N		X		1	1	1	1	1		2		Various x 2	1	2	1	1	1,7	French, French and Portuguese
Nervous (trans. Jittery, Fluttering,		2	Shinayakasa	N		X			2	1	1		1	1	1	Various x 2	2	1	2		1,11	French x 2
Crumple/Crumple		3	Shari	N		X		1	2	1	1	1	1	2	1	Various x 3	2	2	2	1	1,7,11	French x 2, French and Portuguese,
Elastic		4	Koshi?	N		X		2	2	1	1	2	1	3	1	Various x 3, Car Seat	2	3	3	1	1,6,7,11	French x 3, French and Portuguese
Smooth	Rough	8	Numeri	N	X		2	4	1		3 (1x?)	2 (1x?)	1	1 x ?	3, 1 x ?	Shirting, Various x 4, Men's Suiting, Car Seat, Stiffened Cotton	3	3	2	2	2,4,5,6,7,10,11,13	Korean and English (US), Korean, Turkish, French x 2, French and Portuguese, English (US) x 2
Stiff	Soft, Pliable, Flexible	6	Koshi/Hari	N		X	2	2	1		2 (1x?)	1 (1x?)	1	2, 1 x ?	3, 1 x ?	Shirting, Men's Suiting, Various x 2	3	1	2		2,5,10,11,12,13	Korean and English (US), Turkish, English (US) x 3, French
Absorbent		2		N	n/a	n/a		1	1		1		1		2	Shirting, Various	1	1	1		2,11	Korean and English (US), French
Flowing	Clingy	2	Hari	N		X			1		1		1		2	Shirting, Various	1	1	1		2,11	Korean and English (US), French
Even		1	Numeri	N	X			1			1				X	Shirting		X			2	Korean and English (US)
Expensive		1		Y				1			1				X	Shirting		X			2	Korean and English (US)
Shiny/Luster (trans.	Matte	2		N	X			2			2				2	Shirting, Bag Fabrics	1	1			2,3	Korean and English (US), Taiwanese
Flexible	Stiff	2	Koshi/Shinayakasa	N		X	1	1			2			1	1	Shirting, Various	1	1			2,10	Korean and English (US), English (US)
Loose	Dense	1	Hari	N		X		1			1				X	Shirting		X			2	Korean and English (US)
Strong		2	Koshi	N		X		1	1		1		1		2	Shirting, Various		1			2,11	Korean and English (US), French
Fuzzy		1		N	X			1			1				X	Shirting		X			2	Korean and English (US)
Harsh	Soft, Slippery	6		N	X			4	1		2	2	1	3	3	Shirting, Car Seat, Various x 3	1	3	3	1	2,6,8,11,12,13	Korean and English (US), French x 3, English (US) x 2
Sheer		1		N	X			1			1				X	Shirting		X			2	Korean and English (US)
Durable		1		N		X		1			1				X	Shirting		X			2	Korean and English (US)
Tough	Soft	1	Koshi	N		X		1			1				X	Bag Fabrics	X				3	Taiwanese
Matte	Shiny/Luster (trans. Lustrous)	1		N	X			1			1				X	Bag Fabrics	X				3	Taiwanese
Bonny	Dull	1		N				1			1				X	Bag Fabrics	X				3	Taiwanese
Dull	Bonny	1		Y				1			1				X	Bag Fabrics	X				3	Taiwanese
Bright	Somber	1		N	X			1			1				X	Bag Fabrics	X				3	Taiwanese
Somber	Bright	1		Y	X			1			1				X	Bag Fabrics	X				3	Taiwanese
Delicate	Rough	1		N		X		1			1				X	Bag Fabrics	X				3	Taiwanese
Rough	Delicate, Smooth	9	Numeri	N	X		2	5	1		4 (1x?)	2 (1x?)	1	4, 1 x ?	3, 1 x ?	Bag Fabrics, Various x 5, Men's Suiting, Car Seat	4	2	2	1	3,4,5,6,7,8,10,11,13	Taiwanese, Korean, Turkish, French x 3, French and Portuguese, English (US) x 2
Decency	Budge	1		N				1			1				X	Bag Fabrics	X				3	Taiwanese
Budge	Decency	1		N				1			1				X	Bag Fabrics	X				3	Taiwanese
Obstructed	Slippery	1		N	X			1			1				X	Bag Fabrics	X				3	Taiwanese
Simple	Complicated	1		N				1			1				X	Bag Fabrics	X				3	Taiwanese
Complicated	Simple	1		N				1			1				X	Bag Fabrics	X				3	Taiwanese
Elegant	Vulgar	1		Y				1			1				X	Bag Fabrics	X				3	Taiwanese
Vulgar	Elegant	1		Y				1			1				X	Bag Fabrics	X				3	Taiwanese
Luxurious	Plain	1		Y		X		1			1				X	Bag Fabrics	X				3	Taiwanese
Plain	Luxurious	1		Y	X			1			1				1	Bag Fabrics	1				3	Taiwanese
Flamboyant	Quiet	1		N				1			1				X	Bag Fabrics	X				3	Taiwanese
Quiet	Flamboyant	1		N				1			1				X	Bag Fabrics	X				3	Taiwanese
Practical	Fancy	1		N				1			1				X	Bag Fabrics	X				3	Taiwanese
Fancy	Practical	1		N				1			1				X	Bag Fabrics	X				3	Taiwanese
Unique	Ordinary	1		N				1			1				X	Bag Fabrics	X				3	Taiwanese
Ordinary	Unique	1		Y				1			1				X	Bag Fabrics	X				3	Taiwanese
Classic	Modern	1		N				1			1				X	Bag Fabrics	X				3	Taiwanese
Modern	Classic	1		N				1			1				X	Bag Fabrics	X				3	Taiwanese
Cozy	Unbearable	2		Y				1	1		1		1		2	Bag Fabrics, Various	2		1		3,11	Taiwanese, French
Unbearable	Cozy	1		Y				1			1				X	Bag Fabrics	X				3	Taiwanese
Fashionable	Conservative	1						1			1				X	Bag Fabrics	X				3	Taiwanese
Conseravative	Fashionable	1						1			1				X	Bag Fabrics	X				3	Taiwanese
Natural	Artificial	1		N		X		1			1				1	Bag Fabrics	1				3	Taiwanese
Artificial	Natural	1		N		X		1			1				X	Bag Fabrics	X				3	Taiwanese
Technical	Handwork	1		N				1			1				X	Bag Fabrics	X				3	Taiwanese
Handwork	Technical	1		N				1			1				X	Bag Fabrics	X				3	Taiwanese
Exquisite	Coarse	1		Y				1			1				X	Bag Fabrics	X				3	Taiwanese
Coarse	Exquisite, Fine	3	Numeri	N	X		2	1			3			1	2	Bag Fabrics, Various x 2	2		1		3,9,10	Taiwanese, English, English (US)
Directional	Non-Directional	1		N		X		1			1				X	Bag Fabrics	X				3	Taiwanese
Non-Directional	Directional	1		N		X		1			1				X	Bag Fabrics	X				3	Taiwanese
Bumpy	Flat	1	Numeri	N	X			1			1				1	Various				X	4	Korean

TERM	SUGGESTED OPPOSING TERMS (ANTONYMS)	FREQUENCY AND RELEVENCE			REFERS TO:		ARE EVALUATORS:				IS TERMINOLOGY CHOSEN BY:			BLIND TET Y/N?		FABRIC TYPE(S) EVALUATED	SORTING METHOD:				APPEARS IN TEXT(S):	ORIGINAL LANGUAGE OF TEXT/TERM(S):
		Incidence s Of Term	Related HESC Term	Is Term Hedonic? (Y/N)	Surface	Handle	Trained	Un-trained	Both	Given Training for Heighten ed	"Expert"	Untrained Evaluators	Both	Y	N		Bipolar Scale	Unipolar Scale	Grouping (inc. Difference /Triads)	Other		
Rugged		1		N				1			1				X	Various				X	4	Korean
Prickly		3		Y	X			2	1		3	1	1	1	3	Various x 3	1		2	1	4,11,12	Korean, French, English (US)
Lumpy		1	Numeri	N	X			1			1				X	Various				X	4	Korean
Acute		1		N				1			1				X	Various				X	4	Korean
Tender		1		Y				1			1				X	Various				X	4	Korean
Sparse		1		N				1			1				X	Various				X	4	Korean
Dense	Loose	1	Fukurami/Koshi	N		X		1			1				1	Various				1	4	Korean
Tight		1		N		X	1				1			?	?	Men's Suiting	X				5	Turkish
Full		1	Fukurami	N		X	1				1			?	?	Men's Suiting	X				5	Turkish
Pliable	Stiff	2	Hari/Koshi	N		X	1				1			1 x ?	1 x ?	Men's Suiting	1				5,13	Turkish, English (US)
Pleasant		2		Y	X			1	1			1	1	1	1	Car Seat, Various	1	1	2		6,11	French x 2
Silk		1		N				1				1		X		Car Seat		X	X		6	French
Hard	Soft	4	Koshi	N		X	1	1	1			2	1	2	1	Car Seat, Various x 2	2	1	2		6,10,11,13	French x 2, English (US) x 2
Satin		1		N				1				1		X		Car Seat		X	X		6	French
Velvet		2		N				1	1			1	1	1	1	Car Seat, Various	1	1	2		6,11	French x 2
Wool		1		N				1				1		X		Car Seat		X	X		6	French
Mellow		2		Y				1	1			1	1	1	1	Car Seat, Various	1	1	2		6,11	French x 2
Synthetic		2		N				1	1			1	1	1	1	Car Seat, Various	1	1	2		6,11	French x 2
Unpleasant		2		Y				1	1			1	1	1	1	Car Seat, Various	1	1	2		6,11	French x 2
Cotton/Cottony		2		N				1	1			1	1	1	1	Car Seat, Various	1	1	2		6,11	French x 2
Limp	Crisp, Springy	4	Hari	N		X	1	1	1		1	1	1	2	1	Car Seat, Various x 2	2	1	2		6,10,11,13	French x 2, English (US) x 2
Relief		2	Numeri	N	X			1	1			1	1	X		Car Seat, Various	1	1	2		6,11	French x 2
Rib		1	Numeri	N	X			1				1		X		Car Seat		X	X		6	French
Sleek	Rugous	1	Numeri	N	X			1				1		X		Various		X		X	7	French and Portuguese
Rugous (trans. [illegible], wrinkled)	Sleek	1						1				1		X		Various		X		X	7	French and Portuguese
Pilous (trans. [illegible])		1		N				1				1		X		Various		X		X	7	French and Portuguese
Fluffy		1		N	X			1				1		X		Various		X		X	7	French and Portuguese
Shape		1	Koshi?	N		X		1				1		X		Various		X		X	7	French and Portuguese
Grainy		2	Numeri	N	X			1	1		1		1	1	1	Various x 2	1		1	1	8,11	French x 2
Raspy		1	Shari	N	X			1			1			X		Various				X	8	French
Silky		3	Numeri	Y	X		2	n/a	1,(1 x n/a)	n/a	2		1	1	2	Various x 3	2		2		9,10,11	English, English (US), French
Animal		1		N	X			1			1				X	Various			X		9	English
Protecetive		1		N				1			1				X	Various			X		9	English
Mossy		1	Fukurami	N	X			1			1				X	Various			X		9	English
Scratchy		3	Shari	Y	X		1	1, 1 x n/a	1,(1 x n/a)	n/a	1	1	1	2	2	Various x 3	2		2		10,11,12	English (US) x 2, French
Crisp	Limp	1	Shari	N		X	1	1			1			X		Various	X				10	English (US)
Fine	Coarse	1	Numeri	N		X	1				1			X		Various	X				10	English (US)
Firm	Sleazy	1	Hari	N		X	1				1			X		Various	X				10	English (US)
Sleazy	Firm	1	Shinayakasa	N		X	1				1			X		Various	X				10	English (US)
Snagging		1		N	X				1				1		X	Various	X		X		11	French
Floating		1	Shinayakasa	N		X			1				1		X	Various	X		X		11	French
Baby		1		N	?	?			1				1		X	Various	X		X		11	French
Raw		1		N	X				1				1		X	Various	X		X		11	French
Boardy		1	Koshi?	N		X			1				1		X	Various	X		X		11	French
Ribbed		1		N	X				1				1		X	Various	X		X		11	French
Crepe		1		N		X			1				1		X	Various	X		X		11	French
Downy		1	Fukurami	N		X			1				1		X	Various	X		X		11	French
Granite Like		1		N	?	?			1				1		X	Various	X		X		11	French
Irregular		1		N	X				1				1		X	Various	X		X		11	French
Bulky		1	Fukurami	N		X			1				1		X	Various	X		X		11	French
Comfortable		1		Y					1				1		X	Various	X		X		11	French
Irritating		1		Y	X				1				1		X	Various	X		X		11	French
Jeans		1		N		X			1				1		X	Various	X		X		11	French
Wooly		1		N	X				1				1		X	Various	X		X		11	French
Malleable		1	Shinayakasa	N		X			1				1		X	Various	X		X		11	French
Flannelette		1		N	X				1				1		X	Various	X		X		11	French
Peach-like		1		N	X				1				1		X	Various	X		X		11	French
Weighting		1		N		X			1				1		X	Various	X		X		11	French
Pilling		1		N	X				1				1		X	Various	X		X		11	French
Fleece		1	Fukurami	N	X				1				1		X	Various	X		X		11	French
Satiny		1	Numeri/Shinayakasa	N	X				1				1		X	Various	X		X		11	French
Solid		1	Hari/Koshi	N		X			1				1		X	Various	X		X		11	French
Spongy		1	Fukurami	N		X			1				1		X	Various	X		X		11	French
Cloth (trans. Calico)		1		N		X			1				1		X	Various	X		X		11	French
Velvety		1	Fukurami/Numeri	N	X				1				1		X	Various	X		X		11	French
Dry		1	Shari	N	X				1				1		1	Various	X		X		11	French
Starchy		1	Shari/Hari	N	X			1				1		X	X	Various			X		12	English (US)
Clammy		1		Y	X			1				1		X	X	Various			X		12	English (US)
Plush		1	Fukurami	N	X			1				1		X	X	Various			X		12	English (US)
Non-Stretchy	Stretchy	1	Koshi?	N		X															13	English (US)
Springy	Limp	1	Hari	N		X															13	English (US)
Compact	Open	1		N		X															13	English (US)
Open	Compact	1		N		X															13	English (US)
Stretchy	Non-Stretchy	1	Koshi?	N		X															13	English (US)

Reference For The Above Chart (Quoted Verbatim From Private Communication With Douglas Atkinson)

1. F. Philippe, L. Schacher, D. C. Adolphe, C. Dacremont, 2003. The Sensory Panel Applied to Textile Goods – a new marketing tool. Journal of Fashion Marketing and Management Vol. 7 No. 3 pp. 235-248

2. H. Kim, G. Winakor,1996. Fabric Hand as Perceived by U.S. and Korean Males and Females. Clothing and Textiles Research Journal, Vol. 14, No. 2, pp. 133-144

3. S.- H. Hung, M.-C. Chuang A Study on the Relationship between Texture Image and Textile Fabrics of Bags. thesis, Institute of Applied Arts National Chiao-Tung University, Hsinchu, Taiwan 1999

4. H.-J. Suk, S.-H. Jeong, T.-H. Yang and D.-S. Kwon, TACTILE SENSATION AS EMOTION ELICITOR. Kansei Engineering International Vol.8 No.2 pp.147-152 (2009)

5. V. Sular, A. Okur, Handle Evaluation of Men's Suitings Produced In Turkey. Fibers and Textiles in Eastern Europe Vol. 16, No.2 pp. 61-68 (2008)

6. D. Picard, C. Dacremont, D. Valentin, A. Giboreau, Perceptual Dimensions of Tactile Textures. Acta Psychologica Vol. 114 pp. 165-184 (2003)

7. C. Nogueira, M. E. Cabeco-Silva, L. Schacher, D. Adolphe, Textile Materials: Tactile Describers. Journal of Food Technology 7 (3) pp. 66-70 (2009)

8. L Pelletier, I Soufflet, C Dacremont, How to Describe the Handle of Fabrics? A Focus on Grainy, Harsh, Rough and Raspy Perception. SPISE 2007, dch.hcmut.edu.vn

9. W. Moody, R. Morgan, P. Dillon, C. Baber and A. Wing, Factors Underlying Fabric Perception, in: Proceedings of the Conference on Eurohaptics, 2001, pp. 192–201

10. G. Winakor, C. J. Kim, Fabric Hand: Tactile Sensory Assessment, Textile Research Journal Vol. 50 No. 10 pp. 601-610 (1980)

11. I. Soufflet, M. Calonniera and C. Dacremont, A comparison between industrial experts' and novices' haptic perceptual organization: a tool to identify descriptors of the handle of fabrics, Food Quality and Preference Vol. 15 pp. 689-699 (2004)

12. J. Laughlin, Perception of Fabrics: A Texturalcentric study of the visual and tactile responses of adult and elderly women, International Journal of Clothing Science and Technology Vol. 3, No. 5, pp. 20-31 (1991)

13. ASTM Standard D123, 2009, "Standard Terminology Relating to Textiles," ASTM International, West Conshohocken, PA, 2009, DOI: 10.1520/D0123-09, www.astm.org.

Appendix II. Words used by two or less out of 28 participants and hence discarded

animal	three-dimensiona	cushiony	horrific	outgoing	stubborn
appealing	ugh	damaged	huggable	papery	substantial
attractive	uncomfortable	deceiving	hydrophobic	patchy	subtle
bendable	useful	deceptive	hypnotic	pattern	suffocating
breezy	wool	decorative	I like it	pimpled	summery
bright	70' feel	deep	impractical	playability	symbolic
brittle	a lot going on	denim	imprinted	pleasurable	terrible
common	acrylic	dense	indecent	plush	tickly
cosy	air	detailed	indented	pollution	touchable
creasable	alive	different feel and	inelastic	polyester	towel
crinkly	angular	different on sides	insulated	porous	translucent
cuddly	artistic	dimensional	insulating	posh	trashy
dark	arty	dimply	insulation	predictable	trendy
dry	authentic	disco	interwoven	pure	twanky
dull	beautiful	disgusting	intricate	purposeful	unattractive

easy	bitty	domestic	inviting	quality	uncommon
elegant	black	Double-layered	ironed	real	undesirable
fashionable	blue	drape	jagged	regular	uninspiring
foldable	bounces	drapy	jeans	reinforced	uninviting
frail	bouncy	easy on the eye	lasting	relaxing	unusual
fun	breaking	enduring	latex	reliable	useless
functional	breathable	enjoyable	levels	repetitive	velvet
fuzzy	brutal	entrancing	lightweight	repulsive	visible
girly	busy	even	lined	responsive	vulgar
glossy	captivating	everywhere	long-lasting	rich	watery
good	carpet	exciting	looks cool	ridges	wavy
grippy	carpety	explosive	loud	rigging	waxed
grooved	changeable	eye catching	lustrous	ripped	waxy
hardwearing	checked	familiar	Machine-made	ripply	wearable
itchy	classy	feather	makes you want to	rugged	weaved
jaggy	clean	feels wet	man-made	rug-like	webbed

335

knitted	clear	fibrous	manufactured	safe	weighty
leathery	clinical	flat	masculine	scrunches	welcoming
lovely	cloth	flimsy	mathematical	secretive	well-made
matte	clothing	floppy	mesh	sensory	wet
matted	cloud	flowy	messy	shaggy	what the hell
meshy	cloudy	fluid	mice	sharp	white
metallic	coloured	folded	mismatched	simple	wild
noisy	comfy	formatted	mmm	slick	winter
old-fashioned	composite	fragmented	modern	slidy	wintery
plastic	confident	free-flowing	moist	slight	withstanding
practical	confused	frictionless	mouldable	smelly	woolen
random	constraining	frustrating	movement	sown	worn
retro	convenient	funky	multi-layered	spooky	wow
ridged	cooling	funny	neat	squashy	wrinkles
robust	corset	futuristic	netting	squeezable	you can wear it
sandy	cotton	glides	netty	squicky	yucky

sexy	Cotton-like	glitter	nice material	squidgy	
skin-like	covering	gooey	nothing about it	squiggly	
sneaky	crisp	grab no	nude	standing-out	
sparkly	crisscrossy	grabby	offensive	steady	
spongy	crumples	groovy	oh boy	steam	
stitched	crumply	heavyweight	old generation	stippled	
surprising	curtain	hideous	open	stripes	
tactile	curtains	hip	organic	stripy	
tangly	curved	homely	organised	structured	

Appendix III. Four Fabrics Used For Testing iShoogle

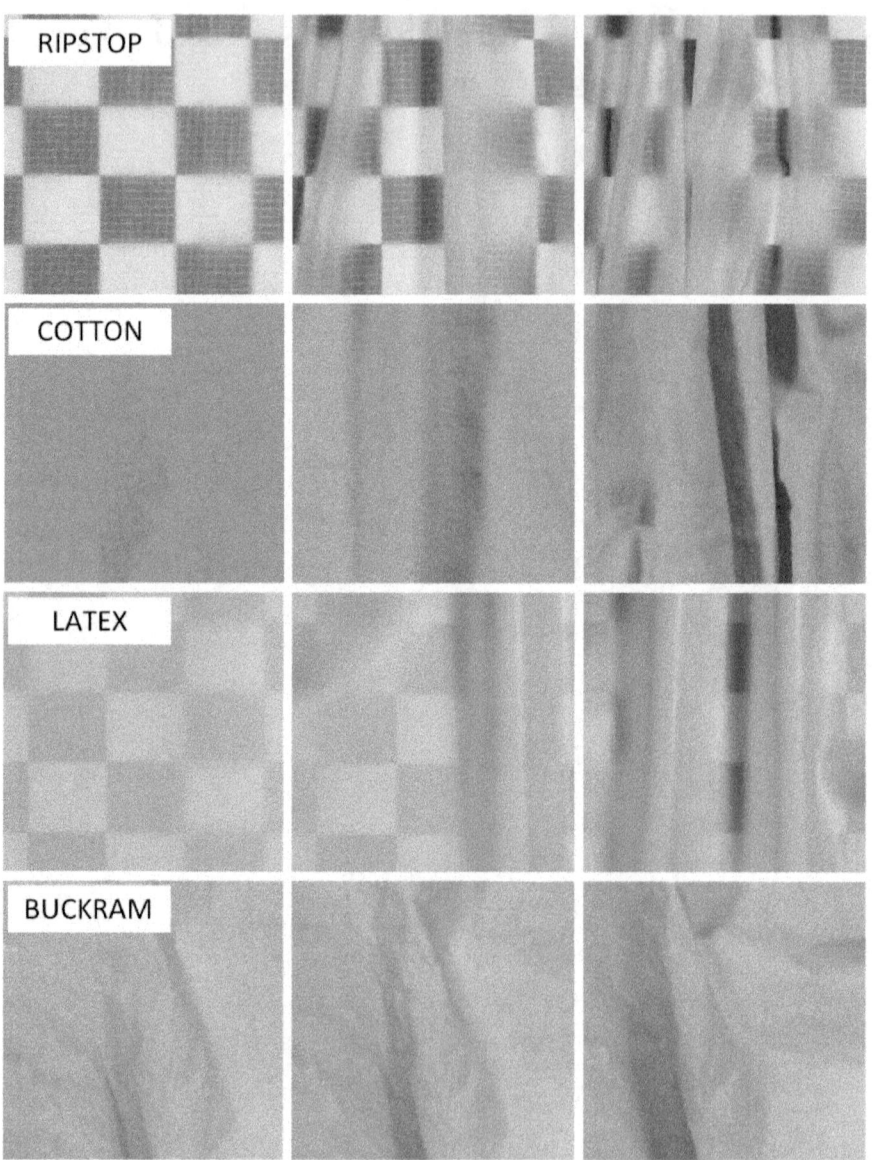

Appendix IV. Area Independent Method For Creating Annotation Scheme For A New Area Of Research

The process we followed to create a gesture dictionary for handling fabrics can be reused to create annotation schemes and dictionaries in other areas of HCI. We took the following steps:

1. We identified areas of literature and expert handbooks to review, where researchers explored and described gesture spaces of similar problems. We found that interaction with digitally enhanced physical objects via digital means was often associated with the same problems and constraints. We also used the vocabulary used in describing handling physical objects translated or simulated via digital means described in Section 3.2.

2. From the literature we wrote down all the annotation items: description tags (Pinch, Stroke), parameters (slow, circular) and modifiers (one hand, on the edge). From these annotative elements we created an extensive annotation scheme that stored a large amount of information, often excessive and redundant. At this stage some additional annotation items could be added if they appeared to be suitable for the explored gesture space.

3. This initial dictionary with redundant tags should be used on a small sample of participant data or a pilot study. Preferably this step would be performed by two or more independent researchers and their results compared as seen in Section 3.4.3.

4. Once data from the pilot are annotated, they need to be eyeballed and clustered. To reduce redundancy in the annotation scheme and make it faster to use, one would discard the units of description (tags, parameters and modifiers) that were used by only one person, were difficult to recognise on the video recording, or that were

disagreed upon among researchers. From the remaining items, an annotation scheme should be created as described in Figure *21*.

5. If the explored gesture space is described in too much detail and the annotation scheme is too large to use in a practical way for quick and efficient annotations, this process could be repeated iteratively until a satisfactory result is obtained.

6. The annotation dictionary should be finalized and represented in a visual way to enable other researchers to use it for the purposes of cross-referencing annotations and replicating studies as described in Section 3.5.2.

The weaknesses of this approach are that it can be over-trained on the pilot data and can be influenced by subjective opinions of the researchers. The process can be also time consuming. To counter over-training we recommend to pilot-annotate multiple fragments of video from a variety of participants, representing the variety of gathered data. The process of simplifying tags should be critical, because it is possible that some annotation items were not annotated because of accidental factors, such as camera angle. For example seeing the manipulation only from above it is impossible to see gestures where user reaches underneath the fabric (could be aided by performing the experiment on a glass table with a camera underneath). Other scenarios where gestures were impossible to accurately annotate were: a participant leaned their head low to see fine details of the fabric and obscured the view of the camera with their head; a participant lifted the fabric from the table and performed gestures out of frame and with camera being not in focus. To combat the subjectivity, we recommend involving more than one person in the process of annotation, analysis and simplifying tags.

We believe that this process was successful in establishing an annotation dictionary to describe the gestures used to assess qualities of fabrics. Other researchers should be able to follow our guidelines and achieve comparably satisfactory results in other unexplored gesture spaces.

9. Bibliography

American Association of Textile Chemists and Colorists (1993). *Evaluation Procedures: Fabric Hand: Subjective Evaluation.* Raleigh, NC: American Association of Textile Chemists and Colorists.

Abrams, R. A., Davoli, C. C., Du, F., Knapp, W. H., & Paull, D. (2008). Altered vision near the hands. *Cognition, 107*(3), 1035-1047.

Alexander, C. (1964). *Notes on the Synthesis of Form.* Cambridge, MA: Harvard University Press.

Atkinson, D., Orzechowski, P., Petreca, B., Bianchi-Berthouze, N., Watkins, P., Baurley, S., . . . Chantler, M. (2013). *Tactile perceptions of digital textiles: a design research approach.* Paper presented at the Proceedings of the SIGCHI Conference on Human Factors in Computing Systems.

Bensaid, S., Osselin, J.-F., Schacher, L., & Adolphe, D. (2006). The effect of pattern construction on the tactile feeling evaluated through sensory analysis. *Journal of the Textile Institute, 97*(2), 137-145.

Blackler, A. L., Popovic, V., & Mahar, D. P. (2002). Intuitive use of products. In D. Durling & J. Shackleton (Eds.), *Common Grounds* (pp. 120-135). Staffordshire: Staffordshire University Press.

Brandt, B., Brown, D., Burns, L., Cameron, B., Chandler, J., Dallas, M., . . . Salusso, C. (1998). Development of an interdisciplinary method for the study of fabric perception. *Journal of the Textile Institute, 89*(1), 65-77.

Buxton, B., & Billinghurst, M., Guiard, Y., Sellen, A., & Zhai, S. (2011). *Human Input to Computer Systems: Theories, Techniques and Technology.* Unpublished. See http://www.billbuxton.com.

Cadoz, C. (1994). The gesture as man-machine communication channel. *TSI-Technique et Science Informatiques, 13*(1), 31-62.

Cierniak, G., Scheiter, K., & Gerjets, P. (2009). Explaining the split-attention effect: Is the reduction of extraneous cognitive load accompanied by an increase in germane cognitive load? *Computers in Human Behavior, 25*(2), 315-324.

Citrin, A. V., Stem, D. E., Spangenberg, E. R., & Clark, M. J. (2003). Consumer need for tactile input: An internet retailing challenge. *Journal of Business Research, 56*(11), 915-922.

Civille, G. V., & Dus, C. A. (1990). Development of terminology to describe the handfeel properties of paper and fabrics. *Journal of Sensory Studies, 5*(1), 19-32.

Dillon, P., Moody, W., Bartlett, R., Scully, P., Morgan, R., & James, C. (2001). Sensing the fabric: To simulate sensation through sensory evaluation and in response to standard acceptable properties of specific materials when viewed as a digital image. In Brewster, S. & Murray-Smith, R. (Eds.), *Haptic Human-Computer Interaction* (pp. 205-218). Heidelberg: Springer.

Dragicevic, P., Ramos, G., Bibliowitcz, J., Nowrouzezahrai, D., Balakrishnan, R., & Singh, K. (2008). *Video browsing by direct manipulation.* Paper presented at the Proceedings of the SIGCHI Conference on Human Factors in Computing Systems.

Garland, R. (1991). The mid-point on a rating scale: Is it desirable. *Marketing Bulletin, 2*(1), 66-70.

Giboreau, A., Navarro, S., Faye, P., & Dumortier, J. (2001). Sensory evaluation of automotive fabrics: the contribution of categorization tasks and non verbal information to set-up a descriptive method of tactile properties. *Food Quality and Preference, 12*(5), 311-322.

Häubl, G., & Trifts, V. (2000). Consumer decision making in online shopping environments: The effects of interactive decision aids. *Marketing Science, 19*(1), 4-21.

Henze, N., Rukzio, E., & Boll, S. (2011). *100,000,000 taps: Analysis and improvement of touch performance in the large.* Paper presented at the Proceedings of the 13th International Conference on Human Computer Interaction with Mobile Devices and Services.

Hoggan, E., Kaaresoja, T., Laitinen, P., & Brewster, S. (2008). *Crossmodal congruence: The look, feel and sound of touchscreen widgets.* Paper presented at the Proceedings of the 10th International Conference on Multimodal interfaces.

Hummels, C., Overbeeke, K. C., & Klooster, S. (2007). Move to get moved: a search for methods, tools and knowledge to design for expressive and rich movement-based interaction. *Personal and Ubiquitous Computing, 11*(8), 677-690.

Israel, J. H., Hurtienne, J., Pohlmeyer, A. E., Mohs, C., Kindsmuller, M., & Naumann, A. (2009). On intuitive use, physicality and tangible user interfaces. *International Journal of Arts and Technology, 2*(4), 348-366.

Janzen, D., & Saiedian, H. (2005). Test-driven development: Concepts, taxonomy, and future direction. *Computer* (9), 43-50.

Karrer, T., Wittenhagen, M., & Borchers, J. (2012). *Draglocks: handling temporal ambiguities in direct manipulation video navigation.* Paper presented at the Proceedings of the SIGCHI Conference on Human Factors in Computing Systems.

Kawabata, S., & Niwa, M. (1991). Objective measurement of fabric mechanical property and quality: Its application to textile and clothing manufacturing. *International Journal of Clothing Science and Technology, 3(1)*, 7-18.

Knight, H.-M. C. (2008). *An architecture for sensate robots: real time social-gesture recognition using a full body array of touch sensors.* (Unpublished MEng dissertation). Massachusetts Institute of Technology, Cambridge, MA.

Kouprie, M., & Visser, F. S. (2009). A framework for empathy in design: Stepping into and out of the user's life. *Journal of Engineering Design, 20*(5), 437-448.

Kurtenbach, G., & Hulteen, E. A. (1990). Gestures in human-computer communication. In Laurel, B. (Ed.) *The art of human-computer interface design* (pp. 309-317). Boston, MA: Addison Wesley.

Lee, H.-H., Kim, J., & Fiore, A. M. (2010). Affective and cognitive online shopping experience effects of image interactivity technology and experimenting with appearance. *Clothing and Textiles Research Journal, 28*(2), 140-154.

Levin, A. M., Levin, I. R., & Heath, C. E. (2003). Product category dependent consumer preferences for online and offline shopping features and their influence on multi-channel retail alliances. *Journal of Electronic Commerce Research, 4*(3), 85-93.

Magnenat-Thalmann, N., Volino, P., Bonanni, U., Summers, I. R., Bergamasco, M., Salsedo, F., & Wolter, F.-E. (2007). From physics-based simulation to the touching of textiles: The HAPTEX project. *International Journal of Virtual Reality, 6*(3), 35-44.

Martonjak, L. (2011). *How does sound affect user experience when handling digital fabrics using a touchscreen device?* (Unpublished MSc dissertation), University College London, London.

Mayer, R. E., Hegarty, M., Mayer, S., & Campbell, J. (2005). When static media promote active learning: Annotated illustrations versus narrated animations in multimedia instruction. *Journal of Experimental Psychology: Applied, 11*(4), 256.

Methven, T., Orzechowski, P., & Chantler, M. (2011). A Comparison of Crowd-Sourcing vs. Traditional Techniques for Deriving Consumer Terms. Paper presented at Digital Engagement.

Mohs, C., Hurtienne, J., Israel, J. H., Naumann, A., Kindsmüller, M. C., Meyer, H. A., & Pohlmeyer, A. (2006). *IUUI–intuitive use of user interfaces.* Paper Presented at the Usability Professionals Conference.

Moody, W., Morgan, R., Dillon, P., Baber, C., & Wing, A. (2001). *Factors underlying fabric perception.* Paper presented at EuroHaptics.

Moreno, R., & Mayer, R. (2007). Interactive multimodal learning environments. *Educational Psychology Review, 19*(3), 309-326.

Mulder, A. (1996). *Hand gestures for HCI.* (Hand Centered Studies of Human Movement Project Technical Report.)

Orzechowski, P., Padilla, S., Atkinson, D., Baurley, S., & Chantler, M. (2012). *Are single images sufficient to communicate qualities of texture-rich products?* Paper presented at Perception.

Orzechowski, P., Padilla, S., Atkinson, D., Chantler, M. J., Baurley, S., Berthouze, B.-N., . . . Petreca, B. (2012). *Archiving and simulation of fabrics with multi-gesture interfaces.* Paper presented at the Proceedings of HCI.

Orzechowski, P. M. (2010). *Interactive mobile presentation of textiles.* Paper presented at the Proceedings of the 12th International Conference on Human Computer Interaction with Mobile Devices and Services.

Orzechowski, P. M., Atkinson, D., Padilla, S., Methven, T. S., Baurley, S., & Chantler, M. (2011). *Interactivity to enhance perception: does increased interactivity in mobile visual presentation tools facilitate more accurate rating of textile properties?* Paper presented at the Proceedings of the 13th International Conference on Human Computer Interaction with Mobile Devices and Services.

Orzechowski, P. M., Padilla, S., Atkinson, D., Chantler, M., Baurley, S., Bianchi-Berthouze, N., . . . Petreca, B. B. (2012). *iShoogle: a textile archiving and simulation tool.* Paper presented at the Proceedings of the 26th Annual BCS Conference on Human Computer Interaction (HCI 2012).

Padilla, S. (2008). *Mathematical models for perceived roughness of three-dimensional surface textures.* (Unpublished doctoral dissetation). Heriot-Watt University, Edinburgh.

Padilla, S., & Chantler, M. J. (2011). *ShoogleIt. com: Engaging online with interactive objects.* Paper presented at Digital Engagement.

Padilla, S., Halley, F., & Chantler, M. J. (2011). *Improving product browsing whilst engaging users.* Paper presented at Digital Engagement.

Padilla, S., Orzechowski, P. M., & Chantler, M. J. (2012). *Digital tools for the creative industries.* Paper presented at Digital Futures.

Peck, J., & Wiggins, J. (2006). It just feels good: Customers' affective response to touch and its influence on persuasion. *Journal of Marketing, 70*(4), 56-69.

Randell, C., Andersen, I., Moore, H., & Baurley, S. (2005). *Sensor Sleeve: Sensing Affective Gestures.* Paper presented at the Ninth International Symposium on Wearable Computers– Workshop on On-Body Sensing.

Rime, B., Shiaratura, L. (1991). Gesture and speech. In Feldman, R.S. & Rime, B. (Eds.), *Fundamentals of Nonverbal Behavior* (pp. 239 281). New York: Cambridge University Press.

Schifferstein, H. N., & Cleiren, M. P. (2005). Capturing product experiences: A split-modality approach. *Acta Psychologica, 118*(3), 293-318.

Schiphorst, T. (2009). *soft(n): toward a somaesthetics of touch.* Paper presented at the CHI on Human Factors in Computing Systems.

Scilingo, E. P., Lorussi, F., Mazzoldi, A., & De Rossi, D. (2003). Strain-sensing fabrics for wearable kinaesthetic-like systems. *IEEE Sensors Journal, 3*(4), 460-467.

Shaari, N., & Suleiman, N. (2009). *Assistive clothing for disabled people based on kansei approach using indigenous clothing construction.* Paper presented at the International Association of Societies of Design Research Conference.

Solomon, G. E. (1997). Conceptual change and wine expertise. *The Journal of the Learning Sciences, 6*(1), 41-60.

Soufflet, I., Calonnier, M., & Dacremont, C. (2004). A comparison between industrial experts' and novices' haptic perceptual organization: A tool to identify descriptors of the handle of fabrics. *Food Quality and Preference, 15*(7), 689-699.

Spence, C. (2011). Crossmodal correspondences: A tutorial review. *Attention, Perception, & Psychophysics, 73*(4), 971-995.

Steininger, S., Lindemann, B., & Paetzold, T. (2001). *Labeling of Gestures in SmartKom—Concept of the Coding System.* Paper presented at the Gesture Workshop.

Still, J. D., & Dark, V. J. (2010). Examining working memory load and congruency effects on affordances and conventions. *International Journal of Human-Computer Studies, 68*(9), 561-571.

Sutcliffe, A. (2013). *Human-computer interface design.* New York: Springer.

Takahashi, C., Diedrichsen, J., & Watt, S. J. (2009). Integration of vision and haptics during tool use. *Journal of Vision, 9*(6), 3.1-3.13.

Vroomen, J., & Gelder, B. (2000). Sound enhances visual perception: cross-modal effects of auditory organization on vision. *Journal of Experimental Psychology: Human Perception and Performance, 26*(5), 1583-1590.

Wagner, S. M., Nusbaum, H., & Goldin-Meadow, S. (2004). Probing the mental representation of gesture: Is handwaving spatial? *Journal of Memory and Language, 50*(4), 395-407.

Watanabe, K., & Shimojo, S. (2001). When sound affects vision: effects of auditory grouping on visual motion perception. *Psychological Science, 12*(2), 109-116.

Whitworth, B., & Ahmad, A. (2014). *The social design of technical systems: Building technologies for communities.* The Interaction Design Foundation.

Wong, A., Marcus, N., Ayres, P., Smith, L., Cooper, G. A., Paas, F., & Sweller, J. (2009). Instructional animations can be superior to statics when learning human motor skills. *Computers in Human Behavior, 25*(2), 339-347.

Wu, D., Wu, T.-I., Singh, H., Padilla, S., Atkinson, D., Bianchi-Berthouze, N., . . . Baurley, S. (2011). The affective experience of handling digital fabrics: Tactile and visual cross-modal effects. In D'Mello, S., Graesser, A., Schuller, B., & Martin, J.C. (Eds.), *Affective computing and intelligent interaction* (pp. 427–436). Berlin Heidelberg: Springer.

Yee, W. (2009). Potential limitations of multi-touch gesture vocabulary: Differentiation, adoption, fatigue. In Jacko, J.A. (Ed.) *Human-Computer Interaction. Novel Interaction Methods and Techniques* (pp. 291-300). Berlin Heidelberg: Springer.

www.ingramcontent.com/pod-product-compliance
Lightning Source LLC
Chambersburg PA
CBHW060820170526
45158CB00001B/35